BLOOD SISTERS

Also by Sarah Gristwood

Non-Fiction

Arbella
Bird of Paradise
Elizabeth and Leicester
The Ring and the Crown (co-author)

Fiction

The Girl in the Mirror

SARAH GRISTWOOD

Blood Sisters

The Hidden Lives of the Women
Behind the Wars of the Roses

Harper
Press

HarperPress
An imprint of HarperCollins*Publishers*
77–85 Fulham Palace Road,
Hammersmith, London W6 8JB
www.harpercollins.co.uk

Published by Harper*Press* in 2012

1

A catalogue record for this book
is available from the British Library

ISBN 978-0-00-730929-0

Typeset in Minion by Palimpsest Book Production Limited,
Falkirk, Stirlingshire

Printed and bound in Great Britain by
Clays Ltd, St Ives plc

MIX
Paper from
responsible sources
FSC™ C007454

CONTENTS

PART ONE
1445–1461

PART TWO
1461–1471

LIST OF ILLUSTRATIONS

de bourgogne a Ihesu Crist by Nicolas Finet, c.1470. British Library Add.7970, f.1v (© The British Library Board)

Elizabeth of York by unknown artist, oil on panel, late 16th century; after unknown artist c. 1500 (© National Portrait Gallery, London)

The birth of Caesar from *Le fait des Romains*, Bruges, 1479. British Library Royal 17 F.ii, f.9 (© The British Library Board)

The Devonshire Hunting Tapestry – Southern Netherlands (possibly Arras), 1430–40 (© Victoria and Albert Museum, London)

Procession at the Funeral of Queen Elizabeth, 1502 (© The Trustees of the British Museum)

The preparations for a tournament. Illustration for René of Anjou's *Livre des Tournois*, 1488–89? Bibliothèque nationale de France, Francais 2692, f.62v–f.63 (Bibliothèque nationale de France)

Margaret of Burgundy's crown, Aachen Cathedral Treasury (© Domkapitel Aachen (photo: Pit Siebigs))

Song 'Zentil madona': from Chansonnier de Jean de Montchenu, 1475?, Bibliothèque nationale de France, MS Rothschild 2973, f.3v–f.4 (Bibliothèque nationale de France)

The Tower of London from the Poems of Charles of Orleans, c.1500. British Library, Royal 16 F. II f.73 (© The British Library Board)

Elizabeth of York's signature on a page of 'The Hours of Elizabeth the Queen', c.1415–20. British Library Add 50001, f.22 (© The British Library Board)

Wheel of Fortune illumination from the *Troy Book*, c.1455–1462. British Library Royal 18 D.II, f.30v (© The British Library Board)

N

*North
Sea*

Edinburgh

• Dumfries   • Newcastle on Tyne

Raby Castle

Middleham Castle

*Irish
Sea*

York   • Hull
Towton

Bosworth   • King's Lynn

Ludlow •   *Grafton Manor*   Norwich
        Warwick   Cambridge   • Bury St Edmunds
Pembroke Castle   Ipswich •

        • Oxford
        London
• Bristol

        Winchester   Canterbury •   Dover
Exeter   Southampton   Calais
                Portsmouth

                                        Agincourt

English Channel

Plymouth

                        • Antwerp
                Bruges • Ghent
                        • Brussels

Rouen

Paris
                Seine
                        • Troyes

Rennes •

Angers   *Loire*   BURGUNDY
                                • Dijon

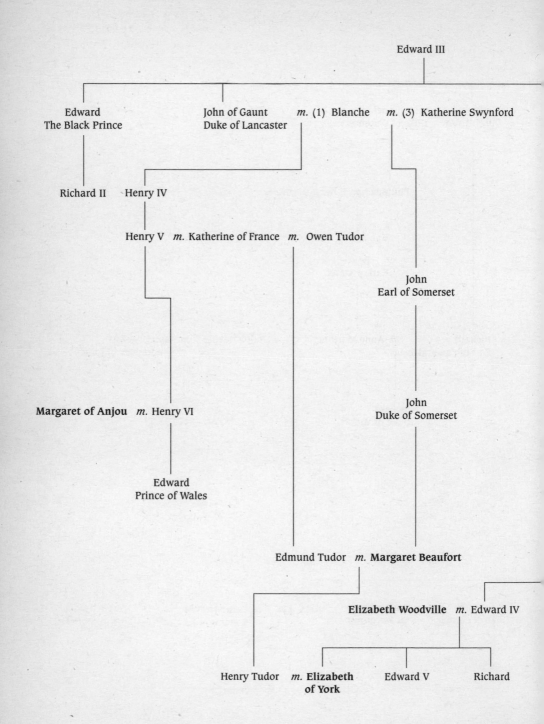

Edward III

Edward
The Black Prince

John of Gaunt   *m.* (1) Blanche   *m.* (3) Katherine Swynford
Duke of Lancaster

Richard II   Henry IV

Henry V   *m.* Katherine of France   *m.* Owen Tudor

John
Earl of Somerset

John
Duke of Somerset

Margaret of Anjou   *m.* Henry VI

Edward
Prince of Wales

Edmund Tudor   *m.* **Margaret Beaufort**

Elizabeth Woodville   *m.* Edward IV

Henry Tudor   *m.* **Elizabeth
of York**   Edward V   Richard

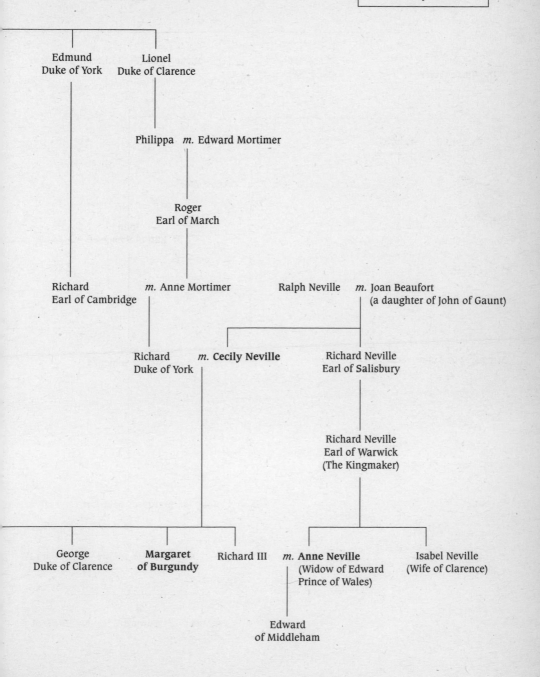

Simplified
Family Tree

Edmund
Duke of York

Lionel
Duke of Clarence

Philippa   *m.* Edward Mortimer

Roger
Earl of March

Richard
Earl of Cambridge

m. Anne Mortimer

Ralph Neville   *m.* Joan Beaufort
(a daughter of John of Gaunt)

Richard
Duke of York

m. **Cecily Neville**

Richard Neville
Earl of Salisbury

Richard Neville
Earl of Warwick
(The Kingmaker)

George
Duke of Clarence

**Margaret
of Burgundy**

Richard III   *m.* **Anne Neville**
(Widow of Edward
Prince of Wales)

Isabel Neville
(Wife of Clarence)

Edward
of Middleham

A NOTE ON NAMES

Of the seven women whose stories I explore, the fashions of the times mean that two are called Elizabeth and three, Margaret. I have therefore referred to the York princess who married the Burgundian ruler as Margaret 'of Burgundy', while giving Margaret of Anjou the French appellation she herself continued sometimes to use after marriage – Marguerite. The family originally spelt as 'Wydeville' has been given its more familiar appellation of 'Woodville', and other spellings and forms have sometimes been modernised. The quotations at the top of each chapter have been drawn from Shakespeare's history plays.

REIGNS

Henry IV   1399–1413   Lancaster
Seized the throne from his cousin Richard II

Henry V   1413–22   Lancaster

Henry VI   1422–61   Lancaster
Succeeded to the throne before he was a year old, and at first
   ruled in name only

Edward IV   1461–70 (first reign)   York
Seized the throne from Henry VI

Henry VI   October 1470–April 1471
               ('Readeption')   Lancaster

Edward IV   1471–83 (second reign)   York

Edward V   April–June 1483   York

Richard III 1483–85   York

Henry VII   1485–1509   Lancaster

Henry VIII 1509–47   Tudor

PROLOGUE

February 1503

She had died on her thirty-seventh birthday and that figure would be reiterated through the ceremony. Thirty-seven virgins dressed in white linen, and wreathed in the Tudor colours of green and white, were stationed in Cheapside holding burning tapers; thirty-seven palls of rich cloth were draped beside the corpse. The king's orders specified that two hundred poor people in the vast and solemn procession from the Tower of London to Westminster should each carry a 'weighty torch', the flames flickering wanly in the February day.[1]

For Elizabeth of York had been one of London's own. Her mother Elizabeth Woodville had been the first English-born queen consort for more than three centuries, but where Elizabeth Woodville had been in some ways a figure of scandal, her daughter was less controversial. She had been a domestic queen, who gave money in return for presents of apples and woodcocks; and bought silk ribbons for her girdles, while thriftily she had repairs made to a velvet gown. Elizabeth rewarded her son's schoolmaster, bought household hardware for her newly married daughter, and tried to keep an eye out for her sisters and their families. The trappings of the hearse showed she was a queen who had died in childbirth, a fate feared by almost every woman in the fifteenth century.

She had been, too, a significant queen: the white rose of York who had married red Lancaster in the person of Henry VII and ended the battles over the crown. Double Tudor roses, their red petals firmly encircling the white, were engraved and carved all over the chapel where she would finally be laid to rest.

The records describe how on her death Henry 'took with him certain of his secretest, and privately departed to a solitary place to pass his sorrows and would no man should resort to him but such his Grace appointed'; leaving behind orders 'for 636 whole masses' to be said. 'Also then were rung the bells of London every one, and after that throughout the Realm with solemn dirges and Masses of Requiems and every Religious place, colleges, and Churches.' The loss of his queen was 'as heavy and dolorous to the King's Highness as hath been seen or heard of'. It was the end of the partnership which had given birth to the Tudor dynasty.

Elizabeth had been at the Tower when she 'travailed of child suddenly' and was there delivered on Candlemas Day of a baby daughter who may have come prematurely. The records of her own Privy Purse expenses show boatmen, guides, horses sent suddenly to summon a doctor from the country; linen purchased to swaddle a new baby who would outlive her mother only by days. 'And upon the 11th day of the said month being Saturday in the morning, died the most gracious and virtuous princess the Queen, where within the parish church of the foresaid Tower her corpse lay 11 days after.'

Mourning garments were hastily ordered for her ladies, and while these were being prepared they put on their 'most sad and simplest' clothes. Elizabeth's body would, immediately after death, have been disembowelled; prepared with spices, balm and rosewater; tight wrapped in waxed cloth. '60 ells of Holland cloth . . . likewise gums, balms, spices, sweet wine, and wax, with which being cered, the king's plumber closed her in lead', before the body was placed in a wooden chest, covered in black and white velvet with a cross of white damask. On the Sunday night the body was ready for removal to the chapel. The queen's sister Lady Katherine Courtenay acted as chief mourner at the requiem mass, a ritual repeated daily as long as the body lay in the Tower.

It was Wednesday 22 February when the coffin was placed on a bier covered in black velvet and drawn by six horses, themselves decked in black. The cushions of black velvet and blue cloth of gold must have helped secure the coffin in place, and helped the gentleman ushers who knelt, braced against the horses' motion, at either end of the moving construction. Above the coffin was an effigy of the queen, clothed in 'the very Robes of Estate', with her hair about her shoulders and her sceptre in her right hand. The funeral effigy of a royal personage symbolised the dual nature of a king or queen; the immortal office and the mortal body.

The banners at the corners of the bier were painted on a white background, to show this was the funeral of a woman who died in childbed, while behind the bier came the ladies of honour, each mounted on a palfrey; the chariots bearing other senior ladies; a throng of servants and citizens of London. In front of the bier went the choirs, and the English and foreign male dignitaries. Companies of foreign merchants – French, Spanish, Venetian – bearing their country's arms stood among the crafts guilds and fellowships of London who held thousands of torches along the way. Bells rang, choirs sang, and incense scented the cold air from each parish church as the body passed by. From the Tower to Temple Bar; to Charing Cross and then on to Westminster; the same route that had been taken for Elizabeth's coronation.

In the churchyard of St Margaret's, where the peers 'took their mantles', the body was once again censed and then borne into the Abbey shoulder high. There it rested while, after the service, the Dirige, conducted by the abbot and nine bishops, Lady Katherine, escorted by her nephew the Marquess of Dorset and by the Earl of Derby, led the lords and the ladies to a supper of fish in the Queen's Great Chamber. Watched that night by her ladies and men of all ranks, lit by hundreds more heavy tapers, Elizabeth's corpse waited for the next day. Body and soul could not be left unprotected through the dark night hours: each one of those tapers might serve to drive a demon away.

The long list of services offered for the dead woman reflects the importance of the church rites in the daily life of the fifteenth century. Lauds were said at six the next morning, followed by Our Lady's Mass at seven; the Mass of the Trinity; and then the Requiem Mass. As the ceremony came towards its close the mourners, in order of precedence, laid lengths of rich fabric across the effigy. The blue and green, the bright strands of metal in the weave, must have stood out against the funereal scene. After the sermon the ladies left, for men to do the real physical work of burial. The queen's chamberlain and ushers broke their staves of office and cast them into the grave with ritual tears, in token that their service to Elizabeth of York was ended. Perhaps the emotion was real – Elizabeth had been a gentle mistress, and loyal to those who served her and family.

Following the funeral alms were given to 'bed-rid folks, lazars, blind folks'; to churches, to hospitals, to charitable foundations. And, with more than 9000 yards of black cloth coming out of the Great Wardrobe, King Henry had handed out 'the greatest livery of black gowns that ever was seen in our day'. Her funeral had cost some £3000; twice that of her father, and five times that of her eldest son. Henry must indeed have loved Elizabeth, even though in the political sphere his concern had been to avoid any suggestion that it was from her bloodline that he derived his legitimacy.

The funeral had been – as was customary for a female corpse – a predominantly female ceremony; partly because the one mourned was a woman; partly because concern for the dead was always firstly a female duty. But Elizabeth's mother-in-law, Lady Margaret Beaufort, was absent. Instead, she occupied herself in laying down a set of ordinances for royal mourning to be used for future deaths – costume and comportment, prescribed precisely, 'apparel for princesses and great estates', moving down the scale in their order. A queen was to wear a surcoat with a train before and behind; the king's mother (though Margaret was technically only a countess) was 'to wear in every thing like to the queen'. It was often said that Margaret's concern for rank and dominance came between her and Elizabeth; if so, they were not the only mother-in-law and daughter-in-law in this story to have had problems.

Elizabeth Woodville – the beautiful widow who had captured the heart of King Edward IV – had been bitterly resented by Edward's mother Cecily Neville. Cecily had been the matriarch of the Yorkist clan, mother also to Richard III; just as Margaret Beaufort was a leader of the Lancastrians – another mother of kings who could never quite forget that Fortune had snatched her own queen's crown away. Cecily's daughter Margaret, too, was living in Burgundy, but as the sister of two Yorkist monarchs she never lost her urge to take a hand in the affairs of England.

Poor Anne Neville, Richard III's wife, had been too shadowy a figure to have quarrelled with her mother-in-law. But the final woman in this story had quarrelled with half the world – Marguerite of Anjou, Henry VI's wife, the Lancastrian queen under whose determined rule the 'Wars of the Roses', the Cousins' War, had first got under way.

The events that caused the Cousins' War, and finally brought into being the Tudor dynasty, were above all a family saga – 'a drama in a princely house'. And the circle of women behind the conflicts and resolutions of the late fifteenth century were locked into a web of loyalty and betrayal as intimate and emotional as that of any other domestic drama, albeit that in this a kingdom was at stake.

The business of their lives was power; their sons and husbands the currency; the stark events of these times worthy of Greek tragedy. Cecily Neville had to come to terms with the fact that her son Edward IV had ordered the execution of his brother George, Duke of Clarence, and the suspicion that her other son Richard III had murdered his nephews. Elizabeth Woodville is supposed to have sent her daughters to make merry at Richard III's court while knowing that he had murdered her sons, those same Princes in the Tower. Elizabeth of York, as the decisive battle of Bosworth unfolded, could only await the results of what would prove a fight to the death between the man some say she had incestuously loved – her uncle Richard III – and the man she would in the end marry, Henry VII.

The second half of the fifteenth century is alive with female energy, yet the lives of the last Plantagenet women remain relatively unexplored. The events of this turbulent age are usually described in terms of men, under a patriarchal assumption as easy as that which saw Margaret Beaufort give up her own blood right to the throne in favour of her son Henry; or passed the heiress Anne Neville from one royal family to the other as though she were as insentient an object as any other piece of property.

Of the seven women who form the backbone of this book, the majority have already been the subject of at least one biographical study. The aim of this work, however, is to interweave these women's individual stories, to trace the connections between them – connections which sometimes ran counter to the allegiances established by their men – and to demonstrate the way the patterns of their lives often echoed each other. It tries to understand their daily reality: to see what these women saw and heard, read, smelt, even tasted. The bruised feel of velvet under the fingertip, or the silken muzzle of a hunting dog. The discomfort of furred ceremonial robes on a scorching day: a girl's ability to lose herself in reading a romantic story.

The stamping feet of the 'maid that came out of Spain' and danced before Elizabeth of York, and the roughened hands of Mariona, the laundrywoman listed in Marguerite of Anjou's accounts who kept the queen's personal linen clean. The tales of Guinevere and Lancelot, popularised in these very years by a man who knew these women; along with the ideal of the virginal saints whose lives they studied so devotedly. To ignore these things and to focus too exclusively on the wild roller coaster of military and political events results in a distorted picture, stripped of the context of daily problems and pleasures.

The attempt to tell the story of these years through women is beset with difficulties, not least the patchy nature of the source material. To insist that the women were equal players with the men, on the same stage, is to run the risk of claiming more than the known facts can support. The profound difference between their ideas and those of the modern world must first be acknowledged; but so too, conversely, must recognisable emotions – Elizabeth of York's frantic desire to find a place in the world, Margaret Beaufort's obsessive love for her son. It is the only way we can imagine how it felt to be flung abruptly to the top of Fortune's wheel and then back down again. And though the tactics of the battlefield are not the subject of this book, each one meant gain or loss for wives, daughters and mothers whose destiny would be decided, and perhaps unthinkably altered, in an arena they were not allowed even to enter.

The Tudor wives of only a few decades later have a much higher profile, and yet the stories of these earlier figures are even more dramatic. These women should be a legend, a byword. In a time not only of terror but of opportunity, the actions of the women forged in this furnace would ultimately prove to matter as much as the battlefields on which cousin fought cousin.[2] Their alliances and ambitions helped get a new world under way. They were the mothers and midwives if not actually of modern England, then certainly of the Tudor dynasty.

PART ONE

1445–1461

ONE

Fatal Marriage

O peers of England, shameful is this league,
Fatal this marriage, cancelling your fame
Henry VI Part 2, 1.1

It was no way for a queen to enter her new country, unceremoniously carried ashore as though she were a piece of baggage – least of all a queen who planned to make her mark. The *Cock John*, the ship that brought Marguerite of Anjou across the Channel, had been blown off course and so battered by storms as to have lost both its masts. She arrived, as her new husband Henry VI put it in a letter, 'sick of ye labour and indisposition of ye sea'. Small wonder that the Marquess of Suffolk, the English peer sent to escort her, had to carry the seasick fifteen-year-old ashore.[1] The people of Portchester in Hampshire, trying gallantly to provide a royal welcome, had heaped carpets on the beach where the chilly April waves clawed and rattled at the pebbles, but Marguerite's first shaky steps on English soil took her no further than a nearby cottage, where she fainted. From there she was carried to a local convent to be cared for.

This would be the woman whom Shakespeare, in *Henry VI Part 3*, famously dubbed the 'she-wolf' of France, her 'tiger's heart wrapped in a woman's hide'. The Italian-born chronicler

Polydore Vergil,[2] by contrast, would look back on her as 'imbued with a high courage above the nature of her sex . . . a woman of sufficient forecast, very desirous of renown, full of policy, counsel, comely behaviour, and all manly qualities'. But then Vergil was writing for the Tudor monarch Henry VII, sprung of Lancastrian stock, and he would naturally wish to praise the wife of the last Lancastrian king, the woman who had fought so hard for the Lancastrian cause. Few queens of England have so divided opinion; few have suffered more from the propaganda of their enemies.

Marguerite of Anjou was niece by marriage to the French king Charles VII, her own father, René, having been described as a man of many crowns but no kingdoms. He claimed the thrones of Naples, Sicily, Jerusalem and Hungary as well as the duchy of Anjou; titles so empty, however, that early in the 1440s he had settled in France, his brother-in-law's territory. At the beginning of 1444 the English suggested a truce in the seemingly endless conflict between France and England known as the Hundred Years War; the arrangement would be cemented by a French bride for England's young king, Henry VI. Unwilling to commit his own daughters, Charles had proffered Marguerite. Many royal and aristocratic marriages were made to seal a peace deal with an enemy, the youthful bride a passive potential victim. But in this case, the dealmaking was particularly edgy.

In the hope of ending the long hostilities the mild-mannered Henry VI – so unfitting a son, many thought, to Henry V, the hero of Agincourt – had not only agreed to take his bride virtually without dowry but to cede the territories of Anjou and Maine, which the English had long occupied. This concession would be deeply unpopular among his subjects. Nor did the thunder and lightning that had greeted Marguerite's arrival augur well to contemporary observers.

The new queen had been ill since setting out from Paris several weeks before. She progressed slowly towards the French coast, distributing Lenten alms and making propitiatory offerings at each church where she heard mass, dining with dignitaries and taking leave of her relations one by one along the way. But gradually, in the days after her arrival England, she recovered her health in a series of convents, amid the sounds and scents of Church ritual with all their reassuring familiarity. On 10 April 1445 at Southampton, one 'Master Francisco, the Queen's physician' was paid 69s 2d 'for divers aromatic confections, particularly and specially purchased by him, and privately made into medicine for the preservation of the health of the said lady'.

If Suffolk's first concern had been to find medical attention for Marguerite, his second was to summon a London dressmaker to attend her before the English nobility caught sight of her shabby clothes: 'to fetch Margaret Chamberlayne, tyre maker, to be conducted into the presence of our lady, the Queen . . . and for going and returning [from London to Southampton], the said Margaret Chamberlaune was paid there by gift of the Queen, on the 15th of April, 20s.' Among the various complaints the English were preparing to make of their new queen, one would be her poverty.

Before Marguerite's party set out towards the capital there was time for something a little more courtly, if one Italian contemporary, writing to the Duchess of Milan three years later, is to be believed. An Englishman had told him that when the queen landed in England the king had secretly taken her a letter, having first dressed himself as a squire: 'While the queen read the letter the king took stock of her,[3] saying that a woman may be seen very well when she reads a letter, and the queen never found out it was the king because she was so engrossed in reading the letter, and she never looked at the king in his squire's dress, who remained on his knees all the time.' It was the same trick that Henry VIII would play on Anne of Cleves almost a century later – a game from the continental tradition of chivalry.[4]

Henry VI, if the Milanese correspondent is to be believed, saw 'a most handsome woman, though somewhat dark' – and not, the Milanese tactfully assured his duchess, 'so beautiful as your Serenity'. At the French court Marguerite had already acquitted herself well enough to win an admirer in the courtly tradition, Pierre de Brezé, to carry her colours at the joust; and to allow the Burgundian chronicler Barante to write that she 'was already renowned in France for her beauty and wit and her lofty spirit of courage'. The beauty conventionally attributed to queens features in the scene where Shakespeare's Marguerite first meets Henry VI: it was the lofty spirit that, in the years ahead, was to prove the difficulty. Vergil too wrote that Marguerite exceeded others of her time 'as well in beauty as wisdom'; and though it is not easy to guess real looks from the conventions of medieval portraiture, it is hard not to read determination and self-will in the swelling brow and prominent nose that are evident in images of Marguerite of Anjou – in particular the medallion by Pietro di Milano.

The royal couple met officially five days after Marguerite had landed, and had their marriage formalised just over a week later in Titchfield Abbey. The first meeting failed to reveal either the dangerous milkiness in the man, or the capacity for violence in the young woman. But the first of the problems they would face was – as Marguerite moved towards London – spelt out in the very festivities.

Her impoverished father had at least persuaded the clergy of Anjou to provide funds for a white satin wedding dress embroidered with silver and gold marguerites; and to buy violet and crimson cloth of gold and 120 pelts of white fur to edge her robes. As her party approached the city she was met at Blackheath by Henry's uncle, the Duke of Gloucester, with five hundred of his retainers and conducted to his luxurious river-side 'pleasaunce' at Greenwich. Gloucester had in fact opposed the marriage, seeing no advantage in it for England.

Marguerite's entry into London on 28 May, after resting a night at the Tower, was all that it should have been. A coronet of 'gold rich pearls and precious stones' had been placed on the bride's head, nineteen chariots of ladies and their gentle-women accompanied her, and the conduits ran with wine white and red. The livery companies turned out in splendid blue robes with red hoods, while the council had ordered the inspec-tion of roofs along the way, anticipating that eager crowds would climb on to them to see the new queen pass by.

The surviving documentation details a truly royal provision of luxury goods for Marguerite's welcome. A letter from the king to his treasurer orders up 'such things as our right entirely Well-beloved Wife the Queen must necessarily have for the Solemnity of her Coronation'. They included a pectoral of gold embellished with rubies, pearls and diamonds; a safe conduct for two Scotsmen and their sixteen servants, 'with their gold and silver in bars and wallets'; a present of £10 each to five minstrels of the King of Sicily (the nominal title of Marguerite's father) 'who lately came to England to witness the state and grand solemnity on the day of the Queen's coronation'; and 20 marks reward to one William Flour of London, goldsmith, 'because the said Lord the King stayed in the house of the said William on the day that Queen Margaret, his consort, set out from the Tower'.

The ceremonies were 'royally and worthily held', the cost reckoned at an exorbitant £5500. All the same, Marguerite had had to pawn her silver plate at Rouen to pay her sailors' wages; and as details of the marriage deal began to leak out, the English would feel justified in complaining that they had bought 'a queen not worth ten marks'. In the years ahead, they would discover they had a queen who – for better or worse – would try to rewrite the rules, and indeed the whole royal story.

As Marguerite rode into her new capital, the pageantry with which she was greeted spelt out her duty. It was hoped that through her 'grace and high benignity':

> Twixt the realms two, England and France
> Peace shall approach, rest and unite,
> Mars set aside, with all his cruelty . . .

This was a weight of expectation placed on many a foreign royal bride. Earlier in the fifteenth century the Frenchwoman Christine de Pizan had written in *The Treasury (or, Treasure) of the City of Ladies* that women, being by nature 'more gentle and circumspect', could be the best means of pacifying men: 'Queens and princesses have greatly benefitted this world by bringing about peace between enemies, between princes and their barons, or between rebellious subjects and their lords.' After all, the Queen of Heaven, Mary, interceded for sinners. Marguerite would be neither the first nor the last to find herself uncomfortably placed between the needs of her adopted country and that of her birth. The Hundred Years War had been a conflict of extraordinary bitterness. This bitterness Marguerite, by her very presence as a living symbol, was supposed to soothe; but it was a position of terrifying responsibility.

Her kinsman the Duke of Orléans wrote that Marguerite seemed as if 'formed by Heaven to supply her royal husband the qualities which he required in order to become a great king'. But the English expectations of a queen were not those of a Frenchman, necessarily. Marguerite's mother, Isabelle of Lorraine, had run the family affairs while René of Anjou spent long years away on campaign or in captivity. Her grandmother, Yolande of Aragon, in whose care she spent many of her formative years, had acted as regent for her eldest son, Marguerite's uncle; and she had been one of the chief promoters of Joan of Arc, who had helped sweep the French Dauphin to victory against the English. Those English, by contrast, expected their queens to take a more passive role. Uncomfortable memories still lingered of Edward II's wife Isabella, little more than a century before: the 'she-wolf of France', as Marguerite too would be dubbed, who was accused of having murdered her husband to take power with her lover. Had Marguerite's new husband been a strong king, the memories might never have surfaced – but Henry showed neither inclination nor ability for the role he was called on to play.

Henry VI had succeeded while in his cradle, and had grown up a titular king under the influence of his older male relatives. Perhaps that had taught him to equate kingship with passivity. For although Henry had now reached adulthood he still, at twenty-three, showed no aptitude for the reins of government. There has always been debate over what, if anything, was actually wrong with Henry. Some contemporaries describe him as both personable and scholarly; others suggest he may have been simple-minded, or had inherited a streak of insanity. But what is certain is that he was notably pious, notably prudish – described by a papal envoy as more like a monk than a king – and seemed reluctant to take any kind of decision or lead. He was the last man on earth, in other words, to rule what was already a turbulent country. At the end of *Henry IV Part 2* Shakespeare vividly dramatises the moment at which the new Henry V, this Henry's father, moves from irresponsible princedom to the harsh realities of kingship. There was, however, no sign of Henry VI reaching a similar maturity. It was a situation which left Marguerite herself to confront the challenges of monarchy.

It is difficult to conjure up a picture of Marguerite or her husband in the first few years of their marriage. Anything written about them later is coloured by hindsight, and the early days of Marguerite's career tend to be lost in the urgent clamour of events just ahead. But there is no reason to doubt that her expectation was that of a normal queenship, albeit more active than the English were accustomed to see. Though her husband's exchequer may have been depleted, though English manners might not compare to those across the Channel, her life must at first have been one of pleasant indulgence.

Christine de Pizan gives a vivid picture of life for a lady at the top of the social tree. 'The princess or great lady awaking in the morning from sleep finds herself lying in her bed between soft, smooth sheets, surrounded by rich luxury, with every possible bodily comfort, and ladies and maids-in-waiting at hand to run to her if she sighs ever so slightly, ready on bended knee to provide service or obey orders at her word.' The long list of estates granted to Marguerite as part of her dower entitlement forms an evocative litany:

> To be had, held and kept of the said Consort of Henry, all the appointed Castles, Honours, Towns, Domains, Manors, Wapentaches, Bales, county estates, sites of France, carriages, landed farms, renewed yearly, the lands, houses, possessions and other things promised, with all their members and dependencies, together with the lands of the Military, Ecclesiastic advocacies, Abbotcies, Priories, Deaneries, Colleges, Capellaries, singing academies, Hospitals, and of other religious houses, by wards, marriages, reliefs, food, iron, merchandize, liberties,

free customs, franchise, royalties, fees of honour . . . forests, chaises, parks, woods, meadows, fields, pastures, warrens, vivaries, ponds, fish waters, mills, mulberry trees, fig trees . . .

It is the same genial picture of a queen's life that can be seen in a tapestry that may have been commissioned for Marguerite's wedding – there are Ms woven into the horses' bridles, and marguerites, her personal symbol, are sported by the ladies. It depicts a hunting scene bedecked with flowers and foliage, the ladies in their furred gowns, hawk on wrist, wearing the characteristic headdress of the time, a roll of jewelled and decorated fabric peaking down over the brow and rising behind the head. Hunting, with 'boating on the river', dancing and 'meandering' in the garden were all recreations allowed by Christine de Pizan in a day otherwise devoted to the tasks of governance (if relevant), religious duties and charity. Visiting the poor and sick, 'touching them and gently comforting them', as she wrote, sounds much like the work of modern royalty. 'For the poor feel especially comforted and prefer the kind word, the visit, and the attention of the great and powerful personage over anything else.' Letters show Marguerite asking the Archbishop of Canterbury to treat 'a poor widow' with 'tenderness and favour'; and seeking alms for two other 'poor creatures and of virtuous conversation'.

But Marguerite had been brought up to believe that queen-ship went beyond simple Christian charity.[5] Not only did she have the example of her mother and grandmother, but her father was one of the century's leading exponents of the chiv-alric tradition, obsessed with that great fantasy of the age, the Arthurian legends. Indeed, when Thomas Malory wrote his English version of the tales, the *Morte d'Arthur*, completed in 1470, his portrayal of Queen Guinevere may have been influ-enced by Marguerite. It may have been on the occasion of

Marguerite's betrothal that René organised a tournament with knights dressed up as Round Table heroes and a wooden castle named after Sir Lancelot's Joyeuse Garde. A bound volume of Arthurian romances was presented to the bride.

René was the author not only of a widely translated book on the perfect management of the tournament, but also of the achingly romantic *Livre de Coeur de L'Amour Epris*. He may have illustrated it, too; and if so, it has been suggested that his figure of Hope – who repeatedly saves the hero – may have been modelled on Marguerite. Queens in the Arthurian and other legends of chivalry were not only active but sometimes ambiguous creatures. Ceremonious consorts and arbiters of behaviour, they were also capable of dramatic and sometimes destructive action: it was Guinevere who brought down Camelot.

The two visions of queenship came together in the Shrewsbury – or Talbot – Book, a wedding present to Marguerite from John Talbot, Earl of Shrewsbury. Although one of England's most renowned military commanders, he would not play much part in the political tussles ahead. On the illuminated title page, Henry and Marguerite are seated crowned and hand in hand, her purple mantle fastened with bands of gold and jewels, the blue background painted with gold stars. At her feet kneels Talbot, presenting his book which she graciously accepts, the faintest hint of a smile lurking under her red-gold hair. All around are exquisite depictions of the daisy, her symbol. The image is at once benign and stately, an idealised picture of monarchy – for all that the facing page, tracing Henry VI's genealogical claim to be king of France as well as of England, hints at political controversy. An anthology of Arthurian and other romances, poems and manuals of chivalry, the book also includes Christine de Pizan's treatise on the art of warfare and one on the art of government – a guide not only to conducting one's emotional life but also to running a country.

Henry had had his palaces refurbished for his bride – the queen's apartments must have fallen out of use in his minority. Marguerite employed a large household and paid them handsomely, exploiting all the financial opportunities open to a queen to enable her to do so. Regulations for a queen's household drawn up in the year of her arrival listed sixty-six positions, including a countess as senior lady with her own staff, a chamberlain, three chaplains, three carvers, a secretary, a personal gardener, pages of the beds and of the bakery, two launderers and various squires. Less than ten years later, the council had to suggest that the size of the queen's household should be cut *down* to 120. She had, however, brought no relations and few French attendants with her, something which had been a problem with previous consorts. But what at first looked like a blessing meant that she would attach herself to new English advisers, ardently and unwisely.

On the journey from France Marguerite had learned to trust her escort Suffolk – the pre-eminent noble whom the Burgundian chronicler Georges Chastellain called England's 'second king'. She never saw any reason to change her mind – or to hide her feelings. Suffolk for his part, perhaps from a mixture of genuine admiration and intelligent politics, flattered and encouraged the young queen, even writing courtly verses playing on her name, the marguerite or daisy:

> For wit thee well, it is a paradise
> To see this flower when it begins to spread
> With colours fresh enewed, white and red.

Although by the standards of courtly love poetry these phrases were mere convention, there were inevitably those who suspected something more than a platonic relationship between the girl in her teens and the man in his late forties – and suggested that a betrayal of England's king might be allied to betrayal of England as a country. More than a century later, the idea of a romantic liaison between Marguerite and Suffolk was still sufficiently alive that Shakespeare has Suffolk, on their first meeting in France, falling for her beauty before he learns her identity. But even Shakespeare's Suffolk mixes self-interest with sexual attraction, hoping to rule the king through Marguerite – and in reality, the queen had become close not only to the duke but also to his wife (born Alice Chaucer, granddaughter of the poet), which surely argues against an affair.

Suffolk had not been the only noble adviser to approve the French marriage. It had also had the endorsement of Cardinal Beaufort, the king's great-uncle and one of the men who had governed the country during his minority, who shared Suffolk's personal regard for Marguerite. In addition she enjoyed the support of the cardinal's Beaufort relatives (the Somerset line that were Margaret Beaufort's family). But against the marriage had been the king's uncle Humfrey, Duke of Gloucester; and though Gloucester was now ageing and increasingly marginalised, his was in many ways the voice of the Francophobe English people.

All too soon, within weeks of Marguerite's arrival and coronation, the matter of England's ceding Maine and Anjou came to a head. It was said that Henry had promised to give back the territories 'at the request of his wife', as one angry reporter, Dr Thomas Gascoigne, put it: '. . . that aforesaid queen of ours begged the King of England that [the lands] so be given to her father at the urging of William de la Pole, duke of Suffolk, and his wife who earlier had promised to request it.' And Gascoigne's voice was but one among many.

In a sense he was right. In a letter to her uncle the king of France in late 1445 Marguerite promised: 'And as to the deliverance which you desire to have of the Comté of Maine, and other matters contained in your said letters, we understand that my said lord has written to you at considerable length about this: and yet herein we will do for your pleasure the best that we can do . . .' A letter of Henry's own volunteers to give up territory in Maine, at least partly because of 'our dear and well-beloved companion the queen, who has requested us to do this many times'. Reconciliation, and encouragement to implement the peace process, was what a queen was supposed to work at. Even the pageants had said so.

Popular blame for the loss of these lands fell largely on the head of Suffolk, the official negotiator of the marriage deal; but the situation did nothing for Marguerite's popularity. Neither did the enmity of the old Duke of Gloucester. As Polydore Vergil wrote: 'This woman, when she perceived the king her husband to do nothing of his own head but to rule wholly by the Duke of Gloucester's advice . . . determined to take upon herself that charge and, little by little, deprive the duke of that great authority which he had lest she also might be reported to have little wit who would suffer her husband, now of mature years, to be under another man's government . . .' And Christine de Pizan had urged that a wife's task should always be to preserve 'the honour of her husband'. But it seems also likely that Marguerite had no conception of faction as an avoidable evil, or of the idea that the monarchy in England was supposed to be above such disputes. In the French court faction was the modus operandi, and it was normal for the crown to align itself with one or another party. The difficult relationship between England and France underpinned the first years of Marguerite of Anjou's queenship. But it also dominated the lives of the women from the English families on either side of the political divide.

TWO

The Red Rose and the White

The red rose and the white are on his face,
The fatal colours of our striving houses
Henry VI Part 3, 2.5

Contemporary commentators never spoke of the 'Wars of the Roses'.[6] The name itself is a much later invention, variously credited to the historian David Hume in the eighteenth century and the novelist Sir Walter Scott in the nineteenth. The idea of the two roses was in currency not long after the event, and the white rose was indeed a popular symbol for the house of York, one party in the conflict, but the red rose was never widely identified with their opponents, the house of Lancaster, until the moment when Henry VII, poised to take over the country in 1485, sought an appropriate and appealing symbol – soon merged, in the first days of his kingship and after his marriage to Elizabeth of York, into the red and white unifying 'Tudor rose'.

In some ways, moreover, the attractive iconography of the two roses does history a disservice, implying a neat, two-party, York/Lancaster divide. In reality the in-fighting which tore the ruling class of England apart for more than three decades was never just a dispute between two families, as clearly separate as the Montagues and the Capulets. The 'Wars of the Roses' are more accurately called the 'Cousins' War', since all the protagonists were bound together by an infinite number of ties. And these conflicts should really be seen in terms of politics – secret alliances, queasy coalitions, public spin and private qualms. It was a world in which positions were constantly shifted and alliances changed from day to day.

In 1445, the last undisputed king of England had died almost seventy years before. He had been the powerful and prolific Edward III, latest in the long line of Plantagenet kings who had ruled England since the Norman Conquest. But in 1377 Edward was succeeded by his grandson (the son of his dead eldest son), the ten-year-old Richard II. Richard was deposed in 1399 by his cousin, Shakespeare's Bolingbroke, who became Henry IV and was succeeded by his son Henry V, who in turn was succeeded by his son Henry VI. So by 1445 this Lancastrian line had successfully held the throne for almost half a century.

There had, however, been an alternative line of succession in the shape of the Yorkists – descended, like the Lancastrians, from Edward III's younger sons. The white rose Yorkists had arguably a better claim than the Lancastrians, depending on the attitude taken to a woman's ability to transmit rights to the throne: while the Lancastrian progenitor, John of Gaunt, had been only Edward's third son, the Yorkists were descended in the female line from his second son Lionel, as well as in the male line from his fourth son, Edmund. And there was no denying the fact that, because Henry V had died so early and Henry VI had therefore succeeded as a nine-month-old baby, men had begun to cast their eyes around and think of their opportunities. There was no denying, either, that even now Henry seemed both reluctant and unfitted to assume his destined role. If Henry – now mature, now married – were indeed to prove himself a strong king, the Lancastrian line should hold the throne indefinitely. If not, however, there was that other possibility: the more so since the present Duke of York, while still loyal to the crown, was an able and active man (an ally of Humfrey Duke of Gloucester) and married to a woman – Cecily Neville – as forceful as himself.

In 1445, the year Marguerite of Anjou arrived in England, neither Anne Neville nor Margaret of Burgundy had yet been born, let alone Elizabeth of York. Elizabeth Woodville – about eight years old, though no one had bothered to record her precise date of birth – was growing up in rural obscurity. Indeed, out of our seven protagonists only Cecily Neville was a woman of full maturity. Margaret Beaufort was just a toddler, though her bloodline meant she was already a significant figure, a prize for whom others would compete. While Cecily would become the matriarch of the ruling house of York, Margaret's bloodline was an important carrier of the Lancastrian claim. In fact, at this moment she (or any son she might bear) might be considered heir presumptive to the throne until children came to her kinsman Henry VI.

Margaret Beaufort had been born in 1443 at Bletsoe in Bedfordshire. Her mother was a comparatively obscure widow who already had children by her first husband, Sir Oliver St John. Margaret's father, however, was the Earl (later Duke) of Somerset, and from him she inherited a debatable but intriguing relationship to the throne.

Her grandfather, the first Earl of Somerset, had been one of John of Gaunt's sons by his mistress Katherine Swynford. John's nephew, Richard II, had confirmed by binding statute that all the children of the pair were rendered legitimate by their subsequent marriage, and able to inherit dignities and estates 'as fully, freely, and lawfully as if you were born in lawful wedlock'. When John of Gaunt's eldest son (by Blanche of Lancaster) seized Richard's throne, and had himself declared Henry IV, this first Earl of Somerset became half-brother to the king. But when in 1407 Somerset requested a clarification of the position laid down in that earlier legitimation, the resultant Letters Patent confirmed his entitlement to estates and noble rank with one very crucial proviso – '*excepta dignitate regali*', excepting the dignities of the crown.

Less controversially, Margaret was also heiress to great lands. But by the time of her birth, the anomalies of her family's position – royal, but yet possibly excluded from ruling – had been compounded by her father's chequered career.

Somerset had been captured as a young man in the wars with France, and held captive there for seventeen years. When he returned to England only a few years before Margaret's birth, he set about trying to assume the position to which he felt his blood entitled him – but, as the author of the Crowland Abbey chronicles put it, 'his horn was exalted too greatly on high'.[7] In 1443 his position – his closeness in blood to a king short of relatives – had led to his appointment as commander of England's army in fresh hostilities against the French. But the campaign was a disaster and Somerset was summoned home in disgrace, his daughter having been born while he was away. Only a few months later, in May 1444, he died, the Crowland chronicler asserting ('it is generally said') that he had committed suicide – a heinous sin in the fifteenth century. The rumours surrounding his death only added to the dubiousness of the baby Margaret's position, and perhaps later increased her well-documented insecurities.

Somerset's brother Edmund, who succeeded to the title, was able to ensure that the Beaufort family retained their influence – not least because of the friendship he would strike up with the new queen. It was this friendship which would bring him into conflict with the Duke of York, and with York's wife Cecily.

Born in 1415 to the powerful Ralph Neville, Earl of Westmorland, and known as the beautiful 'Rose of Raby' after the family stronghold, Cecily was the daughter of his second marriage, to Joan Beaufort – of the same notably Lancastrian family as Margaret Beaufort. But the political divisions of later years had not yet taken shape and indeed, though Cecily would become the Yorkist matriarch, her father had supported the Lancastrian usurpation of Richard II by John of Gaunt's son, Henry IV.

Joan Beaufort was John of Gaunt's daughter by Katherine Swynford – in later years Cecily, John of Gaunt's granddaughter, might have found it galling that Margaret Beaufort could be regarded as inheriting John of Gaunt's Lancastrian claim when she was only his great-granddaughter. The vital difference was that Margaret's claim had come through her father and her father's father – through the male line.[8]

By the time Cecily was born in May 1415, the Neville family was enormous. Joan Beaufort had two daughters from her first marriage, and when she married Ralph he had a large family already. They went on to produce ten more surviving children. By contrast Cecily's husband, Richard of York, had just one sister. His marriage would bring him an almost unparalleled number of in-laws, but in the fifteenth century in-laws figured as potentially trustworthy allies and were more a blessing than a curse. Certainly the Nevilles would – in many ways, and for many years – do Richard proud.

Richard had been born in 1411, grandson to Edward III's fourth son, Edmund. In 1415 his father (another Richard) was executed for his involvement in a plot against Henry V. The child eventually became Ralph Neville's ward. By that time the boy had inherited the dukedom of York from a childless uncle; and later another childless uncle died, this time on his mother's side, leaving Richard heir to the great Welsh and Irish lands of the Mortimer family.

Whether or not there were any thought that he might be king-in-waiting, York was an undoubted catch and it was inevitable that Ralph Neville would hope to keep this rich matrimonial prize within his own family. York's betrothal to Cecily took place just a year after he came into the Nevilles' care. The following year Ralph himself died, and York's wardship passed into the hands of Cecily's mother, Joan. Full, consummated marriage would have been legal when Cecily was twelve, in 1427, and had certainly taken place by 1429 when permission was received from the papacy for them jointly to choose a confessor.[9]

In medieval terms, Cecily was lucky. She would have known Richard well and he was only four years her elder. And since Richard, like Joan, had moved into the glittering world of the court, it seems probable that Cecily would have done so, too – unless separations are to be deduced from the fact that their first child was not born for several years, though after that they came with notable frequency.

Cecily gave birth to that first child – a daughter, Anne – in 1439 and a first son, Henry, in February 1441 at Hatfield: then the property of the Bishop of Ely, but frequently available to distingushed visitors or tenants. But Henry did not live long; just as well, perhaps, that Cecily had the distraction of an imminent move to France, where York had been appointed governor of the English territories, still haunted by the spectre of Joan of Arc, the holy Maid, burnt there only a decade before. In Rouen, the capital of English Normandy, the couple set up home in such state that an officer of the household had to be appointed to overlook Cecily's expenditure,[10] which included lavishly jewelled dresses and even a cushioned privy. Their second son, the future Edward IV, was born there in April 1442; another son, Edmund, in May 1443; and a second daughter, Elizabeth, the following year.

There is no evidence from that time of rumours concerning Edward's paternity. But in the years ahead there would be debate about the precise significance of his date of birth[11] and where Richard of York had been nine months before it; about the hasty and modest ceremony at which he was christened; and about his adult appearance and physique, which were singularly different from Richard's. It is true that Edward was christened in a private chapel in Rouen Castle, while his younger brother Edmund was christened in the far more public arena of Rouen Cathedral – but that may have meant no more than that Edward seemed sickly; all the likelier, of course, if he were premature. It is also true that Edward, the 'Rose of Rouen', was as tall and physically impressive as his grandson, Henry VIII, while Richard of York was dark and probably small. But perhaps Edward simply took after his mother, several of whose other children would be tall too.[12]

York himself showed no sign of querying his son's paternity;[13] while the fact that he and the English government held lengthy negotiations concerning a match between Edward and a daughter of the French king hardly suggests suspicion about his status. This was not, moreover, the first time an allegation of bastardy had been levelled at a royal son born abroad – John of Gaunt, born in Ghent, had been called a changeling. In the years ahead Cecily's relationship with her husband would give every sign of being close and strong. And then there is the question of the identity of her supposed lover – an archer called Blaybourne. For a woman as status-conscious as Cecily – the woman who would be called 'proud Cis' – that seems especially unlikely. There are certainly queries as to how the story spread. The Italian Dominic Mancini,[14] visiting England years later at a time when it had once again become a matter of hot debate, said that Cecily herself started the rumour when angered by Edward. A continental chronicler has it relayed by

Cecily's son-in-law Charles of Burgundy.[15] But sheer political expedience apart, time and time again it will be seen how slurs could be cast on women (four out of the seven central to this book) through claims of sexual immorality.

Certainly Cecily was still queening it in Rouen as Duchess of York when, in the spring of 1445, the young Marguerite of Anjou passed through the city on her way to England and marriage with Henry VI. It may have been here that the thirty-year-old woman and the fifteen-year-old girl struck up a measure of friendship that would survive their husbands' future differences – one example among many of women's alliances across the York/Lancaster divide. But at this point Marguerite's role was far the grander, even if beset with difficulty.

THREE

A Woman's Fear

If it be fond, call it a woman's fear;
Which fear, if better reasons can supplant,
I will subscribe, and say I wronged the duke.
Henry VI Part 2, 3.1

When Marguerite arrived in England, her recent acquaintance Cecily was not far behind her. In that autumn of 1445, her husband's posting in France came to an end; Richard and Cecily returned home and settled down. In May 1446 another daughter, Margaret (the future Margaret of Burgundy), was born to them, probably at Fotheringhay in Northamptonshire, while the two eldest boys were likely to have been given their own establishment, at Ludlow – a normal practice among the aristocracy. But the couple were now embittered and less wealthy, since the English government had never properly covered their expenses in Normandy.

York had hoped to have been appointed for another spell of office but was baulked, not least by Beaufort agency – the cardinal and his nephew Somerset. It was this, one chronicler records, that first sparked the feud between York and the Beauforts, despite the fact that the latter were Cecily's mother's family. The Burgundian chronicler Jean de Waurin[16] says also that Somerset 'was well-liked by the Queen. . . . She worked on King Henry, on the advice and support of Somerset and other lords and barons of his following, so that the Duke of York was recalled to England. There he was totally stripped of his authority. . . .' York now had a long list of grievances, dating back a decade to the time when a sixteen-year-old Henry VI had begun his own rule without giving York any position of great responsibility.

If York belonged to the 'hawks' among the country's nobility, so too did the king's uncle, Humfrey of Gloucester. By the autumn of 1446 King Charles was demanding the return of ever more English holdings in France, and Henry VI, under Marguerite's influence, was inclined to grant it. But Humfrey, who would be a powerful opponent of this policy, would have to be got out of the way. In February 1447 – under, it was said, the aegis of Marguerite, Suffolk and the Beaufort faction – Gloucester was summoned to a parliament at Bury St Edmunds, only to find himself arrested by the queen's steward and accused of having spread the *canard* that Suffolk was Marguerite's lover. He was allowed to retire to his lodgings while the king debated his fate but there, twelve days later, he died. The cause of his death has never been established and, though it may well have been natural, inevitably rumours of murder crept in – rumours, even, that Duke Humfrey, like Edward II before him, had been killed by being 'thrust into the bowel with an hot burning spit'.

Gloucester had been King Henry's nearest male relative and therefore, despite his age, heir. His death promoted York to that prominent, tantalising position. The following month Cardinal Beaufort died too. The way was opening up for younger men – and women. Marguerite did not miss her opportunity and over the next few years could be seen extending her influence through her new English homeland, often in a specifically female way.

A letter from Margery Paston, of the Norfolk family whose communications tell us much about the events of these times, tells of how when the queen was at Norwich she sent for one Elizabeth Clere, 'and when she came into the Queen's presence, the Queen made right much of her, and desired her to have a husband'. Marguerite the matchmaker was also active for one Thomas Burneby, 'sewer for our mouth [food taster]', telling the object of his attention that Burneby loved her 'for the womanly and virtuous governance that ye be renowned of'. To the father of another reluctant bride, sought by a yeoman of the crown, she wrote that, since his daughter was in his 'rule and governance', he should give his 'good consent, benevolence and friendship to induce and excite your daughter to accept my said lord's servant and ours, to her husband'. Other letters of hers request that her shoemaker might be spared jury service 'at such times as we shall have need of his craft, and send for him'; that the game in a park where she intended to hunt 'be spared, kept and cherished for the same intent, without suffering any other person there to hunt'. For a queen to exercise patronage and protection – to be a 'good lady' to her dependants – was wholly acceptable. But Marguerite was still failing in her more pressing royal duty.

In contrast to that of the prolific Yorks, the royal marriage, despite the queen's visits to Thomas à Becket's shrine at Canterbury, was bedevilled by the lack of children. A prayer roll of Marguerite's, unusually dedicated to the Virgin Mary rather than to the Saviour, shows her kneeling hopefully at the Virgin's feet, probably praying for a pregnancy. One writer had expressed, on Marguerite's arrival in England, the Psalmist's hope that 'Thy wife shall be as the fruitful vine upon the walls of thy house'; and the perceived link between a fertile monarchy and a fertile land only added to the weight of responsibility. As early as 1448 a farm labourer was arrested for declaring that

'Our Queen was none able to be Queen of England . . . for because that she beareth no child, and because that we have no prince in this land.'

The problem was probably with Henry, whose sexual drive was not high. The young man who famously left the room when one of his courtiers brought bare-bosomed dancing girls to entertain him may also have been swayed by a spiritual counsellor who preached the virtues of celibacy. But it was usually the woman who was blamed in such circumstances, and so it was now. A child would have aligned the queen more clearly with English interests, and perhaps removed from her the pressure of making herself felt in other, less acceptable, ways. Letters written by the king were now going out accompanied by a matching letter from the queen, and it was clear who was the more forceful personality.

Henry VI had never managed to implement his agreement to return Anjou and Maine to France, and in 1448 a French army had been despatched to take what had been promised. The following year a temporary truce was broken by a misguided piece of militarism on the part of Somerset, now (like his brother before him) England's military commander in France and (like his brother before him) making a woeful showing in the role. The French retaliation swept into Normandy. Rouen – where York and Cecily had ruled – swiftly fell, and soon Henry V's great conquests were but a distant memory. York would have been more than human had he not instanced this as one more example of his rival's inadequacies, while Suffolk (now elevated to a dukedom) did not hesitate to suggest that York aspired to the throne itself. In 1449 York was sent to occupy a new post as governor of Ireland – or, as Jean de Waurin had it, 'was expelled from court and exiled to Ireland'. Cecily went with him and there gave birth to a son, George, in Dublin. The place was known even then as a graveyard of reputations; still, given the timing, they may have been better off there in comfortable exile. English politics were becoming ever more factionalised, and some of the quarrels could be seen swirling around the head of Margaret Beaufort, only six years old though she might have been.

After her father's death wardship of the valuable young heiress, with the right to reap the income of her lands, had been given to Suffolk – although, unusually for the English nobility, the baby was at least left in her mother's care. Her marriage, however, was never going to be left to her mother to arrange. By 1450 she was a pawn of which her guardian had urgent necessity.

Most of the blame for the recent disasters in England's long war with France had been heaped on Suffolk's head (though there was enmity left over and to spare for Marguerite, whose father[17] had actually been one of the commanders in the French attack). Suffolk was arrested in January 1450; immediately, to protect the position of his own family, he arranged the marriage of the six-year-old heiress Margaret to his eight-year-old son John de la Pole. Presumably in this, as in everything else, Suffolk had Queen Marguerite's support.

The marriage of two minors, too young to give consent, and obviously unconsummated, could not be wholly binding: Margaret herself would always disregard it, speaking of her next husband as her first. None the less, it was significant enough to play its part; when, a few weeks later, the Commons accused Suffolk of corruption and incompetence, and of selling out England to the French, prominent among the charges was that he had arranged the marriage 'presuming and pretending her [Margaret] to be next inheritable to the Crown'.

Suffolk was placed in the Tower, but appealed directly to the king. Henry, to the fury of both the Commons and the Lords, absolved him of all capital charges and sentenced him to a comparatively lenient five years' banishment. Shakespeare has Marguerite pleading against even this punishment,[18] with enough passion to cause her husband concern and to have the Earl of Warwick declare it a slander to her royal dignity. But in fact the king had already gone as far as he felt able in resisting the pressure from both peers and parliament, who would rather have seen Suffolk executed. And indeed, when at the end of April the duke finally set sail, having been granted a six-week respite to set his affairs in order, their wish was granted. Suffolk was murdered on his way into exile, his body cast ashore at Dover on 2 May.

It had been proved all too clearly that Henry VI, unlike his immediate forbears, was a king unable to control his own subjects. Similarly, Marguerite had none of the power which, a century before, had enabled Isabella of France to rule with and protect for so long her favourite and lover Mortimer. It has been said that when the news of Suffolk's end reached the queen – broken to her by his widow, Alice Chaucer – she shut herself into her rooms at Westminster to weep for three days. In fact, king and queen were then at Leicester, which casts some doubt on the whole story – but tales of Marguerite's excessive, compromising grief would have been met with angry credence by the ordinary people.

It was said at the time that, because Suffolk had apparently been murdered by sailors out of Kent, the king and queen planned to raze that whole county. Within weeks of his death came the populist rising led by Jack Cade, or 'John Amend-All' as he called himself, a colourful Yorkist sympathiser backed by three thousand mostly Kentish men. The rebels demanded an inquiry into Duke Humfrey's death, and that the crown lands and common freedoms given away on Suffolk's advice should all be restored. They also made particular complaint against the Duchess of Suffolk; indeed, her perceived influence may have been the reason that, the following year, parliament demanded the dismissal of the duchess from court.

By the middle of June the rebels were camped on Blackheath, just south of London. In early July they entered the city and were joined by many of the citizens. Several days of looting and riot changed that; and Cade fled to Sussex, where he was killed. But the rebellion had exposed even more cruelly than before the weakness of the government. The royal pardons offered to the rebels were declared, as was customary if in this case unlikely, to have been won from Henry by 'the most humble and persistent supplications, prayers and requests of our most serene and beloved wife and consort the queen'.

As if the Cade rebellion were not enough, the authorities also had a stream of bad news from France with which to contend. In May the Duke of Somerset had been forced to follow the surrender of Rouen by that of Caen.

By the time Cherbourg fell, on 12 August 1450, England had, as one Paston correspondent put it, 'not a foot of ground left in Normandy'. But Somerset's favour with the queen survived his military disasters. It was Marguerite who protected him, on his return to London, from demands that he should be charged as a traitor; but this flamboyant partisanship was itself a potential source of scandalous rumour, despite the fact that Somerset's wife, Eleanor Beauchamp, was also close to the queen.

In the vacuum left by Suffolk's death two leading candidates arose to fulfil the position of the king's chief councillor. One was indeed the Duke of Somerset, Margaret Beaufort's uncle. The other was Cecily's husband Richard Plantagenet, Duke of York, now making a hasty unannounced return from Ireland and intensely aware of his position both as the king's ranking male kinsman and as the progenitor of a flourishing nursery: 'the issue that it pleased God to send me of the royal blood', as he put it pointedly.

York's dissatisfaction was no doubt partly personal – he had been left seriously out of pocket by his experiences abroad – but at the start of the 1450s he could be seen at the same time as heading a call for genuine reform. Six years into Marguerite's queenship the crown of England was in a lamentable state; its finances were so bad that the Epiphany feast of 1451 had reputedly to be called off because suppliers would no longer allow the court food on credit, while the king's officials had recently been petitioning parliament for several years' back wages. This was certainly no new problem – the financial position had been serious a decade before Marguerite arrived in England – but it was now worse than ever. By 1450, the crown was almost £400,000 in debt.

The military campaign in France had been disastrously expensive, and the war inevitably caused disruption to trade – but the costs of maintaining the royal court were also now conspicuously far greater than the revenues available, especially under the influence of a high-spending queen;[19] while there was widespread suspicion that her favourites were being allowed to feather their nests too freely. On her arrival in England parliament had voted Marguerite the income usually bestowed on queens – 10,000 marks, or some £6700; but the parlous state of her husband's finances meant that those sums due her from the Exchequer were often not forthcoming. The surviving accounts show her making determined efforts to claim her dues, but they also show formidable expenditure – not just the £73 she gave to a Venetian merchant for luxury cloth, or the £25 to equip a Christmas 'disguising' at the Greenwich 'pleasaunce' (Humfrey, Duke of Gloucester's former residence which Marguerite had now adopted as her own), but sums of money clearly used to reward, in cash or in kind, her allies.

The parliament of May 1451 heard a petition for York to be named heir presumptive to the childless Henry VI, and his and

Cecily's sons after him. Everything known about her would suggest that Cecily stood right alongside her husband, whose supporters were by the beginning of 1452 claiming that the king 'was fitter for a cloister than a throne, and had in a manner deposed himself by leaving the affairs of his kingdom in the hands of a woman who merely used his name to conceal her usurpation, since, according to the laws of England, a queen consort hath no power but title only'.

The charge is to some degree substantiated by the number of grants made 'by the advice of the council of the Queen' as revealed in accounts of the Queen's Wardrobe department for 1452–3; and while some have queried whether the enmity between Marguerite and York was as instinctive and as early as has popularly been supposed, there is no doubt that by this point real conflict was on the way. By February 1452 both sides were raising troops. On 2 March the two armies drew up, three miles apart, near Blackheath.

Neither party, however, was yet quite ready to fight. A royal delegation of two bishops and two earls was sent to command York, in the king's name, to return to his allegiance. Prominent among York's demands was that Somerset be arrested and York himself acknowledged as the king's heir. Back in the royal camp, so one account goes, the bishops saw to it that the queen was kept occupied while they spoke to the king, who was persuaded to agree to all the demands. But the next morning there was a dramatic scene when Marguerite intercepted the guards who were leading Somerset away and instead took him to the king's tent so that York, arriving a few minutes later to make his peace with his monarch, found himself also confronting a furious queen. Somerset was clearly in as much favour as ever; York felt he had been fooled. He had no option, however, but to make a humiliating public pledge of his loyalty before being allowed to withdraw to his estates in Ludlow. Armed conflict had been averted for the moment, but the divisions in the English nobility were deeper than ever. The resentful York and his adherents remained a threat for a king and a court party anxious to strengthen their position in any possible way; and one of the ways most favoured by the age was marriage. In February 1453 Margaret Beaufort's mother was commanded to bring her nine-year-old daughter – Somerset's niece – to court.

During the first years of Marguerite's queenship Margaret had been raised at her own family seat of Bletsoe,[20] as well as at Maxey in the Fens. Her mother had remarried, and there is evidence from her later life both that Margaret developed an enduring closeness to her five St John half-siblings and that she shared several of her mother's traits: piety, a love of learning, and a desire for money and property. On 23 April 1453, she and her mother attended the annual celebration to honour the Knights of the Garter that marked St George's Day; on 12 May the king put through a generous payment of 100 marks for the 'arrayment' of his 'right dear and well beloved cousin Margaret'. But Margaret Beaufort had not been invited to court just for a party. The king had decided both to dissolve her marriage to Suffolk's son, and to transfer her wardship to two new guardians: his half-brothers Edmund and Jasper Tudor. These were the sons of Henry's mother, Katherine de Valois, by her second, secret, alliance with a young Welshman in her service, the lowly Owen Tudor – or 'Tydder', as enemies spelt it slightingly. More to the point, they were half-brothers whom the still childless Henry had begun to favour.

It seems certain that when the king had the marriage with Suffolk's son dissolved, he already had it in mind to marry Margaret and her fortune to Edmund, the elder of his two half-brothers. This could take place in just over two years' time, as soon as she turned twelve and reached the age of consent. It is possible Henry envisaged this move as a step to making Edmund his heir, though of course Edmund's own lineage gave him no shadow of a claim to the English throne. He certainly had royal blood in his veins – but it was the blood of the French royal house. Marriage might allow him to absorb Margaret's claim to the throne of England – a claim which, of course, would be inherited by any sons of the marriage. And the fact that Henry had neither children nor royal siblings meant that even comparatively distant claims were coming into prominence.

The formal changes in her marital situation required some participation from the nine-year-old Margaret herself. She would later imagine it as a real choice and an expression of manifest destiny, praying to St Nicholas to help her choose between the two husbands; but she was essentially fooling herself. Her account of a dream vision the night before she had to give her answer was given in later life to her chaplain, John Fisher. As she lay in prayer, about four in the morning, 'one appeared unto her arrayed like a Bishop, and naming unto her Edmund, bade take him unto her husband. And so by this means she did incline her mind unto Edmund, the King's brother, and Earl of Richmond.' Perhaps that 'by this means she did incline her mind . . .' is the real story – perhaps Margaret, even then, was trying to invent a scenario to mask the unpalatable fact that she would have had no choice in the matter. Or perhaps the story was only later Tudor propaganda, designed to reinforce the message that they were a divinely ordained dynasty.

FOUR

No Women's Matters

Madam, the king is old enough himself
To give his censure. These are no women's matters.
Henry VI Part 2, 1.3

The court party were about to get another, unexpected, boost
– one that, ironically, made Margaret Beaufort's marriage a
matter of a little less urgency. That spring of 1453 the king was
at long last able to announce – to his 'most singular consolation', as the official proclamation had it – that his 'most dearly
beloved wife the Queen [was] *enceinte*'.

Marguerite can have had no doubt to whom to give thanks
for her pregnancy. Having already made a new year's offering
of a gold tablet with the image of an angel, bedecked with jewels,
she had recently been on pilgrimage to Walsingham, where the
shrine of Our Lady was believed to be particularly helpful to
those trying to conceive. On the way back she had stayed a night
at Hitchin in Hertfordshire with Cecily Neville, who that summer
wrote to Marguerite[21] praising 'that blessed Lady to whom you
late prayed, in whom aboundeth plenteously mercy and grace,
by whose mediation it pleased our Lord to fulfil your right
honourable body of the most precious, most joyful, and most
comfortable earthly treasure that might come unto this land'.

Cecily was not writing only to congratulate Marguerite – nor even to lament the infirmity of her own 'wretched body'. She was indeed recovering from the birth of her son Richard, of which Thomas More[22] wrote that it was a breech birth and the mother could not be delivered 'uncut'. But it was her husband's fall from favour that caused her to be 'replete with such immeasurable sorrow and heaviness as I doubt not will of the continuance thereof diminish and abridge my days, as it does my worldly joy and comfort'. She would have sued to Marguerite earlier had not 'the disease and infirmity that since my said being in your highness presence hath grown and groweth' caused her 'sloth and discontinuance'. In this long, elaborate and convoluted letter Cecily renewed the plea she had made at Hitchin: that her husband the Duke of York should no longer be 'estranged from the grace and benevolent favour of that most Christian, most gracious and most merciful prince, the king our sovereign lord'.

It is not known whether York had asked Cecily to intercede, or whether she did so on her own initiative. The lists of gifts made by Marguerite each year show presents being made to Cecily and her servants; this can be interpreted as a less politically coded conduit to the husband, or as an expression of female alliance. Either way, Cecily's letter may have had some effect. When a great council was summoned that autumn York did, belatedly, receive an invitation to attend; one of the signatories on the document was Marguerite's confessor.

The council was summoned by Margaret Beaufort's uncle, Somerset, on 24 October. Recently, several important things had happened. On 19 October the French king's forces had entered Bordeaux, leaving England only Calais as a foothold in France and ending the Hundred Years War with France's resounding victory. On the 13th Queen Marguerite had given birth to a healthy baby boy, named Edward after Edward the

Confessor, whose feast day it was. But while proclamations of the joyous news were read around the country, at court the joy was muted. For the man to whom the news should have been most welcome of all, the baby's father, Henry VI, had been for some weeks in a catatonic stupor.

It had been the middle of August when the king, after complaining one evening of feeling unusually sleepy, had woken the next morning with lolling head, unable to move or to communicate with anybody. Over the days and weeks ahead, as his physicians and priests tried the full panoply of fifteenth-century remedies – bleedings, purgings and cautery on the one hand, exorcism on the other – he seemed not entirely to lose consciousness but to be utterly incapable. Modern medicine has tentatively diagnosed his condition as catatonic schizo-phrenia, or a depressive stupor, triggered by the news from France or just possibly by the fact of Marguerite's pregnancy. Every effort was made at first to conceal the king's condition, not only from the country at large but specifically from York.

It was in this climate that, as custom dictated, Marguerite had withdrawn into her apartments at Westminster to await her child's birth; it was an all-female world which not even her priest was allowed to enter. Never can withdrawal from the wider world have seemed less timely. After the birth – and the churching or ceremony of religious purification some forty days later at which Marguerite, wearing a robe trimmed with more than five hundred sables, was attended by the duchesses not only of Suffolk and Somerset but also of York – she had to accept the fact that Henry in his catatonic state could make no sign of acknowledging the baby as his. This represented both a personal slight and a practical problem if the name of the little prince were to be invoked as nominal authority for a council to rule during his father's incapacity.

There would, perhaps inevitably, be rumours about the

baby's paternity – whispers that Marguerite had been guilty of adultery with the Duke of Somerset. If it were indeed the news of Marguerite's pregnancy that had triggered the king's collapse, the question is whether he was horrified by the first indisputable evidence of his own sexuality or, conversely, by awareness that the child could not be his and that his wife must have been unfaithful.

By the traditions of courtly love, adultery could be a forgivable, even laudable, route to emotional fulfilment. Guinevere was guilty of adultery with Lancelot while her husband Arthur, soon to fall into his own magic sleep below the lake, stood by; but because Guinevere was Lancelot's true lover, she was able to be redeemed. In the world of practical politics, however, it was a different story. When chroniclers such as Robert Fabian wrote that 'false wedlock and false heirs fostered' were the 'first cause' of the ills in the body politic, they were making an equation between private morality and public wellbeing which would have seemed reasonable to any contemporary.

The whispers of unfaithfulness would rise to a crescendo of public debate towards the end of the decade, when Marguerite's Yorkist enemies found it convenient both to discredit the Lancastrian heir and to cast a slur on Marguerite herself in the field in which women were above all judged: her chastity. As Catherine de' Medici would later warn Elizabeth I, her sexuality was always the way in which a powerful woman could be most successfully attacked. Christine de Pizan similarly suggested that a queen had less freedom of sexual action than a lower-ranking woman, for 'the greater a lady is, the more is her honour or dishonour[23] celebrated through the country'. But the birth of Prince Edward transformed Marguerite, the first of several women in this story for whom their sons would be the ones to play. She would now not be prepared to sit back and allow others to rule – as her husband all too patently could not – the country.

In January 1454 it was reported that the queen, 'being a manly woman, using to rule and not be ruled', had drawn up a bill of five articles 'whereof the first is that she desires to have the whole rule of the land', so a Paston correspondent wrote. There was no very recent precedent in England for a woman's rule, or indeed a formal regency. Though several of the early Norman queens[24] had acted as regent, memories of the last woman to hold the reins of power, Isabella of France a century before, were not reassuring. Marguerite's mother-in-law Katherine de Valois had taken no part in government during Henry VI's minority.

But across the Channel there was precedent aplenty. Maybe it helped that the French had regularised their position by 'discovering' an ancient tradition that a woman could not inherit. The Salic law, while it debarred a woman from the throne itself, conversely enabled her to get near the throne without seriously imperilling the status quo. Marguerite's family tradition was of women taking control when necessary; but there was severe disapproval for a woman who crossed the indefinable boundary and seemed to seek rule openly. Perhaps Marguerite's very bid, influenced by the experience of her continental family, would have repercussions when, almost thirty years later, the governors of England came to consider a Woodville queen's position during another prospective regency.

Discussions as to how the country should be ruled dragged on for weeks, in parliament and in the council chamber, which suggests that Marguerite's claim was not instantly dismissed. At the end of February, both she and York were scheduled to make grand public arrivals in London. The mayor and aldermen agreed to turn out in scarlet to give the queen a formal welcome on Wednesday – and to do the same for the Duke of York on Friday. In the end, however, in the last days of March it was decided that the country would be governed during the king's incapacity by a council of nobles with York as 'protector' at their head. It was solution to which all the men involved – even Henry VI's half-brothers Edmund and Jasper Tudor – could agree.

York was described also as 'defensor' of the realm – a military role that could only have been held by a man. While Somerset was disempowered – arrested in the queen's apartment – Marguerite was sent to Windsor to be with her husband: a wife, not a force in the land. She seemed, however, to accept the decision, even when the council's money-saving reforms reduced her household and thus her power base. It is hard, indeed, to know what else she could have done. Certainly she could not stress Henry's incapacity: she had no authority to act other than through him. Although some lords refused to serve on York's council on the grounds that they were 'with the queen', either physically or otherwise, the normal business of administration seemed – except only for the continued opposition of Somerset – to be going comparatively smoothly.

Then, on Christmas Day 1454, Henry recovered his senses. On 28 December the queen brought her son to him and told him the baby's name, and, in the words of the Paston letters, 'he held up his hands and thanked God therefore'. Another account has it that he also, unhelpfully, said the child 'must be the son of the Holy Spirit', which could not but fan the flames of doubt about the boy's paternity.

The king's recovery was hailed with relief by all; in reality, it only presented a new set of problems. York had been a capable governor, but the king's recovery also resurrected Somerset, boiling with fury, while the weakened Henry would henceforth be more susceptible than ever to petticoat government. York could only ride back to his own estates for safety and with him, in spirit if not in person, came Cecily's brother Richard Neville, Earl of Salisbury, and Neville's eldest son, the Earl of Warwick – the man who has gone down in history as 'the Kingmaker' and whose wife would two years later give birth to the most obscure female protagonist in this story, Anne.

Up until the 1450s the Neville family had continued to support the Lancastrian government, to which they were linked by the connections of Joan Beaufort. Cecily, married to York, must have found herself isolated within her own family. This situation had now begun to change, largely because of the repercussions of a feud with another great northern family, the Percy earls of Northumberland. The two divisions of the Neville family were coming to be on opposite sides. Cecily, the former 'Rose of Raby', was now closest to the Nevilles of Middleham, Salisbury and Warwick, who were aligning themselves with her husband; while her half-nephew Ralph, who held the Raby land and the Westmorland title, remained Lancastrian. Whatever the cause, the change of allegiance in at least some of her kin must have been welcome to Cecily.

In May 1455 the queen and Somerset held another great council charged with protecting the king 'against his enemies'. It is from this month that many historians date the start of the 'Cousins' War'. The stand-off between the two parties quickly gave way to armed conflict as the king (supported by Somerset, though not by the queen, who had retreated to Greenwich with her baby) rode out of London at the head of a royal army and York likewise mustered his forces. The battle of St Albans was no major military engagement – an hour-long fracas through the market place and the town's main street – but it was notable for two things. Contemporaries were shocked, not only that the victorious Yorkist soldiers had looted their way through an English town, but that the king had been slightly wounded by an arrow from one of his English subjects. A number of lords and gentlemen on the royal side were slain, among them the Duke of Somerset, cut down by an axe outside the Castle Inn. Once again Marguerite had lost her great ally (and Margaret Beaufort her uncle, and the head of her family).

York's and the Nevilles' was the victory. But the battle of St Albans was significant in yet another way. There may have been no clear-cut turning-point in Marguerite of Anjou's progress towards political activism, but this was surely the moment when the process was completed.[25]

With a few exceptions, the battlefield was not part of a lady's experience in the fifteenth century. Some thirty years before, legend had it, Margaret's grandmother Yolande had donned silver armour and led her troops against the English at the battle of Baugé. But though the century of Joan of Arc may have given lip service to the idea of the woman warrior, even Isabella of Castile, Katherine of Aragon's mother, who was often pictured leading her own troops into battle, in fact confined herself to strategy and the supply of arms, planning and provisioning. Certainly most of the ladies whose husbands or sons were involved in wars would not have heard about events for days or even weeks afterwards. News travelled only at a horse's pace; and in an age before mass media (before, even, the dissemination of official printed reports) they may never have known as much about the progress of each battle as is known today. The history of the 'Wars of the Roses' has usually been told in terms of the men who alone could take part in its physical conflicts. But the lives of the women behind them could be affected no less profoundly.

As the Yorkists took over the reins of government, there was no overt breach of loyalty – everything was done in the king's name. Past wrongs were blamed on the dead Somerset and his allies. But Marguerite at least was mistrustful and unhappy, again leaving the court to take refuge in the Tower with her baby. The fact that Henry resumed his role as king almost as York's puppet must have frightened as well as angered her. That autumn the king fell ill again, though this time only for three months, and from November 1455 to February 1456 York resumed his protectorship of the country.

But as York set about a policy of financial retrenchment, the queen was working to try and make the king's rule more than nominal. 'The queen is a great and strong laboured woman, for she spares no pain to sue her things to an intent and conclusion to her power', wrote one observer, John Bocking, a connection of the Paston family. Early in 1456, as the king's recovery put an end to York's protectorship, Marguerite herself left London, taking her baby son to the traditional Lancastrian stronghold of Tutbury. She had decided to take action, rallying support and persuading the king to remove the court from London to the Midlands, where her own estates lay. In September of that year her chancellor was entrusted by the king with the Privy Seal, which gave her access to the whole administration of the country.

Marguerite portrayed herself always as the king's subordinate and adjunct, which was what was needed in the short term but in the long term both acted to the detriment of her authority and left her vulnerable to charges of exceeding her brief. It was as Marguerite managed to accrue more power to herself that the rumours really began to circulate about her sexual morality – as if the two things were two sides of the same unnatural coin.[26] It was increasingly said that the prince was not the king's son but perhaps Somerset's – or not even hers, but a changeling. In February 1456 one John Helton, 'an apprentice at court', was hanged, drawn and quartered 'for producing bills asserting that Prince Edward was not the queen's son'.

The pageants that welcomed Marguerite into the city of Coventry on 14 September that year reflected the confusion about her role. In most of them she was represented as traditionally female – wife and mother – and praised particularly for her 'virtuous life'. (Considering the aspersions that had been cast on her sexual virtue, a point was being made there, if, as is possible, Marguerite herself had any hand in framing the images.) She was hailed, hopefully if inappropriately, as a 'model of meekness, dame Margaret' – and though the ending made a show of the famously sword-wielding and dragon-slaying St Margaret, it was not before six famous conquerors had promised to give the saint's less well-armed namesake their protection; of which, as a female, she clearly stood in need.

But that autumn the king called a council from which (so a correspondent of the Pastons' wrote) the Duke of York withdrew 'in right good conceit with the king, but not in great conceit with the Queen'.

By the beginning of 1457 – with the business of appointing a council for Marguerite's baby son, with her order of a huge stock of arms for the Midlands castle of Kenilworth – the balance of power was running in favour of the queen. And when she paid another visit to Coventry, at the insistence of her officials she was escorted back out of the city by the mayor and sheriffs with virtually the same ceremonies that would have been accorded to the king, or so the city recorder noted with shock: 'And so they did never before the Queen till then.' Only the parade of the king's sword was missing.* But while Marguerite was acting so determinedly, others of

---

* Eighteen years later Ferdinand of Aragon was shocked to hear that his wife Isabella had not only had herself proclaimed hereditary monarch of Castile, but paraded through Segovia with a drawn sword carried before her. 'I have never', he protested, 'heard of a queen who usurped this masculine attribute.'

her sex were still too young to play their role in the country's history.

In Warwick Castle, on 11 June 1456, the Earl of Warwick's wife Anne Beauchamp had given birth to their second daughter, Anne. Anne Beauchamp had come unexpectedly (and not without familial strife) into a vast inheritance, and since the Warwicks never produced sons her daughters Isabel and Anne Neville[27] were early marked out as the greatest heiresses of their day. Anne would have a future as chequered as any in the fifteenth century – but at the moment, geographically close though they may have been to Queen Marguerite, her father and her family were prominent in the Yorkist cause. Meanwhile in far-off Wales, at Pembroke Castle, the young Lancastrian Margaret Beaufort was also about to have to take control of her own destiny.

FIVE

Captain Margaret

Where's Captain Margaret to fence you now?
Henry VI Part 3, 2.6

In 1455, shortly after her uncle Somerset had been killed in the queen's cause, Margaret Beaufort had reached her twelfth birthday. Until this time, in the absence of evidence to the contrary, she had probably been left in her mother's care, but when the king's half-brother Edmund Tudor was sent to Wales as the king's representative late that year he would almost certainly have been able to take Margaret with him as his wife. Popular opinion would have suggested that, even though it was now legal, consummation of the marriage should be delayed – the more so since Margaret was slight and undeveloped for her age. But other factors weighed more heavily with Edmund: fathering a child on Margaret would give him a life interest in her lands; and though there was now a Lancastrian heir, there was still not a spare. She became pregnant in the first half of 1456, some time before her thirteenth birthday. It would at best have been an anxious time for her, but worse was to follow. Edmund did not live to see the birth of his child. Captured at Carmarthen by an ally of the Duke of York's, he was soon released but caught plague there and died in November.

Isolated in plague-ridden Wales and heavily pregnant, a terrified Margaret had only one ally close at hand – her brother-in-law Jasper Tudor, who, himself only in his early twenties, was called to take on this quasi-paternal role. She fled to his stronghold of Pembroke and it was there that on 28 January 1457 she gave birth to a boy.

The ceremony that was supposed to surround the birth of a possible heir to the throne was described in ordinances Margaret Beaufort herself laid down in later life for the birth of her first grandchild; and though there was obviously more ritual involved in the confinement of a queen than in that of a mere great lady, the essential goals were the same. The woman went apart, some weeks before the birth, into carefully prepared rooms: 'Her Highness's pleasure being understood as to what chamber it may please her to be delivered in, the same to be hung with rich cloth or arras, sides, roof, windows and all, except one window, which must be hanged so that she have light when it pleases her.' She took communion, then progressed in state to her apartments; took wine and sweet-meats with her (male) officers and then bade them farewell. As she entered her chamber she passed into a female world, where 'women are to be made all manner of officers, butlers, sewers and pages; receiving all needful things at the chamber door'. It was meant to create a protective environment for mother and child alike – perhaps conditions as near womb-like as possible.

After the birth a new mother was not allowed outdoors until she went for her 'churching' or purification some forty days later, accompanied by midwives and female attendants, bearing a lighted candle, to be sprinkled with holy water. Christine de Pizan gives a description of the lying-in of a mere merchant's wife, who arranged that awe-struck visitors should walk past an ornamental bed and a dresser 'decorated like an altar' with silver vessels before even reaching her own bedchamber: 'large and handsome', with tapestries all around, and a bed made up with cobweb-fine display sheets, and even a gold-embroidered rug 'on which one could walk'. 'Sitting in the bed was the woman herself, dressed in crimson silk, propped up against large pillows covered in the same silk and decorated with pearl buttons, wearing the headdress of a lady.' But it seems likely that Margaret Beaufort's circumstances militated against any such pleasurable feminine display.

We know that women were as anxious then as now to take any precaution they could against the perils of childbirth: from a favourite midwife to the Virgin's girdle. Even in a lower sphere of society, Margaret Paston was so eager to get the midwife she wanted that the woman – though incapacitated by a back injury – had to reassure her she'd be there, even if she had to be pushed in a barrow. What we do not know is to just what degree the conditions of the year or the remoteness of the place changed things for Margaret. But we know the birth did not go easily.

The labour was long and difficult. Both Margaret and the child were expected to die, and were there to be a choice some Church authorities urged that those in attendance should prioritise the unbaptised baby, even it were not a valuable boy. There seems little doubt that her physical immaturity was part of the problem – as her confessor John Fisher would later put it: 'It seemed a miracle that of so little a personage anyone should have been born at all.' She herself thought so, at least: in later years she would combine forces with her daughter-in-law Elizabeth of York to ensure that her young granddaughter and namesake Margaret was not sent to Scotland too early lest her new husband, the king of Scotland, would not wait to consummate the marriage 'but injure her, and endanger her health'.

There seems little doubt that Margaret Beaufort was indelibly marked by her early experiences – perhaps physically,[28] since neither of her two subsequent marriages produced any children, and certainly mentally.* Contemporaries remarked on her sense of vulnerability. The image of Fortune's wheel was impossible for contemporary commentators to avoid:

> But Fortune with her smiling countenance strange
> Of all our purpose may make sudden change.

So ran the jingle. Margaret's confessor would say, in the 'Mornynge Remembraunce' sermon he preached a month after her death, that 'she never was yet in that prosperity but the greater it was the more always she dread the adversity'. That whenever 'she had full great joy, she let not to say, that some adversity would follow'. (However, the other early Tudor biographer, the court poet Bernard André,[29] claimed that she was 'steadfast and more stable than the weakness in women suggests'.)

Even the trauma she had suffered did not long subdue the young mother's determination. There are few early proofs of Margaret Beaufort's character, but, if the tale is true, this is surely one of them. The sixteenth-century Welsh chronicler Elis Gruffydd claimed that Jasper had the baby christened Owen; it was Margaret who forced the officiating bishop to christen him again with a name allied to the English throne – Henry.

---

* Perhaps, even, it would not be surprising if Margaret the devout turned with a sense of angry recognition to the religious theories of the day that held maidenhood, virginity, to be the most perfect time of a woman's life – attempted, in her later rejection of the married state, almost to recreate it. Certainly the iconography was all around – the Virgin Mary, the Maid of Orléans, the Pearl Maiden of poetry, even Galahad and the Grail. The nobly born virgin martyrs – St Catherine of Alexandria, Cecilia, Barbara, Agnes, Agatha, and St Margaret – had become the most popular saints in the England of the day.

The next few weeks – the beginning of her official period of mourning – would be spent at Pembroke caring for her delicate baby. But his birth demanded speedy action. In March, almost as soon as she was churched and received back into public life, she and her brother-in-law Jasper were travelling towards Newport and the home of the Duke of Buckingham. A new marriage had to be arranged for her,[30] and an alliance that would protect her son. The choice was Henry Stafford, a mild man some twenty years older than she but, crucially, the second son of the Duke of Buckingham, a staunchly Lancastrian magnate almost as powerful as his brother-in-law the Duke of York – Anne, Duchess of Buckingham was Cecily Neville's sister. A dispensation was needed, since the pair were second cousins; by 6 April it had been granted, although the actual marriage ceremony would not take place until Margaret's mourning was complete, on 3 January 1458.

The bride, still only fourteen, would keep the grander title her first marriage had won her, Countess of Richmond, but she brought with her estates now enriched by her dowager's rights. Her son Henry Tudor would at first probably have remained in Wales in his uncle's care. But the arrangement appears to have been a happy one, with Margaret and her new husband visiting Jasper and baby Henry at Pembroke; the elder Buckinghams welcoming their new daughter-in-law (Duchess Anne would bequeath Margaret several choice books); and – despite the absence of any further children – every sign of contentment, at least, between the pair. Margaret would seem to have found a safe haven – except that events would not leave any haven tranquil and unmolested for long.

In the spring of 1458 the adversarial parties in the royal dispute were brought to the ceremony of formal reconciliation known as a 'Loveday'. It was in everyone's interest that some unity should be restored to the country. Queen Marguerite and the Duke of York walked hand in hand into church to exhibit their amity before God. The pose showed queenly intercession, peacemaking; but it also cast her as York's equal and political match. Ironically, what might sound to modern ears like a tribute to her activities was actually a devaluation of her status: as queen, she was supposed to be above the fray. To remain on that pedestal might keep her immobile; but to step down from it exposed her vulnerability.

The pacific image was, moreover, misleading. In the summer and autumn of 1458 there were fresh clashes between Marguerite and the Yorkists. She had the Earl of Warwick summoned to London to account for acts of piracy he had committed while governor of Calais, to which post he had been appointed the previous year. He arrived with a large force of armed retainers wearing his livery, and his supporters rallied protests in the city against the queen and the authorities. Tensions deepened when Warwick narrowly escaped impalement on a spit as he passed through the royal kitchens. He claimed that the queen had paid the scullion who was wielding it to murder him. Later that year Marguerite left London. She was assembling a personal army – what one report described as 'queen's gallants', sporting the livery badge of her little son.

A random letter preserved in the archives of Exeter Cathedral, concerning a snub to the crown's candidate for the deanery, gives a taste of her mood at this time. It had been reported that some of the cathedral chapter were inclined to set aside the royal recommendations, to which news Marguerite retorted that it would be 'to our great marvel and displeasure if it be so. Wherefore we desire and heartily pray you forthwith that for reverence of us . . . you will . . . be inclined and yield to the accomplishment of my lord's invariable intention and our in this matter.' It is notable that Henry's letter of confirmation was shorter and feebler, and that the officer sent down to see that the royal will was done was Marguerite's own master of jewels. But it is also true, of course, that as a woman she was only ever able to act in the name of her husband or of her tiny son.

The chronicler Polydore Vergil says that the queen (who was 'for diligence, circumspection and speedy execution of causes, comparable to a man') believed a plan was afoot to put the Duke of York on the throne itself: 'Wherefore this wise woman [called] together the council to provide remedy for the disordered state of things. . . .' At a meeting of the council in Coventry in the summer of 1459 York, Warwick and their adherents were indicted for their non-appearance 'by counsel of the queen'. Nominally, of course, the council was the king's council, and it was he who was still ruling the country. But the queen's dominance must have made it hard for many a loyal Englishman to be sure just where his loyalties lay.

The anonymous *English Chronicle* declares that now was the moment when the Yorkists worked hardest to spread rumours. 'The queen was defamed and denounced, that he that was called prince, was not her son, but a bastard gotten in adultery; wherefore she, dreading that he should not succeed his father in the crown of England, sought the alliance of all the knights and squires of Cheshire, to have their benevolence, and held open household among them.'

In the context of armed conflict Marguerite was far from negligible, but here too she could only act by proxy. One chronicle describes how it was 'by her urging' that the king – nominally – assembled an army. But as that army met the York/ Neville forces in the autumn of 1459 at Blore Heath, Marguerite could only wait for news a few miles away. That news included the fact that Thomas, Lord Stanley, whose forces had been promised to her, had in fact held them neutral and outside the fray. It was after this battle that Marguerite reputedly told a local blacksmith to put the shoes of her horse on backwards, to disguise her tracks as she rode away. Shakespeare's Clarence in *Henry VI Part 3* mocks 'Captain Margaret'; but in fact the inability to fight in person would be a problem of female rule even for Elizabeth I in the next century. Christine de Pizan wrote that a baroness should know the laws of arms and the tactics necessary to defend her castle against attack; her queen, however, was expected to take a more passive role. Even at the Paston level a man could be found sending his wife to preserve their claim to the house; and she ordering crossbows. But Margaret Paston was eventually to find that 'I cannot well guide nor rule soldiers', who did not heed her as they would a man.

Nevertheless Marguerite's influence was powerful. When the two armies faced off outside Ludlow a fortnight or so later, one source records that the Lancastrian soldiers would fight 'for the love they bare to the King, but more for the fear they had of the Queen, whose countenance was so fearful and whose look was so terrible that to all men against whom she took displeasure, her frowning was their undoing and her indignation their death'. On this occasion the Yorkist forces ultimately backed off from armed conflict with their monarch, and the resultant flight has come to be called the rout of Ludford Bridge.

Warwick and Salisbury fled to Calais where their family was waiting. With them went Edward, Earl of March, the eldest son of York and Cecily. York himself and his second son, Edmund, fled to Ireland. Cecily and her younger children had most likely remained at Ludlow: a comfortable castle, since the residency there of York's two eldest sons had ensured it was full of the fifteenth-century luxuries of chimneys, window glass and privacy, but now no sanctuary. Several sources record that she and her two youngest sons were taken prisoner there but it was never likely that any personal, physical reprisal would be taken against her, a woman. One chronicle does say that while the town of Ludlow was robbed to the bare walls 'the noble Duchess of York unmanly and cruelly was entreated[31] and [de]spoiled', but the absence of any other sign of outrage suggests that the damage was only to her property.

When a parliament held at Coventry – packed with Marguerite's supporters, and later known as the 'Parliament of Devils' – attainted the Yorkist lords, Cecily went to the city on 6 December and submitted. *Gregory's Chronicle* recorded that: 'The Duchess of York came unto King Harry and submitted her unto his grace,[32] and she prayed for her husband that he might come to his answer to be received unto his grace: and the king full humbly granted her grace, and to all hers that would come with her. . . .' Attainder meant not only that the men were convicted of treason, but that their lands were now the property of the crown. Cecily, however, was given a grant of a thousand marks per annum – income derived from some of those confiscated lands – 'for the relief of her and her infants who had not offended against the king'.[33] Her sister-in-law the Countess of Salisbury was personally attainted;[34] Cecily was not. She was placed in custody; but the custodian was her own sister Anne, Duchess of Buckingham, whose husband had declared for the queen's side and who seems to have kept her own natal Lancastrian sympathies. It is speculated that the comparative leniency with which Cecily was treated was the result of her friendship with Queen Marguerite – though the chronicles also report that 'she was kept full straight with many a rebuke' from her sister – and by January 1460 she was free to move southwards again. All the same, Cecily's fortunes seemed to be at a low ebb.

No wonder the German artist Albrecht Dürer drew Fortune so frequently and in so many different guises, blind and pregnant, wounded or weaponed: the image reflected the arbitrary and ever-changing nature of these times. The poet John Skelton would lament Edward IV himself as Fortune's fool:

She took me by the hand and led me a dance,
And with her sugared lips on me she smiled,
But, what from her dissembled countenance,
I could not beware till I was beguiled . . .

At this moment, the future prominence of Cecily's son had never looked more unlikely.

SIX

Mightiness Meets Misery

then, in a moment, see
How soon this mightiness meets misery
Henry VIII, Prologue

Even by the standards of these tumultuous years, the ups and downs of these few months were extraordinary. In the summer of 1460, Cecily's Yorkist menfolk were back with a fresh army. At Northampton, in July, they again met the forces of the king and queen, and this time the Yorkists were able to seize the person of Henry VI and bring him back to London as their puppet or prisoner, all the while proclaiming their loyalty.

The London chronicler Gregory described Marguerite's flight. 'The queen, hearing this, voided unto Wales but . . . a servant of her own . . . spoiled her and robbed her, and put her so in doubt of her life and son's life also.' But they managed to escape. 'And then she come to the castle of Harlech in Wales [the home of Jasper Tudor], and she had many great gifts and [was] greatly comforted, for she had need thereof . . .' She had only four companions, the chronicler reports in horror (a great lady's household might be a hundred and fifty) and she was often forced to ride pillion behind a fourteen-year-old boy.

Marguerite was not the only woman whose fortunes had changed overnight. Everything was changing, once again, for Cecily, too. In this latest battle, her brother-in-law the Duke of Buckingham had been among the casualties. While Warwick returned to Calais in triumph to fetch his family home, Cecily, with her younger children, moved to London, to await word from her husband. As Queen Marguerite fled westwards, York sent for Cecily (travelling in a chair of blue velvet,[35] 'and four pair coursers therein') to come and meet him in Hereford, to share his triumphal progress, heralded by trumpeters and displaying the royal arms, back towards the city.

It surely says something about their relationship that he wanted her by his side, riding in victory through the green summer countryside. But in fact the very flamboyance of their entry may have worked against them. Citizens and nobles alike were pleased enough to welcome York: a steady hand to keep anarchy at bay. But when it looked as though he would claim the throne itself, it was clear they were no more ready to accept this usurpation than they had been Marguerite's proxy sovereignty. One monastic chronicler, the Abbot of St Albans John Whethamsted, left a long and vivid description of the misstep into which York's 'exaltation of mood' led him; right down to the distribution of the major players around Westminster palace. York strode to the parliamentary chamber and laid his hand upon the throne as if to claim it. He waited for the applause which, however, failed to come and then (the king being 'in the queen's apartments') moved to the principal chamber of the palace, smashing the locks to gain his entry.

People of all 'estates and ranks, age, sex, order and condition' had begun to murmur against York's presumption. By the end of October 1460 a deal had been hammered out by which Henry would keep the throne for his lifetime but would not be succeeded by his son. Instead, York and York's sons would be his heirs, an idea presumably made more plausible by that long whispering campaign suggesting Marguerite's infidelity. Such a prospect, with its huge advancement for her children, must have been welcome to Cecily. But of course Marguerite, whose own young son had been disinherited, was never going to accept it quietly.

Towards the end of the year she took ship northwards from Wales. Marguerite's plan was to appeal for help from the Scots – where, ironically, another woman, Mary of Guelders, was commencing her rule as regent on behalf of her eight-year-old son James, her husband having recently been killed by an exploding cannon while besieging Yorkist sympathisers at Roxburgh. Mary sent an envoy to escort Marguerite and her young son to Dumfries and Lincluden Abbey where they were royally entertained and herself came down to meet them. The two queens spent twelve days together at the abbey; and Mary promised military aid, offering the hospitality of the Scottish royal palaces while it was assembled. Moving into England with a foreign army would do little to increase her popularity, but Marguerite was in no mood to worry.

With Henry's captivity she had now become the undisputed leader of what was beginning to look like a genuine opposition party: stripped of much she had once enjoyed, but liberated for the first time to act openly on her own initiative. The Yorkist lords, according to *Gregory's Chronicle*, tried to lure Marguerite back to London with faked messages from her husband, 'for they knew well that all the workings that were done grew by her, for she was more wittier than the king . . .'.

As the Duke of York moved north to meet the impending Lancastrian threat, Marguerite's name was being invoked by friends and enemies alike – even before she was ready to leave Scotland. York, holed up in his own Sandal Castle, was advised (says the Tudor writer Hall, whose grandfather had been the adviser concerned) not to sally out, but answered it would be dishonour to do so 'for dread of a scolding woman, whose only weapons are her tongue and her nails'. The Lancastrian herald, trying to provoke York into taking a dangerous offensive, sneered that he should allow himself 'to be tamely braved by a woman'.

York should have heeded all the warnings. For now, once again, it would be Cecily's turn to drink a bitter cup. No wonder she, like Margaret Beaufort, would remember the image of Fortune's wheel; and would, perhaps ironically, bequeath a bed decorated with that image to the Tudor dynasty. In the words of an anonymous poem:

> I have see fall to men of high nobleness –
> First wealth, and then again distress,
> Now up, now down, as fortune turneth her wheel

On December 30 the royal forces (under the command of the third Duke of Somerset, Margaret Beaufort's cousin, who shared his father's and uncle's strong Lancastrian loyalty) met the Yorkists at the battle of Wakefield. The Yorkists were defeated; and casualties of the rout included York himself, pulled from his horse in the thick of the fray and his seventeen-year-old son Edmund, with whose death Shakespeare would make such play. Salisbury (whose son had also died) was killed the next day. Their heads were set on spikes on the gates of York city, the duke's capped with a paper crown. Tudor chroniclers like Hall and Holinshed,[36] followed by Shakespeare, had the heads presented to a savagely vengeful Marguerite. But in fact Marguerite left Scotland only after news of the victory, travelling southwards in an outfit of black and silver lent to her by the Scottish queen Mary.

Cecily had lost a husband, a son, a brother, and a nephew.

The news must have reached her and her three youngest children in London, probably at Baynard's Castle, with the taste of the Christmas feasts still in their mouths. A great house like Baynard's Castle with its gardens and terraces, its great hall and its courtyards capable of holding the four hundred armed men the Duke had once brought with him from Ireland, must have seemed a place of refuge in a treacherously shifting world. But the Duke of York's death brought to an end a long and in many ways happy union. It had also narrowly deprived Cecily of her chance of being queen, and she would not forget it easily.

Marguerite's party were once more in the ascendant. As the queen came south with her forces, some time in January or early February 1461, she sent letters – one on her own behalf, and one in the name of her young son – to the authorities of London, demanding the city's loyalty. The one from the seven-year-old prince presents him as the active avenger, heading his army, and mentions his mother only as a potential victim. Marguerite's own letter is obliged to suggest that she is acting in tandem with her young son; but it does present her forcefully: 'Praying you, on our most hearty and desirous wise, that [above] all earthly things you will diligently intend [attend] to the surety of my lord's royal person in the mean time; so that through malice of his said enemy he be no more troubled, vexed, or jeoparded. And, by so doing, we shall be unto you such a lady as of reason you shall largely be content.'

As her army swept ever southwards, her troops pillaged the land[37] and, unable to pay them, she did nothing to prevent it. Their actions did much to sour her subsequent reputation, besides providing fuel for Yorkist propaganda that implicitly linked this catastrophic 'misrule' with the parallel reversal of right order represented by a woman's leadership.

After the second battle of St Albans, on 17 February 1461, the reports were full of mentions of the queen or the queen's party. One source, the Milanese ambassador in France, Prospero di Camulio, seems even to suggest that this time she was in the thick of the fray: 'The earl of Warwick decided to quit the field, and . . . pushed through right into Albano [St Albans], where the queen was with 30,000 men.' The chronicler Gregory wrote that in the midst of the battle 'King Harry went to his queen and forsook all his lords, and trusted better to her party than to his own. . . .' One anecdotal report of a speech Marguerite once made to her men is as heroic in its way as Elizabeth I's at Tilbury: 'I have often broken [the English] battle line. I have mowed down ranks far more stubborn than theirs are now. You who once followed a peasant girl [Joan of Arc] now follow a queen . . . I will either conquer or be conquered with you.'

Marguerite had by now experienced far more warfare than most ladies of her time. She had known the tension beforehand, mounting to fever pitch; the fear that each step of your horse's hoof could bring it down on the sharp point of a hidden caltrop, before men rushed out from ambush to claim you as their prey; and the roads afterwards, crammed with the bodies of horses and with bleeding, dying men who lacked even the strength to crawl away.

When the engagement at St Albans was over King Henry, brought there by Warwick under guard, was found seated under an oak tree, and Marguerite was reunited with her husband. As the couple halted outside London the city officials requested that a carefully chosen delegation of ladies should act in the traditional way as go-betweens, interceding with Marguerite 'for to be benevolent and owe goodwill to the city'. The ladies were Ismanie, Lady Scales[38] who had been among those escorting Marguerite from France and who had remained in her household; the widowed Duchess of Buckingham, Cecily of York's sister, whose husband had been killed the previous summer fighting in the Lancastrian cause; and Jacquetta, dowager

Duchess of Bedford, another member of the party that had escorted Marguerite to England. Of the princely house of Luxembourg, and married in her youth to Henry VI's uncle John, Jacquetta had been widowed in 1435 at the age of nineteen; 'minding also to marry rather for pleasure than for honour, without counsel of her friends' she had promptly taken as her second husband 'a lusty knight, Sir Richard Woodville'. Jacquetta had remained close to the queen; and indeed her eldest daughter Elizabeth[39] may have been one of Marguerite's ladies. Now not only was Jacquetta's own husband with the queen's force, but so too had been her daughter's husband John Grey, father of her two young sons. Grey had recently died at the second battle of St Albans; and it was Elizabeth Woodville's widowhood that would soon propel her into national history.

A letter reported that the delegation had returned to London on 20 February with news that 'the king and queen had no mind to pillage the chief city and chamber of their realm, and so they promised; but at the same time they did not mean that they would not punish the evildoers'. The message was sufficiently ambiguous that there was still panic in the streets, and the ladies were sent out again two days later to request the Lancastrian leaders to enter the city without the main body of their army. The queen conceded; ironically, her decision to send only a small symbolic force into London, and her subsequent withdrawal to Dunstable, would prove to be arguably the biggest mistake of her life. The wheel was about to turn yet again.

The huge overturns of fortune did not come heralded in any way. In the weeks after the battle of Wakefield, Cecily Neville had been so afraid that she had sent her two younger sons, George and Richard, abroad to the safety of Burgundy. Yet almost as she did so her eldest son Edward and the Earl of Warwick, with their armies, were preparing to approach

London from the west. On 27 February they were welcomed into the city, where Edward went to his mother's house of Baynard's Castle.

This time there was no talk of loyalty to King Henry – or of wishing only to rid him of his evil counsellors. On 1 March the Bishop of Exeter, Warwick's brother, asked the eager Londoners whether they felt that Henry deserved to rule, 'whereunto', as the *Great Chronicle of London* reported, 'the people cried hugely and said Nay. And after it was asked of them whether they would have the Earl of March [Edward] for their king and they cried with one voice, Yea, Yea.'

Cecily Neville's eldest son, the 'fair white rose' of York, was still only eighteen but when, three days later, he was acclaimed and enthroned, his huge stature and glowing golden looks made him seem every inch the king. The youthful Edward with his royal bloodline was not only the favourite candidate backed by Warwick and the Neville party, but had recently proved his mettle with his victory at Mortimer's Cross.

But the Yorkists had not yet completely won. London was not England. On 13 March, with Warwick already engaged recruiting men in the Midlands, King Edward marched his army north where Henry and Marguerite still commanded the loyalty of a majority of the nobility. Prospero di Camulio erroneously heard that Marguerite had given her husband poison, after persuading him to abdicate in favour of their son: 'However these are rumours in which I do not repose much confidence.' And very soon, after the dreadful battle of Towton, di Camulio was writing less cautiously.

Fought outside York in wintry weather, on an icy Palm Sunday, Towton is still probably the bloodiest battle ever fought on English soil. No detailed description survives, and the numbers of those involved, as estimated by contemporary reporters and later historians, vary wildly. But what is agreed is that this was a ten-hour endurance test in which men slogged each other to exhaustion; one in which King Edward told his men to give no quarter; and the opposing Lancastrians, with the wind against them, suffered snow and arrows blowing together into their faces.

Before the battle even began both sides were already tired and frozen after a bitter night spent in the biting wind. None the less, the fighting went on until ten o'clock at night, long after it was dark. By dusk the Lancastrian forces had been driven backwards to a deep gully of the river Cock, and many who were not hacked down were drowned as they tried to cross. It was, says the *Great Chronicle of London*, 'a sore and long and unkindly fight – for there was the son against the father, the brother against brother'. Crowland talks of more than thirty-eight thousand dead; and though that is probably an exaggeration, 'many a lady', said *Gregory's Chronicle*, lost her beloved that day.

For others, of course, the news was good. Cecily had word of the victory early, on 3 April, as William Paston wrote: 'Please you to know such tidings as my Lady of York hath by a letter of credence under the sign manual of our sovereign lord king Edward, which letter came unto our said lady this same day . . . at xi clock and was seen and read by me.' The Bishop of Elphin, as he subsequently told the Papal Legate, sets the glad tidings later:[40] 'On Easter Monday, at the vesper hour [sunset], I was in the house of the Duchess of York. Immediately after vespers the Lord Treasurer came to her with an authentic letter . . . On hearing the news the Duchess [returned] to the chapel with two chaplains and myself and there we said "Te Deum" after which I told her that the time was come for writing to your Lordship, of which she approved. . . .'

Now it was Marguerite, her husband and her son who were to flee, leaving York, where they waited for news, with only what they could carry. As Prospero di Camulio wrote: 'Any one who reflects at all upon the wretchedness of that queen and the ruins of those killed and considers the ferocity of the country, and the state of mind of the victors, should indeed, it seems to me, pray to God for the dead and not less for the living.'

PART TWO

1461–1471

SEVEN

To Love a King

Lady Grey: Why stops my lord? Shall I not hear my task?
Edward: An easy task: 'tis but to love a king.

Henry VI Part 3, 3.2

A new regime had come in, a new ruling house held the throne, and everything had changed. But none of the protagonists could fail to be aware that Fortune's wheel could just as easily spin in the opposite direction.

The fortunes of Marguerite of Anjou had for the present turned dramatically for the worse. After the battle of Towton she, her husband and son had fled back to Scotland where they would remain for the next year. The refugees were forced to promise the perpetually contested border town of Berwick to the Scots in return, while any further attempt to recruit French aid was temporarily thwarted by the death that summer of the French king Charles VII. His successor Louis would have to be wooed afresh. Attainted in the first parliament of November 1461 for transgressions and offences 'against her faith and Liegance' to King Edward, Marguerite was being destroyed as only a woman could be. In the words of a contemporary ballad:

> Moreover it is a right great perversion,
> A woman of a land to be a regent –
> Queen Margaret I mean, that ever hath meant
> To govern all England with might and power
> And to destroy the right line was her intent.

Another ballad, composed a couple of years later, had Henry VI lamenting he had married a wife 'That was the cause of all my moan'. The absent Marguerite was now everyone's choice of villain. When the Tudor chronicler Polydore Vergil wrote later that 'By mean of a woman, sprang up a new mischief that set all out of order', he was casting her as another Eve. Even Edward, for whom Henry should surely have been the greatest enemy, wrote of his having been moved 'by the malicious and subtle suggestion and enticing of the said malicious woman Margaret his wife'.

Elizabeth Woodville had certainly suffered: not just the loss of her husband John Grey, but the potential destruction of her whole family. She could no longer count on the security of a home on one of the Grey family's Midland estates. Not only would she have to fight her mother-in-law for her dower rights, but as leading Lancastrians the Woodvilles might well have found themselves ruined when Henry and Marguerite fell.

Margaret Beaufort too had suffered, though to a lesser degree. The armed clashes that brought the Yorkists into power had killed her father-in-law the Duke of Buckingham at Northampton in 1460, and brought the position of his family into question. They had also scattered her family of birth. Her cousin Henry, the latest Duke of Somerset (son to Marguerite's ally), had to flee abroad after Towton with his younger brothers, as did Jasper Tudor. In the autumn of 1461 Jasper followed Queen Marguerite into her Scottish exile and would spend almost a decade, there and in France, trying to rally the Lancastrian cause.

Margaret's husband, Henry Stafford, had fought for the Lancastrians at Towton; he, however, was pardoned by a King Edward determined to heal breaches where possible. The couple were able to establish themselves in the castle of Bourne in the Fen country, part of Margaret's inheritance from her grandmother. The wardship of the four-year-old Henry Tudor was another matter. He was no threat to Edward (or rather, with Henry VI and his son both living, he was not the greatest threat), but he and his lands did present an opportunity.

The boy's lands were transferred to the Duke of Clarence and his wardship handed to the devoted Yorkist Sir William Herbert, the man who had once seized Carmarthen Castle and taken Edmund Tudor into custody. For several years this arrangement seemed a comparatively happy one: Henry, visited by Margaret and her husband, was raised with every advantage as one of Herbert's own family – which, with several young daughters to marry off, they may have planned he would one day become.

As for Cecily Neville, it must have been hard for her to work out where Fortune's wheel had left her. The loss of her husband and her second son, a shattering personal grief, was only weeks behind her; but now another son, her eldest, sat on the throne, opening up a world of possibilities. As Edward set out north again, it was his mother whom he commended to the burghers of London as his representative. The Bishop of Elphin concluded his letter about Cecily's reception of the battlefield news by urging the Papal Legate: 'As soon as you can, write to the King, the Chancellor, and other Lords, as I see they wish it; also to the Duchess, who is partial to you, and [holds] the king at her pleasure.' In the early days of Edward IV's reign, perhaps the bishop was not the only one to consider that Cecily could rule her son as she wished. Edward granted to her the lands held by his father[1] and further subsidised her ever-lavish expenditure. She regarded herself as queen dowager, and played the part. Edward must, after all, have been aware that he had come to the throne by the efforts of her relations, and he was young enough for everyone – perhaps even including his mother – to underestimate his capabilities.[*]

Cecily's youngest daughter – fourteen-year-old Margaret of Burgundy, as she would become – was now installed at Greenwich, the luxurious riverside 'pleasaunce' that had been remodelled by Henry VI's uncle Humfrey, Duke of Gloucester. Her two older sisters were already established elsewhere. Anne, the Yorks' eldest child, had been matched in 1445 when she was six with Henry Holland, son of the great Duke of Exeter who, however, was committed to the Lancastrian cause. By the time she reached adulthood the couple were estranged[2] to the point where Anne notoriously found consolation elsewhere, with a Kent gentleman called Thomas St Leger. The next sister, Elizabeth, had recently been married to John de la Pole, Duke of Suffolk (who, as a child, had nominally been married to Margaret Beaufort). John's father had been the great minister of Henry VI murdered in 1450; his mother the duchess was the mighty Alice Chaucer, a natural Lancastrian who, however, doubtless saw this Yorkist alliance as being in the interests of her family's safety. Elizabeth quickly began to produce a string of children – at least five sons and four daughters – and with her husband converted to the

---

[*] If we want a suggestion of what Cecily might have hoped her relation to Edward would be, we could look to the letter Alice Chaucer's husband Suffolk had left for his son: 'I charge you, my dear son, always as ye be bounden by the commandment of god to do, to love, to worship your lady and mother, and also that ye obey always her commandments, and to believe her counsels and advices in all your works . . .'

Yorkist side her future looked uncontroversial, the more so since John showed no aptitude for nor interest in active political office. But Margaret, two years younger than Elizabeth, was, crucially, still unmarried when her brother Edward came to the throne – and available to be offered in marriage as England's princess.

Under the former regime, Greenwich had been used by Queen Marguerite, who had decorated it with her daisy emblem and added new windows, a great chamber, an arbour in the gardens and a gallery overlooking them. The daisies were equally fitting for this other Margaret. The whole family would come to use Greenwich regularly, but for the moment Edward seized on it primarily as a suitable and healthy residence for his three youngest siblings, and Margaret's closeness to her brothers Richard and George would play an important part in English affairs through into the Tudor period.

Here Margaret, described by the chronicler Jean de Haynin as notably tall 'like her brother Edward' and having 'an air of intelligence and wit', would have continued her education. A well-to-do girl's training in the fifteenth century usually centred on the religious and the practical – reading, in case she had to take over business responsibilities; some knowledge of arithmetic; and an understanding of household and estate management that might extend to a little property law. The technical skill of writing was rarer: even Margaret's adult signature was rough and unformed. And though a girl might be expected to read the psalms in Latin from an early age, to be able to write the language was so unusual that even the learned Margaret Beaufort, says her confessor Fisher, had later to regret that she had not been taught to do so.

But perhaps this York Margaret benefited to some degree from being brought up with her brothers and their tutors. In later life her own books would be in French – which language she obviously was taught – and her collection of books (at least twenty-five, an impressive number for a woman), together with her habit of giving and receiving them as gifts, demonstrates considerable literary interest. Caxton would later – tactfully, but presumably also truthfully – acknowledge her help in correcting his written English. It was under her auspices that he published the first book to be printed in English, a translation from French of the tales of Troy, and he wrote of how she had 'found a defaut in my English which she commanded me to amend'. Those books that Margaret later owned would be wonderfully illuminated in the lively contemporary style with flowers and fruit, animals and birds. Perhaps she got a full measure of enjoyment out of the gardens at Greenwich, but perhaps, too, the spirit of Duke Humfrey, a famed bibliophile, lingered on.

Margaret's pronounced religiosity may have come from her mother, but although in later life she would give particular support to the practical orders of religion, and had as ardent a passion for relics of the saints as any other medieval lady, she seems to have had a more intellectual interest in the subject than Cecily Neville did. If there were to be a darker, almost hysterical, element in her religious faith, perhaps it only shows that the travails of her family, at her most impressionable age, had not left her untouched.

Anne Neville's father the Earl of Warwick was now the man most thought to be the real power behind the throne; though in fact there is much to suggest that, from Warwick's viewpoint, Edward found his own feet much too quickly. The commons 'love and adore [Edward] as if he were their god', wrote one Italian observer. All the same, Warwick, having helped the new king to his throne, was riding high, restless and busy. Meanwhile his wife and daughters probably spent some of their time at the great northern stronghold of Middleham, at the court and on the countess's own family estates in the West Midlands; a countess had her own household, distinct from her husband's, but this female-led world was not recorded as extensively.

Not that Anne's world was always female. Edward's younger brother Richard spent three years being brought up in Warwick's household; and in 1465 he and Anne were recorded as being at the feast to celebrate the enthronement of Anne's uncle George Neville as Archbishop of York. By this point it would have been evident that the nine-year-old Anne would be a significant heiress, whether or not the thirteen-year-old Richard was mature enough to take note. The continental chronicler Waurin recorded that even now Warwick contemplated marrying his daughters to the king's two brothers. Marriage was in the air for others, too. The young King Edward was about to make a choice based (most unusually for the times) on 'blind affection', as Polydore Vergil describes it disapprovingly.

The story of how Elizabeth Woodville is supposed to have originally met Edward IV is one of the best known from history. But very little is known for certain about Elizabeth's life before she made her royal match because no one was watching. Where fact was absent, fiction rushed in.

The sixteenth-century chronicler Hall had Edward hunting in the forest of Wychwood near Grafton, in Northamptonshire, and coming to the Woodville home for refreshment. Other traditions say Whittlebury Forest, where an oak was long celebrated for the legend that Elizabeth had stood under it – bearing her petition to be granted the lands owed to her under the terms of her dowry, and accompanied by the pleading figures of the two little boys she had borne her dead husband – in order to catch the king's attention as he rode by. Either way Elizabeth, Hall said, 'found such grace in the King's eyes that he not only favoured her suit, but much more fantasised her person. . . . For she was a woman . . . of such beauty and favour that with her sober demeanour, lovely looking and feminine smiling (neither too wanton nor too humble) beside her tongue so eloquent and her wit so pregnant . . . she allured and made subject to her the heart of so great a king.'

After Edward, Hall said, 'had well considered all the lineaments of her body and the wise and womanly demeanour that he saw in her' he tried to bribe her into becoming his mistress (under the more flattering courtly appellation of his 'sovereign lady') in the hope of later becoming his wife. Whereupon she answered that 'as she was unfitted for his honour to be his wife then for her own honesty she was too good to be his concubine', an answer that gave rise to a 'hot burning fire' in the king so that he become quite determined to marry her. The same technique worked again when Anne Boleyn practised it on Elizabeth's grandson Henry VIII, whose likeness to Edward has been much remarked.

Thomas More described the same scenario, which Shakespeare would echo almost exactly – the king struck by this woman 'fair and of good favour, moderate of stature, well-made, and very wise' who claimed that if she was too 'simple' to be his wife she was too good to be his concubine; virtuously refusing Edward's advances, but 'with so good manner, and words so well set, that she rather kindled his desire than quenched it'. Hearne's 'Fragment', written in the early sixteenth century by someone who was probably at Edward's court in its later years, similarly recorded that Edward 'being a lusty prince attempted the stability and constant modesty of divers ladies and gentle-women' but, after resorting at 'diverse times' to Elizabeth, became impressed by her 'constant and stable mind'.

Mancini, writing in 1483, even has Edward holding a dagger to her throat; again, as both More and Hall described the scene, 'she remained unperturbed and determined to die rather than live unchastely with the king. Whereupon Edward coveted her much the more, and he judged the lady worthy to be a royal spouse. . . .' One of the most dramatic versions appeared in Italy very soon after the time, in Antonio Cornazzano's *De*

Mulieribus Admirandis ('of Admirable Women'). This reverses the scenario, to have Elizabeth holding the king off with a dagger – the very stuff of melodrama.

These are stories that equate the nobility of virtue – which Elizabeth could be allowed – with the blood nobility she did not possess. But how much of them is mere story and how much can be substantiated by historical evidence, is uncertain. The tale of the meeting under the tree may well be a myth, and its dating is confusing. It had been as far back as 1461, after Towton, that Edward had ridden slowly south and first found the Lancastrian Woodville family, with their widowed daughter Elizabeth Grey, licking their wounds. One account suggests that, because the romance started there, when the king left the district two days later he had not only 'pardoned and remitted and forgiven' Elizabeth's father all his offences but 'affectionately' agreed to go on paying Jacquetta her annual dowry of 'three hundred and thirty three marks four shillings and a third of a farthing'.

Woodville was indeed pardoned in June 1461, in December of which year the king also agreed that Jacquetta should receive her dowry; and Jean de Waurin early claimed that it was Edward's love for Woodville's daughter that had got the man his pardon. But the actual dates suggest a more prolonged and pragmatic sequence of events.

It is not until 1463 that Elizabeth Woodville next appears in the records, and then it is in the context of a property dispute over her dowry from her first husband. Indeed, in mid-April 1464 she was still negotiating for her dower lands as if she had no idea she was about to become queen.

It is possible that Elizabeth did indeed stand by the side of the road, but in 1464 rather than 1461; however, since her father had been appointed to Edward's council in 1463 she would surely have had better ways to put her plea. Elizabeth may simply have met Edward at court after Woodville had been restored to favour. Caspar Weinreich's *Chronicle* of 1464 claims that: 'The king fell in love with [a mere knight's] wife when he dined with her frequently.' This would make sense. In the early 1460s his advisers mooted various foreign marriages for the new king, and Edward seemed quite content that negotiations should begin. This suggests that he was indeed several years into his reign before he met Elizabeth and changed his mind.

Hall and More have Edward first determining to marry Elizabeth and then taking secret counsel of his friends; but the more popular, and more dramatic, version talks of a marriage made in total secrecy. Robert Fabian, contemporary compiler of the *New Chronicles of England and France* and probably also of the *Great Chronicle of London*, describes a wedding at Grafton early in the morning on May Day 'at which marriage no one was present but the spouse, the spousess, the Duchess of Bedford her mother, the priest, two gentlewomen and a young man to help the priest sing'.

After the ceremony, he says, the king 'went to bed and so tarried there upon three or four hours', returning to his men at Stony Stratford as though he had merely been out hunting but returning to Grafton where Elizabeth was brought every night to his bed, 'in so secret manner that almost none but her mother was council.' May Day is a suitably romantic date – as Malory put it: 'all ye that be lovers, call unto your remembrance the month of May, like as did Queen Guinevere'. It is also Beltane, an important date in the pagan calendar, and in the future accusations would be made that witchcraft had been used to produce so unexpected a match.

The ceremony was certainly sufficiently covert that Richard III's first parliament would later be able to denounce it as an 'ungracious pretensed marriage' by which 'the order of all politic rule was perverted' – one which had taken place privately 'and secretly, without Edition of Banns, in a private Chamber, a profane place'. The secrecy of this marriage did not in fact make it illegal (other reasons would be brought in to support that allegation); indeed, the mere consent of the two parties before witnesses might have been enough. But it did seem odd, at a time when the Church was endeavouring to regulate marriage ceremonies – all the odder in view of the very different style in which a king's wedding would usually be celebrated.

Elizabeth's mother Jacquetta would be blamed for her part in making this marriage; but there were two mothers in this story. Whether Cecily heard before the event and failed to dissuade her son, or learned of the marriage afterwards, she was furious. More's account of her arguments against Elizabeth goes on for pages, urging the vital importance of marrying for foreign alliance, and complaining 'that it was not princely to marry his own subject, no great occasion leading thereunto, no possessions, or other commodities, depending thereupon, but only as it were a rich man would marry his maid, only for a little wanton dotage upon her person'.

Her person, of course, was very much the question. The medieval ideal of female beauty favoured golden hair, dark eyebrows, pale skin, a high forehead, small but slightly full lips, and eyes that were sparkling and usually grey. As for the rest of the body, to quote one contemporary writer, Geoffrey of Vinsauf, 'Let the upper arms, as long as they are slender, be enchanting. Let the fingers be soft and slim in substance, smooth and milk-white in appearance, long and straight in shape . . . Let the snowy bosom present both breasts like virginal gems set side by side. Let the waist be slim, a mere handful . . . let the leg show itself graceful, let the remarkably dainty foot wanton with its own daintiness.'

The depiction or description of queens at this time often owed more to the ideal than to reality. Marguerite of Anjou, for instance, appeared in one illustration with honey-blonde hair, despite the Milanese description of her as dark. Queens were usually shown as blonde because it was attributed to the Virgin Mary. But surviving images of Elizabeth Woodville do suggest a genuine beauty that shines down the centuries as well as conforming to the medieval ideal – beauty enough to eclipse the trying fashion for a high shaven forehead and hair drawn plainly back. A depiction from the 1470s shows her wearing a red dress beneath a blue cloak, like that of the Virgin Mary – red for earthly nature, blue for heavenly attributes – with roses, emblematic of virginity, and gillyflowers, which stood for virtuous love and motherhood. Elizabeth had chosen the deep red gillyflower as her personal symbol; the name itself meant 'queen of delights'.

So even Cecily had to admit that there might be 'nothing to be misliked' in the person of 'this widow'. But she, and many others among Edward's advisers, found plenty more of which to complain. Firstly, of course, there was the simple difference in rank, and the fact that Elizabeth brought no great foreign alliance. Warwick – convinced that only a French marriage would put an end to French support for Marguerite of Anjou – had been in the process of negotiating for Bona of Savoy when Edward broke the news of this other contract. The Italian visitor Mancini would later claim that it was Cecily who declared her son illegitimate since his choice of a woman of lower rank seemingly proved he could not be of the blood of kings.

It is debatable just how far from suitable Elizabeth actually was. Certainly, she was not the princess a king might have been expected to marry. Her mother Jacquetta did come from the cadet branch of the Luxembourg family that gave her connections with the emperors of Germany and the kings of Bohemia. But a woman's status came from her father, and a mother could not share her superior rank with her husband and children. That said, throughout the Middle Ages high-born women had chosen to reflect their maternal heritage, most notably in the arms displayed on their seals; and when the time came for Elizabeth's coronation, much play would be made of her connections with European royalty. Then again, there may have been some popularity value in Elizabeth's very Englishness after the experience with French Marguerite, and even a reconciliatory gain from the Woodville family's attachment to the Lancastrian cause.

Another problem was Elizabeth's widowhood. There was a strong sentiment (More and Mancini both put it higher and make it a custom) that the king's bride should be a virgin, not a widow: even more important if she was to provide the children who would inherit the throne. Decades later Isabella of Castile was still complaining that Edward had refused her for 'a widow of England'; and the king's brother Clarence, said Mancini, went so far as to declare the marriage illegal for this reason. Later, another, more serious, issue would raise its head.[3]

Edward's response to his mother, More says, was 'that he knew himself out of her rule'. Playing to Cecily's well-known religiosity, he added that, 'marriage being a spiritual thing', it should follow the guidance of God who had inclined these two parties 'to love together'[4] rather than be made for temporal advantage. As for Warwick, Edward added, surely he could not be so unreasonable as 'to look that I should in choice of wife rather be ruled by his eye than by my own, as though I were a ward that were bound to marry by the appointment of a guardian'.

Edward was getting tired of his mother's, and his mentor's, governance. And anyway, the deed was done; in the face of mounting rumours Edward admitted as much to his council in September 1464 – even if, said Waurin, in a 'right merry' way that probably indicated embarrassment. Elizabeth was presented to the court on 30 September in the chapel of Reading Abbey. Led in by Edward's brother Clarence and the Earl of Warwick for a ceremony that may have been aimed at replacing the big public wedding that was customary for a queen, she received homage offered on bended knee.

The only Englishwoman to become queen consort[5] since the Norman Conquest, Elizabeth Woodville was crowned the following spring in a ceremony of great magnificence at which her mother's royal kin were carefully given a prominent part. Edward had ordered from abroad 'divers jewels of gold and precious stones, against the Coronation of our dear wife the Queen'; silk for her chairs and saddle; plate, a gold cup and basin at £108 5s 6d; and two cloths of gold. Other expenses show a more homely touch: the bridgemaster of London Bridge bought paint, glue, coloured paper, 'party gold' and 'party silver'. Elizabeth was greeted by a pageant as she crossed the river, coming from Eltham to the south. It included six effigies of virgins with kerchiefs on their heads over wigs made of flax and dyed with saffron; and two of angels, their wings resplendent with nine hundred peacock feathers. Elizabeth made her way to the Tower, where tradition dictated she would spend the first night; next day she was carried in a horse litter to Westminster where she was to spend the night, her arrival heralded by the white and blue splendour of several dozen new-made Knights of the Bath.

Details of the coronation survive in a contemporary manuscript. Elizabeth, clad in a purple mantle, entered Westminster Hall under a canopy of cloth of gold, flanked by bishops and with a sceptre in each hand. Removing her shoes before she entered sacred ground, she walked barefoot followed by her attendants: Cecily's sister, the dowager Duchess of Buckingham; Edward's sisters Elizabeth and Margaret; the queen's own mother; and more than forty other ladies of rank. As the procession moved up to the high altar the queen first knelt, and then prostrated herself, for the solemnities. She was anointed with the holy unction and escorted to her throne 'with great reverence and solemnity'. After mass was sung, the queen processed back into the palace. This, for the queen and to a greater degree for the king, was a ceremony that not only acknowledged but actually created the sacred nature of monarchy.

Elizabeth retired into her chamber before the banquet began: a meal of three 'courses', each of some fifteen or twenty dishes, served with the utmost ceremony. First the queen washed in a basin held by the Duke of Clarence. For the entire duration of the meal the Duke of Suffolk (husband of the king's sister Elizabeth) and the Earl of Essex knelt beside her. To signal each course trumpets were sounded, and a procession of mounted knights made the rounds of the great Westminster Hall. Musicians played 'full melodiously and in most solemn wise', and the festivities ended next day with a tournament. The king had not been present at the ceremonies, and this was an accepted tradition: the queen was always the most important person at her own coronation. But there is another whose name does not appear in the records: the king's mother, Cecily.

It was at this time that Cecily elaborated her title of 'My Lady the King's Mother'[6] – used by her, though more often accorded to Margaret Beaufort – into 'Cecily, the king's mother, and late wife unto Richard in right king of England and of France and lord of Ireland', or, more directly, 'Queen by Right'. Though she spent less time now at court she still kept an apartment – the 'queen's chambers' – in one of the royal palaces. Rather than attempt to dispossess his mother, Edward built a new one for his wife.

According to one report – admittedly made to Elizabeth's

brother – the marriage was, broadly speaking, acceptable in the country: Marguerite, and the turmoil for which she was blamed, had put the ordinary people off foreign royalty. But a newsletter from Bruges reported differently, stating that the 'greater part of the lords and the people in general seem very much dissatisfied'. In court circles it was certainly unwelcome. Woodville ascendancy was bound to upset both the royal family and the great magnate Warwick; the more so, since those who had shed blood for York now saw a household of Lancastrians raised to high status.

EIGHT

Fortune's Pageant

And, being a woman, I will not be slack
To play my part in Fortune's pageant.
Henry VI Part 2, 1.2

In April 1462 the last queen, the deposed Marguerite, had
made her way from Scotland to France; a register of the city
of Rouen, published in July, describes her a few months afterwards being received 'with much honour, by the gentlemen of
the King's suite', and lodging in the house of a Rouen lawyer.
Since the previous year she had been using her old admirer
Pierre de Brezé to negotiate a loan and a fleet with which
to seize the Channel Islands as a bridgehead from France to
England: 'If the Queen's intentions were discovered, her friends
would unite with her enemies to kill her,' de Brezé said.
Foreseeing 'good winnings', the French king Louis (possibly
under pressure from his mother, Marguerite's aunt) did eventually give her aid, with Marguerite, in a gesture which would
have horrified her English subjects, promising to cede him
Calais in return. In the autumn of 1462 she had sailed back
to Scotland, bringing forty ships and eight hundred soldiers
provided by the French king and under de Brezé's command.
Collecting some Scots led by Somerset (and nominally by the

deposed Henry VI), she pushed across the border into northern England where she made 'open war', as the *Great Chronicle of London* put it.

Her campaign was unsuccessful. When the Yorkist guns on England's northern coast were trained upon her she was forced to turn tail: 'And in a carvel, wherein was the substance of her goods, she fled; and as she sailed there came upon her such a tempest that she was fain to leave the carvel and take a fisher's boat, and so went a-land to Berwick; and the said carvel and goods were drowned.' Edward himself rode north to confront her; but the next spring, as *Gregory's Chronicle* describes it, she was still fighting on in the north.

In the summer of 1463 there took place one of the few episodes from these wars which have been converted into story. The Duke of Burgundy's official historian Georges Chastellain may have heard the gist of it from Marguerite herself only a few months later – but Chastellain was a poet and rhetorician as much as a chronicler, for whom the message may have been more important than the facts. As Marguerite and her party were fleeing back towards Bamburgh, so the story runs, she and her son were separated from their followers. Suddenly a band of robbers leaped out of the bushes, seized the baggage, tore the jewels from around her neck and dragged her before their leader. He had drawn his sword to cut her throat when she threw herself on her knees and implored him not to disfigure her body past recognition, for, as she said: 'I am the daughter and wife of a king, and was in past times recognized by your-selves as your queen.' In the best tradition of monster-taming myth, the man, known as Black Jack, in turn fell on his knees before her and then led her and her son to a secret cave in Deepden Woods, where she sheltered until de Brezé found her.[7]

Less romantic, if perhaps also exaggerated, is the fact that, as Chastellain tells it, Marguerite was now so poor she had to borrow a groat from a Scottish archer to make an offering on St Margaret's feast day. Indeed, for five days Chastellain claims, she and her husband and son were forced to subsist on a single day's ration of bread, and 'one herring between the three'.

There is, of course, an air of unreality about Chastellain's story, but there is no doubt that Margaret went back to the continent, leaving her husband behind to roam as a fugitive in the north, hiding in friendly houses. Over the next few years she attempted to rally support from the rulers of Brittany, Burgundy, Germany and Portugal, as well as France. Chastellain describes not only her forcible pleading with the European monarchs but the 'wonder' caused by her arrival in Burgundy, since she had once been the duke's mortal enemy. 'Wherefore were heard divers murmurs against her in many mouths, and many savage comments on the nature of her misfortune.' Marguerite, Chastellain says, arrived in Burgundy:

> poor and alone, destitute of goods and all desolate; [she] had neither credence, nor money, nor goods, nor jewels to pledge. [She] had her son, no royal robes, nor estate; and her person without adornment befitting a queen. Her body was clad in one single robe, with no change of clothing. [She] had no more than seven women for her retinue, and whose apparel was like that of their mistress, formerly one of the most splendid women of the world and now one of the poorest; and finally she had no other provision nor even bread to eat, except from the purse of her knight. . . . It was a thing piteous to see, truly, this high princess so cast down and laid low in such great danger, dying of hunger and hardship.

For all his sympathy, it is hard not to feel that the Burgundian chronicler was relishing the drama of Marguerite's 'lowliness and abasement' as he describes how the English in Calais were trying to capture her, how she had been forced to travel in a farm cart 'covered over with canvas and harnessed with four mares like a poor woman going unknown'. The Burgundian duke tried to dodge her for a time, but when Marguerite sent word that: 'Were my cousin of Burgundy to go to the end of the world I would follow him' he gave way, and after meeting her sent both financial aid and his sister the Duchess of Bourbon as a companion. The two women struck up an eager friendship, with Marguerite recounting amazing adventures. The duchess agreed that if a book were to be written on the troubles of royal ladies, Marguerite's would be acknowledged as the most shocking of catastrophes.

Marguerite was finally forced to retreat to her father's estate at St Michel-sur-Bar, living on an inadequate pension from him and paying visits to her European relatives. Letters from her officers detail the continued extreme shortage of ready money – hardly enough coins to pay the messenger – 'but yet the Queen sustaineth us in meat and drink, so as we be not in extreme necessity'. Early in 1465 she tried again to get help from King Louis, but, realising she was in no position to make demands, he merely mocked her plea. In July that year the fugitive Henry VI was finally captured and, after a humiliating journey south with his legs tied to his horse's stirrups and a straw hat on his head, placed in comparatively lenient imprisonment in the Tower. Here he was at liberty to receive visitors, even though Lancastrian chroniclers complained that he was not kept clean as a king should be. He would remain in captivity for the next five years while – for an England settling into Edward's rule and Elizabeth's queenship – Marguerite on the continent was a threat that refused to go away.

Marguerite's own mood must have been made the more desperate by news that things were going well in England, especially when she learned that it was the daughter of her old friend Jacquetta who had changed sides and supplanted her, with Jacquetta's active connivance. This year, 1465, Elizabeth was asked to become patroness of the college (now Queens') that Marguerite herself had founded in Cambridge 'to laud and honour of sex feminine'. Patronage was an established function of queenship; royally born or not, Elizabeth Woodville was settling into her new role.

Hard on the heels of her coronation came news that Queen Elizabeth was pregnant, and in February 1466 Elizabeth of York was born at Westminster. The physician – or astrologer – Master Dominic had been convinced this would be a prince, says the chronicler Fabian; when the child turned out to be a girl the Archbishop of York was substituted for that of Canterbury at the christening. But there was no other diminution of ceremony. A visitor from Bohemia, one Gabriel Tetzel, who had arrived in the retinue of the lord of Rozmital, left an account of the queen's magnificent churching forty days after the birth.

Tetzel was already convinced that this was 'the most splendid court that one can find in all Christendom' when he saw the procession that headed to Westminster Abbey – forty-two singers, twenty-four heralds, sixty lords before the queen and sixty-two ladies after her. The banquet that followed – or rather banquets, since the king and queen kept their separate state – was a striking display of court etiquette. Some commentators have taken it as an example of the upstart Elizabeth Woodville's personal grandiosity, but in fact it may have been no more than the reverence the English were expected to pay to majesty.

Leo von Rozmital and his party were carefully seated (King Edward would have wanted reports of the occasion to spread abroad) in an alcove of 'a particularly splendid and decorated hall' where Elizabeth sat alone at table on a costly golden chair. 'The queen's mother and the king's sister had to stand below,' said Tetzel. 'And if the queen talked with her mother or with the king's sister, they had to kneel before the queen until she drank water. Not until the first dish was set before her were they allowed to sit down.' Her ladies had, he says, to kneel as long as she was eating – no light undertaking, since the meal lasted three silent hours.

Edward's sister Elizabeth was on the new queen's right, his youngest sister, Margaret, on her left. No mention was made of the king's eldest sister, Anne – and his mother, Cecily, presumably chose to absent herself. After the banquet came the dancing: Margaret took the floor with two dukes 'in stately dances, and made impressive courtesies to the queen such as I have never seen elsewhere; nor have I witnessed such outstandingly beautiful maidens.' Edward's charm offensive, designed to increase his reputation around the European courts, had clearly worked spectacularly well and his queen was proving an adept, new to the task though she might be.

The only surviving accounts for Elizabeth Woodville date from 1466–7, and, though it is tempting to concentrate on the colourful details (£14 for sable furs, £18 7s 6d for medicines), they make it clear that to be a queen was not only to be a diplomatic pawn, a breeding machine (she gave birth to a second daughter, Mary, in August 1467) and a decorative accessory. A major element in the role was to be the head of an important household, the mistress of large and widely dispersed estates, and an employer of labourers, craftsmen and professionals in many different capacities.

Elizabeth's income during this period was £4541 (as opposed to the extravagant Marguerite of Anjou's £7563, fourteen years before) but she ended the year in profit, unlike Marguerite, employing seven maids to Marguerite's ten and paying more cautiously. Marguerite had paid one of her principal ladies-in-waiting, Barbalina, 40 marks a year; Elizabeth paid her principal ladies 20. Her husband did not charge her, as

Marguerite's had done, for the time her household spent living with his; some recompense for the fact that he could not afford to grant her dower lands on the scale her predecessor had enjoyed. Elizabeth was sharp when she needed to be in the pursuance of her rights: an undated letter to Sir William Stonor chastises him for the fact that he had taken it upon himself 'to make masteries within our forest and chace of Barnwood and Exhill, and there, in contempt of us, uncourteously to hunt and slay our deer within the same, to our great marvel and displeasure'. In 1468 instructions of the king's concerning the Pastons' affairs were echoed by letters from the queen to the duchesses of Norfolk and Suffolk; she had already written more directly to the Earl of Oxford on the same point. But there remains the question of when and how the use of her influence might be seen as inappropriate by her contemporaries.

A queen was allowed and even expected to exercise influence[8] – to intercede on behalf of those to whom she owed protection. It was part of the symbiotic relationship the phrase 'good ladyship' implied. But Elizabeth's advancement of her family over the years did leave both herself and her husband vulnerable to attack. Certainly these years saw a cementing of Woodville alliances in a way that seemed threatening to other members of the nobility – not least to Edward's brother Clarence. Five Woodville brothers and five sisters married into the nobility, the men being given influential posts; to say nothing, as they grew, of those two sons by her first marriage. The Milanese envoy's later report that since her coronation Elizabeth 'had always exerted herself to aggrandise her relations . . . they had the entire government of the realm' might have been based on her enemy Warwick's propaganda; but it did reflect the popular perception. When Warwick, turning later against Edward, proclaimed him guilty of turning to a life of 'pastime, pleasure, and dalliance' and choosing unsuitable companions, 'men descended of low blood and base degree', he was using the Woodville connection as a stick with which to beat the king, as well as bringing up the concept of scape-goats – 'evil counsellors' – which the would-be kingmakers of these years had so frequently invoked.

Up to a point Elizabeth had been doing what anyone would have done, and in many ways Warwick and his associates had been just the same. There is a case for suggesting that Edward had consciously elevated the Woodvilles as an alterna-tive power base to Warwick's: one dependent on him, rather than on his mentor, and one which he could control. Elizabeth's family, after all, had now become his. The Woodville rise had been, however, both flamboyant and somewhat roughshod – in 1466 Elizabeth's sister Katherine, for example, was married to the youthful Duke of Buckingham, who, in later years, was said to have bitterly resented a bride he felt was beneath him. One of her brothers, John, no more than twenty, had made a marriage that attracted widespread disapproval with the Duchess of Norfolk, 'a slip of a girl about eighty years old'.* The queen's father had been given the title Earl Rivers. One day the king's fool promenaded through the court, dressed as for passing through water. When the king asked why, he punned that he had had difficulty passing through many parts of the realm because the 'Rivers' were running so high.

There was trouble in the late 1460s because of the prominent part the Woodvilles were said to have played in arranging the

---

* As so often, a look at the personalities offers a slightly different perspective: this Duchess of Norfolk, Katherine Neville, Cecily Neville's elder sister, had been married off by her father in 1412, in the chapel of Raby Castle, to the Duke of Norfolk. She mulcted his estates after he died; then married a servant in the household; then married a third time to a Viscount Beaumont. She would outlive all her husbands, the last included. It is just possible she – probably in her sixties, rather than her late seventies – was not entirely the passive victim here.

marriage between Charles, Duke of Burgundy and Edward's sister Margaret, who since the queen's arrival had been living at court as one of her ladies. Indeed, Crowland says that the enmity between the Woodvilles and Warwick really began when he heard that they ('in conformity with the King's wishes') were promoting the Burgundian match. That comment is probably key: the Woodvilles were only carrying out Edward's wishes. None the less the pageantry associated with such a marriage was a field in which the young Woodvilles, with their continental inheritance from their mother Jacquetta, could shine.

At a legendary tournament at Smithfield in London in June 1467 Elizabeth Woodville's brother Anthony – his horses variously decked out in white cloth of gold; in damasks of purple, green and tawny; in blue and crimson velvet; and in crimson cloth trimmed with sables – fought the 'Bastard of Burgundy', the half-brother of Duke Charles, in a ritual battle carefully brought to an end by the king before the knights could do real damage to each other or to his diplomacy. Anthony Woodville, the ultimate early Renaissance man, told a chivalric tale of how the queen's ladies pounced on him (while he was speaking to his sister on his knees, 'my bonnet off my head, according to my duty') and tied a jewelled band to his leg, with a letter bidding him to attend the tournament – 'the adventure of the flower of Souvenance', or remembrance. The emphasis on courtly parade in the reign of Edward IV deliberately evoked his inheritance from Edward III, and thus provided a king who had seized his crown with an aura of legitimacy. So far did the fifteenth-century chivalric 'revival' go that knights were actually known to set up their shield at crossroads and wait for challengers, in the approved Arthurian style. But the parade was useful also for Edward's queen. In a society that was arguably becoming more patriarchal, the chivalric spectacle provided a platform for women.

Underneath all this pageantry lurked something darker. Louis of France – who had no wish for his two enemies, England and Burgundy, to form any alliance – had been spreading malicious rumours about Princess Margaret's chastity. It was the Milanese ambassador at the French court who passed on stories that she was 'somewhat attached to love affairs and even, in the opinion of many, has had a son'. There is no reason to believe there was any truth in the tale, but Edward's own love affairs and colourful marriage must have lent it some air of plausibility. None the less, the tournament held when Margaret arrived in the Burgundian city of Bruges, known as the Tournament of the Golden Tree, was no less splendid than the one at Smithfield and may have been more genuinely perilous. Burgundy paid full lip service to the courtly ideal, and Charles truly loved warfare. In the end, Margaret had to wave her handkerchief in the time-honoured way to ask him to call off the bloodshed. She was, so John Paston reported, 'received as worshipfully as all the world could devise'.

Elizabeth Woodville's brothers were prominent among the escort who accompanied Margaret across the Channel. In Bruges, Edward Woodville was declared prince of the tourney. Anthony was Margaret's chief presenter at the Burgundian court. The English government had granted expenses to send Margaret off generously equipped with £1000 worth of silks and £160 worth of gold, silver and gilt dishes. She would have needed such finery for the nine-day celebrations, at which the feasting guests delighted in gilded swans and harts carrying panniers of oranges, and unicorns bearing baskets of sweetmeats; monkeys threw trinkets to the company, and a court dwarf on a gilded lion competed for attention with a wild man on a dromedary. John Paston wrote: 'As for the Duke's court as of ladies and gentle-women, knights, squires and gentlemen I heard never of none like to it save King Arthur's court . . . for such gear and gold and pearl and stones they of the Duke's court, neither gentlemen or gentlewomen, they want none.' In Aachen, a crown still survives inscribed 'MARGARIT[A] DE [Y]O[R]K'. Made of silver-gilt, enamel, precious stones and pearls, ornamented with white roses, it is most likely to have been made either to celebrate Margaret's wedding, or else as a votive offering to be worn by the statue of the Virgin that still carries it on major feast days.

There is no reason to doubt that, on the other side of the royal family, Cecily too approved her daughter's marriage. Charles was, in Edward's words, 'one of the mightiest Princes in the world that beareth no crown', and queens (the position to which Cecily aspired) expected to send their daughters away. All the same, it is impossible to separate the acknowledgement of the Yorkist dynasty that Margaret's marriage represented from the success of the Woodville family; while the prominence of the unpopular Woodvilles in its turn helped to ensure that the Lancastrian threat never went away.

These were, after all, still paranoid years. Messengers from abroad, bringing instructions from Marguerite,[9] were being captured. Part of the money for the dowry Margaret took to Burgundy had been raised by a loan from London merchants but one of them, Sir Thomas Cook, was arrested before she left the country. One Cornelius, a shoemaker serving one of Marguerite of Anjou's gentlemen, had been found carrying incriminating letters from Lancastrian exiles and was tortured 'by burning in the feet until he confessed many things'. He named a man called John Hawkins as a Lancastrian supporter; Hawkins, in turn, accused Sir Thomas Cook. But what had set Cook at odds with the Yorkist dynasty? The *Great Chronicle of London* suggests that Elizabeth Woodville's mother, whose insultingly low offer for a fine tapestry he had refused, was seeking her revenge.

Jasper Tudor had never flagged in his support for the cause of Henry VI, and in the summer of 1468 – just weeks after Margaret had set sail for Burgundy – he landed in Wales with three ships provided by the French king Louis. It was too small a force for a serious invasion but it represented, as it was intended to, an embarrassment for King Edward. As one of Edward's chief supporters in Wales, William Herbert was ordered to raise troops and ride against Jasper Tudor. Herbert was also Henry Tudor's guardian, and he took the twelve-year-old boy with him for his first taste of action. Jasper and Henry, uncle and nephew, were on opposite sides of the battlefield, but luckily neither saw dreadful consequences that day. Even so, the thought of the danger in which her son had been put must have been terrifying for Margaret.

Indeed, Margaret Beaufort's position had already been undermined by the actions of her extended family. At the start of his reign Edward had shown her and her husband a certain amount of generosity, granting them the great moated manor house of Woking[10] where they made a luxurious home. It looked as if the Beaufort fortunes were slowly rising again. In 1463 Margaret's cousin Henry, the third Duke of Somerset, had accepted a pardon and received many favours from the new king. But only the next year Somerset had betrayed Edward and been summarily executed. His younger brother and heir, the fourth duke, became a leader of the Lancastrian exiles. After that, the king could hardly be blamed if he looked on all Beauforts warily.

NINE

Domestic Broils

and domestic broils
Clean over-blown, themselves the conquerors
Make war upon themselves, brother to brother
Richard III, 2.4

It would swiftly become apparent that the threat from surviving Lancastrians was not the only one that Edward IV and Elizabeth Woodville faced. The Yorkist dynasty was soon in greater danger from divisions within. Warwick had been growing steadily more dissatisfied both with his position under Edward's rule and with Woodville prominence. As the ally of Edward's father York, and as guiding spirit of Edward's own military takeover, he had naturally expected to play a pre-eminent part in the management of the country. But as the new king settled ever more firmly into the seat of power, Warwick found himself increasingly alienated. And as he began to move against Edward, he found himself an extraordinary ally.

George, Duke of Clarence was likewise disaffected, resentful of his position as a mere adjunct to his brother's regime. For a while he had hoped to find an alternative sphere of influence. There was talk of a second Burgundian marriage, with Clarence marrying Charles of Burgundy's daughter and heiress presumptive Mary. But that came to nothing, perhaps because Edward would have been dubious about giving Clarence access to a foreign crown.

Instead, on 12 July 1469 the nineteen-year-old Clarence, described by contemporaries as 'seemly of person and well-visaged' as well as 'right witty', married Warwick's elder daughter Isabel, just a year younger than he. This was another marriage choice of which his brother the king disapproved. The 'Worcester'[11] chronicle suggests that two years earlier he had forbidden it, and had blocked attempts to secure the papal dispensation necessary for two second cousins to marry. For Edward, the erratic Clarence would be a potential weapon in Warwick's hands. In addition, until the king had a son Clarence was his likeliest heir, so Edward had a strong vested interest in negotiating a marriage for the benefit of the country. Warwick and Clarence had therefore arranged for the marriage to Isabel to take place in the earl's own jurisdiction of Calais, away from Edward's eye.

Clarence's position in the line of succession was obviously of prime importance to his new father-in-law. It was around this time and on the continent among Warwick's allies that rumours of Edward's bastardy can first be traced with certainty – rumours that implied Clarence was the true heir of the Yorkist monarchy. It has been suggested that Clarence's mother Cecily had now told him this was true:[12] that his elder brother had been conceived in adultery. (It was in 1469 that Edward asked his mother to exchange the castle of Fotheringhay, into which she had poured both money and effort, for the somewhat run-down Berkhamsted in Hertfordshire; this could be interpreted as punishment for spreading damaging rumours, or simply for a too-visible partiality on her part.) Certainly Cecily travelled to Sandwich in Kent, the port from which the wedding party was leaving; and she may have done so to give them her blessing. Not only was

Clarence her son but Isabel her goddaughter, an important connection in the fifteenth century. She may, however, have been hoping instead to dissuade Clarence from a plan that could only divide her family.

Warwick and Clarence had issued a proclamation inveighing against certain 'seditious persons' prominent at Edward's court, notably Elizabeth Woodville's father, brothers and mother – interestingly, the only woman named. (To have named the queen herself would have been a little too close to the bone.) The day after the wedding Warwick and Clarence sailed to England, almost certainly leaving their womenfolk to follow later. On 29 July Warwick managed to capture Edward and took him north to imprisonment in Yorkshire. In August Margaret Beaufort, ever the opportunist, visited the London residence of the newly prominent Clarence, hoping to negotiate over those lands of Henry's which he held, and surely to regain custody of her son.

The terrible news hit Queen Elizabeth while on a formal visit to Norwich. It was only four months after the birth of her third daughter, named Cecily for her grandmother. Warwick had captured her father, and her brother John, after the battle of Edgecote and executed them without trial.

Elizabeth returned to London, to live in 'scant state'. Fearful for her husband, she had also to cope with accusations of witchcraft brought against her mother (possibly as a precursor to declaring invalid the marriage Jacquetta had helped to make). As evidence, a Northamptonshire gentleman called Thomas Wake produced 'an image of lead made like a man of arms the length of a man's finger broken in the middle and made fast with a wire'; along with two other images, of a man and a woman, which he claimed Jacquetta had commissioned as a means of binding the king and her daughter together. Witchcraft was a serious allegation – one of the few from which even royal rank would not protect a woman.*

Jacquetta, however, had allies behind her – and not only her relations. Her intercession with Marguerite on behalf of London almost a decade earlier had won her friends in the city, to whose authorities she now appealed for support. The wheel of Fortune was about to spin again. There was not enough support for Warwick's coup. Edward escaped from captivity on 10 September and reached London in October, making a triumphal entry into the city. He commanded that the charges against his mother-in-law be examined, and by January 1470 Jacquetta had been cleared of the 'said slander'. If Thomas Wake had been, as seems likely, a pawn of Clarence and Warwick, Jacquetta had been yet another woman to suffer because of the friction between the York brothers.

In December at Westminster Edward staged a deliberately public reconciliation with his brother Clarence and cousin Warwick; but as John Paston reported, though the two lords claimed now to be the king's best friends, 'his household men have other language, so what shall hastily fall I cannot say'. Cecily and her daughters would probably have been working[13] for a real rapprochement. Efforts were made, too, to reconcile the cousinship: young Elizabeth of York was betrothed to Warwick's nephew, suggesting that if Edward failed to produce a son the crown might pass to his daughter rather than to Clarence in the collateral male line. If this were true, however, it would have pushed Clarence even further in his opposition to Edward – the more so since there was also now discussion of restoring young Henry Tudor to his father's earldom of Richmond, greatly to the detriment of

---

* There had been Henry IV's dowager queen, Joan of Navarre, in 1419 briefly imprisoned on the accusation of it. There had been Eleanor Cobham, Humfrey of Gloucester's wife (and thus once Jacquetta's sister-in-law, in the days when she had been Duchess of Bedford) charged in 1441 by her husband's enemies and sentenced to imprisonment for life, as well as humiliating public penance.

Clarence who had been holding the associated lands.

The peacemaking attempts were in vain. Clarence and Warwick quickly returned north, and perhaps the only one to gain was Marguerite, since Louis of France had responded to the Yorkist confusion by inviting the Lancastrian queen to his court. Here she enjoyed not only a reunion with her father, but the promise of French support. Back in England, in early 1470 more rebellions broke out. In March Cecily invited Edward and Clarence to Baynard's Castle, her London home, in an attempt to bring about an agreement, but to no avail. Warwick and Clarence then instituted fresh uprisings. When Edward rode out to deal with them Margaret Beaufort's husband, the peaceable Henry Stafford, was summoned to arm himself and ride out with him. After Margaret's misguided attempt to negotiate with Clarence the previous autumn, there was need for a proof of loyalty.

In April Warwick, and the wife and daughters who had now joined him and Clarence, were forced to flee. Their confidence in finding safe haven in Warwick's territory of Calais was, however, misplaced: the city was closed against them. This was bad news for everybody but disastrous for the heavily pregnant Isabel who, with probably only her mother and sister as attendants, went into labour on the tiny heaving ship with only two flagons of wine sent by the Calais commander for her relief. Her baby was stillborn.

It was the beginning of May before the party were allowed to make landfall in Normandy, and then perhaps only because Louis had decided that the diplomatic treaties which prevented him from openly helping Warwick permitted him to give refuge to the ladies. Spare a thought for Anne Neville here: besides the general misfortune that had befallen her family, she must have known that her own hopes of making a good marriage had declined dramatically. Until, that is, she heard what fortune – or her father – had in store.

Edward in England now had two enemies in exile: Warwick, and Marguerite of Anjou. As far back as 1467, it was claimed, some believed the earl 'favoured Queen Margaret's party'. Whether or not this was true, it may now have been the serpentine brain of Louis – the 'spider king' whose machinations Machiavelli observed before writing *The Prince* – that conceived the idea of making an alliance between these two, themselves long the bitterest of enemies. And the age knew only one good way of cementing that sort of alliance: marriage.

Marguerite had an unmarried son, Warwick an unmarried daughter. The Milanese ambassador to the French court gives a long account of Louis trying to persuade Marguerite to endorse the Warwick marriage, and of how she had shown herself 'very hard and difficult', keeping the earl on his knees before her as she railed. Another account, *The Manner and Guiding of the Earl of Warwick at Angers in July and August 1470*, agrees that she was 'right dificyle'. Not only, she exploded, had Warwick 'injured her as a queen, but he had dared to defame her reputation as a woman by divers false and malicious slanders'.

Anne's feelings about the plan can only be guessed at. The little that is known of her prospective bridegroom, another Edward, is not attractive. The Milanese envoy reported that, as a child, he talked of nothing but cutting off heads. Hall would describe him as having matured into 'a goodly girlish looking and well featured young gentleman'. Still, by the very nature of diplomacy a high-ranking girl was at least as likely to be married to an enemy as to a friend. And of course it was a splendid match – if Henry VI's throne could but be regained for him. But even in an age when most aristocratic marriages were bargains, few brides (Elizabeth Woodville apart) can have had to face quite such a furious reception from their prospective mother-in-law.

The two accounts vary a little over the timing, but *The Manner and Guiding* claims that Queen Marguerite held out for fifteen days[14] against every argument the king of France could show her. 'Some time she said that she saw never honour nor profit for her, nor for her son the Prince. In other [times] she [al]ledged that and she would, she should find a more profitable party, and of more advantage, with the King of England. And indeed, she showed unto the King of France a Letter which she said was sent her out of England the last week, by the which was offered to her son My Lady the Princess' – that is, Elizabeth of York.

Even when Marguerite had given in, the marriage treaty was packed full of conditions, not least 'that from thence forth the said daughter of the Earl of Warwick [Anne] shall be put and remain in the hands and keeping of Queen Margaret', and that 'the said marriage shall not be perfected to [until] the Earl of Warwick had been with an army over the Sea into England, and that he had recovered the realm of England . . .' . If he failed to do so, Anne was presumably to have been left high and dry. But the Milanese ambassador suggests rather that the marriage had to be delayed by the need to wait for a papal dispensation since this couple, like so many others, were related by blood, in the fourth degree.

Warwick and Clarence set sail, to land in the West Country in mid-September 1470. They claimed always to be doing so in the name of King Henry and 'by the assent of the most noble princess, Margaret, Queen of England' and her son. King Edward was in the north, trying to put down a rebellion organised by Warwick's brother-in-law; having moved his pregnant wife and daughters into the Tower (which Elizabeth, as the contemporary *Warkworth's Chronicle* says, 'well victualled and fortified') for safety while he was away. Soon Marguerite and her son, together with the young Anne at Amboise in France, heard of a great victory.

Warwick's army had moved south. The mayor of London was trying to raise a defence, but a Lancastrian supporter had thrown open Southwark jail and a mob burst out. There is a vivid description of Queen Elizabeth releasing the Tower to the mayor's control: he is leading her family to the waterside, she holding a chest of jewels, while her daughters drag bedsheets stuffed with clothing behind them to the boats which would carry them upriver to Westminster Abbey and sanctuary.

On 1 October the Tower fell. Two days later, though Elizabeth and her daughters would not have known it, Edward, his brother Richard and Elizabeth's brother Anthony commandeered a boat to the Low Countries and eventually sought refuge with Edward's sister, Margaret of Burgundy. The Yorkist regime was over – for the moment, anyway.

TEN

That Was a Queen

Thyself a queen, for me that was a queen,
Outlive thy glory, like my wretched self.
Richard III, 1.3

Warwick's Lancastrian supporters came flooding up from Kent, and three days later the earl himself entered the city and did at least calm the rioting. He also released King Henry from imprisonment, although the befuddled king seemed hardly to care that he had once again reclaimed the throne. Elizabeth Woodville was (in official parlance) no longer queen, Cecily Neville no longer the mother of a king, albeit that another of her sons was prominent on the victorious side. The four-year-old Elizabeth of York and her younger sisters were staying somewhere in the mass of low-lying buildings between Westminster Abbey and the river. They probably lived in the abbot's house, where Abbot Mylling certainly received them with kindness and offered occasional luxuries, while a London butcher provided 'half a beef and two muttons' every week. None the less the official Yorkist narrative of these months, *The Historie of the Arrivall of Edward IV in England*, describes Elizabeth Woodville at least as enduring 'great trouble, sorrow, and heaviness, which she

113

sustained with all manner patience that belonged to any creature'.

Meanwhile in Burgundy Duchess Margaret, in warm remembrance of her Yorkist roots, sent letters to her refugee brothers Edward and Richard, while her husband the duke sent funds. Margaret was concerned above all to heal the rifts in her family, but the appearance of these new exiles was something of an embarrassment to a duke still anxious to keep peace with the rapacious French. It was not until Christmas that the new arrivals were invited to join the Burgundian court, France's hostile intentions towards its neighbour having at last become unmistakeable. Still, Margaret, delighted at being allowed to meet and help her two brothers, was active in raising money for their cause.

For Margaret Beaufort in England, the news of Warwick's take-over had been welcome. The Lancastrians were back, supported by Jasper Tudor who had sailed with Warwick's fleet in September, and young Henry Tudor could be handed over into his uncle's custody. By the end of October, Jasper and Henry were in London and Margaret, reunited with her son, took him to see his restored uncle Henry VI who (as Polydore Vergil later told it) prophesied future greatness for the boy. With her son and husband she then travelled to Woking for what sounds like a joyous holiday before handing her son back to his uncle Jasper, to be trained as a nobleman should be, while she herself resumed negotiations with Clarence about his inheritance.

On 2 November 1470 Elizabeth Woodville, still in sanctuary at Westminster, gave birth to a boy. The arrival of a long-awaited son and heir should have been a moment of the greatest triumph for her, but at this moment now no one could tell what his future would be. A prince should have had a cradle canopied in cloth of gold, an ermine-trimmed blanket and the grandest of christenings. Instead, with his grandmother Jacquetta and the abbot for godparents, the baby Edward was baptised in the Abbey 'like a poor man's child'. In a sense he was indeed temporarily a poor man's child – or at least a poor woman's. Henry VI was restrained about claiming back Yorkist lands; he did, however, seize the dower properties of Elizabeth and Jacquetta.

Elizabeth's treacherous brother-in-law, Clarence, had ridden behind Warwick as he entered London, but as the weeks wore on he was once again becoming increasingly disaffected. The marriage deal between Warwick and Marguerite had neatly cut him out. Curiously, Marguerite, whose return to England would surely have confirmed the authority and permanence of the new regime, was still across the Channel. She and her son, with Warwick's wife and daughters, had spent the autumn at the French court, where the records of Louis' receiver of finance show monies paid out for their maintenance, for their silver-ware, 'for their pleasures'. Marguerite's delay might indicate not only a lack of eagerness to be reunited with her husband, but also that she had never connected with England emotionally. Perhaps, though, it may have been simply that Louis demanded her and Anne's presence as a guarantee of Warwick's honesty – they were hostages, in the nicest possible way.

After the news of Warwick's success, Anne Neville and Edward of Lancaster were finally married in Amboise on 13 December. Her mother and sister were present. It is unclear whether the marriage was immediately consummated, the one way of making it irrevocable – several years later Crowland was still describing Anne as a 'maiden'. On the day after the wedding they left for a ceremonial entry into the city of Paris.

It was well after Christmas before Marguerite set out for Rouen, where she expected to find Warwick waiting to escort her back to England. In fact he had remained in England, having more urgent business to attend to. When she finally realised he was not coming, and travelled to the coast without him, not only were the winds unfavourable but frightening rumours urged caution. It was almost the end of March 1471 before the party attempted to set sail, only to be held up further by those contrary winds.

The delay was fatal. On 11 March Edward, with his brother Richard of Gloucester and his brother-in-law Anthony Woodville, had sailed back to England with a new army. He landed three days later north of the river Humber, winning his welcome into the city of York with the now traditional announcement that he sought only his father's inheritance as Duke of York. Working their way southwards, his forces set up camp outside the town of Warwick where the opposing army was led by Clarence. And there, amazingly, the two elder York brothers were reconciled. It was an extraordinary, dramatic turn of events.

Marguerite of Anjou and her new daughter-in-law must have suffered the bitterness of knowing that, if only they had arrived earlier, the pulls and fractions within the Lancastrian party, the support in the country, might have played out very differently. Anne's sister Isabel had crossed the Channel to England earlier to be with her husband Clarence, the results of whose deliberations now placed her on the opposite side to her father, mother and sister. But the *Arrivall* reports that Edward and Clarence were under pressure from their own female relatives, with 'the high and mighty princess my Lady, their mother; my lady of Exeter, my lady of Suffolk, their sisters . . . and, most specially, my Lady of Bourgoigne [Burgundy]' mediating between the two 'by right covert ways and means'. Other sources too record Margaret's 'great and diligent efforts', her streams of messengers: Crowland says Clarence had been reconciled to his brother 'by the mediation of his sisters, the

Duchesses of Burgundy and Exeter', the former working on the king and the latter on the duke. Some suspected a deal had been under negotiation for months – a deal with Margaret of Burgundy as the go-between.

When Clarence had been in Calais the previous year, says the continental writer Philippe de Commynes,[15] he had been approached by a mysterious Englishwoman 'of few words' who claimed she had come from England to serve the duchess (Clarence's wife Isabel) as waiting woman, and requested a private interview. When they were alone, she produced a letter from Edward offering full forgiveness if he would return to the fold. Clarence gave an ambiguous promise to return and the lady, 'the only contriver of the enterprise', departed as mysteriously as she had arrived.

After the battlefield reconciliation Margaret of Burgundy wrote a description to her mother-in-law: 'Clarence with a small company left his people behind him and approached my lord and brother who saw him coming and Lord Clarence threw himself on his knees so that my lord and brother seeing his humility and hearing his words, lifted him up and embraced him several times and gave him his good cheer. . . .'

For the Earl of Warwick, this was catastrophe – for him and, of course, for all those women still tied to the Lancastrian side. Clarence tried to mediate a deal between his brother and his father-in-law, but to no avail. Edward retook London in a bloodless coup, making sure as he neared the city to send 'comfortable messages to the Queen' – Elizabeth Woodville. Most of the Lancastrians powerful enough to stand against him were heading for the West Country to greet Marguerite – the attempt to rally forces against Edward was led by Sir Thomas Cook, the man with whom Jacquetta had quarrelled over a tapestry. Henry returned without argument to captivity in the Tower, while Edward moved in procession towards

Westminster. His reunion with his family – now the richer by that all-important baby boy, his father's 'most desired treasure' – was a great propaganda opportunity. In the words of a later ballad:

> The King comforted the Queen and the other ladies eke.
> His sweet baby full tenderly he did kiss.
> The young prince he beheld and in his arms did bear.
> Thus his bale turned him to bliss.

But of course things were not quite that sunny, and Fortune's wheel could turn yet again. Despite the blow of Clarence's defection Warwick could never be underestimated, and Marguerite was known to be on the way with a French army. Edward sent his family to his mother's home of Baynard's Castle, where Clarence and Gloucester joined them for the night. It was Holy Thursday, a few days before Easter, but Elizabeth Woodville's feelings must have been less than Christian as she looked at Clarence, the man who had been instrumental in putting her through so much.

Two days later on Good Friday Edward returned to London, to take his family to the Tower for safety while he rode out again. On Easter Day his force met Warwick's at Barnet[16] in a fog so dense that some suggested it must have been raised by witchcraft, or, as the chronicler Fabian put it, 'incantations'. The fighting was intense and bloody, and among the many fatalities was the Earl of Warwick.

Cecily's son had now killed her nephew: the 'Kingmaker' had played his last hand in English politics. When Marguerite and her son at long last landed at Weymouth in Dorset on the evening of 14 April the battle was long decided, although she could not have known it. She had reached Cerne Abbey before, next day, the news arrived that caused her to fall to the ground 'like a woman all dismayed for fear . . . her heart was pierced with sorrow, her speech was in a manner gone, all her spirits were tormented with melancholy'. But she rallied herself and moved through the West Country trying to drum up support, cheered in Bristol by a reception warm enough to give her 'new courage'.

Nor did those on the other side have it altogether easy. In London, the Lancastrians had not given up all hope of the city. The mayor and aldermen had to send a message to Edward begging him to come back to the defence 'of the Queen, then being in the Tower of London, my Lord Prince, and my Ladies his daughters . . . and of the city', all in 'the greatest jeopardy'. The royal women felt the Tower shake as below them the Bastard of Falconbridge, a captain and kinsman of Warwick's, turned his guns on the city; seven hundred men died under his onslaught. But overall the tide was still running the Yorkists' way. Philippe de Commynes heard that one reason London welcomed Edward back was his wife Elizabeth. Not only had she borne a son in Westminster, but Londoners were grateful that she had retreated into sanctuary instead of expecting citizens to risk their lives and livelihoods to defend her position. As well as a private pleasure, she had become a political asset for Edward. The parliament of 1472 would put forward a commendation 'of the womanly behaviour and the great constance of the Queen'.[17] At the times of their marriages, Marguerite of Anjou had looked a more suitable queen of England than Elizabeth Woodville; but now the positions were reversed.

As for the other, Lancastrian, queen, the *Arrivall* tells of the frantic, exhausting progress of Marguerite and her son at the beginning of May, Anne perforce with them, though her state must have been pitiable – a fourteen-year-old cut off from her own family and now no use to her in-laws. On the afternoon of the 3rd the Lancastrian army – powerful now in numbers, but exhausted by a 36-mile march in 'foul country' – arrived at Tewkesbury. The ladies of the party retired to a nearby manor for the night, but Hall describes Marguerite riding around the field next morning to encourage her soldiers.

The Duke of Somerset and Marguerite's son (the Prince of Wales, Anne Neville's husband) led the Lancastrian forces; Edward and Richard of Gloucester (with Edward's friend Lord Hastings, and Elizabeth Woodville's eldest son, now Marquess of Dorset) were at the head of the rather fewer but more experienced Yorkist troops. For the Yorkists it was to be a flamboyant victory, though one so bloody that the fleeing Lancastrians were slaughtered even as they tried to cross the river Severn or seek sanctuary in Tewkesbury Abbey. Among those killed was Marguerite's son – with question marks over whether he died in battle or was put to death afterwards. The deed was long laid at Richard's door despite the lack of evidence; Edward as king would in any case have to bear the ultimate responsibility.

Henry VI, Marguerite's husband, now died too – in the Tower and in Yorkist custody. The *Arrivall* says he died of 'pure displeasure and melancholy'; others, including Fabian and Commynes, say he was killed by Richard. As he struck the fatal blow, the eighteen-year-old Duke of Gloucester is supposed to have said: 'Now there is no heir male of King Edward the Third but we of the House of York!' There is no hard evidence for Richard's involvement, let alone his words, but if they were indeed uttered he was ignoring Margaret Beaufort's son Henry Tudor, possibly because of the legitimation issue or because of doubts about the validity of a claim passed through a woman. But one thing is certain: with no son or husband to promote, Marguerite would now have been considered irrelevant.

She was found three days later, the *Arrivall* reports, 'in a poor religious place, where she had hidden herself, for the security of her person'. She appears to have hidden Anne, too: a list of those taken and presented to the king included 'Lady Margaret, Queen, Lady Anne, Princess'. Whether or not Anne felt personal loss at her husband's death, as an example of the turning of Fortune's wheel her past year had been close to unrivalled. She now passed into the charge of her brother-in-law Clarence, who had been pardoned by his brother the king. Crowland reports that when Edward made his triumphal entry into London Marguerite was 'borne in a carriage before the king', as the Roman emperor would have done to Shakespeare's Cleopatra. The last few days had brought the loss of those closest to her and the wreck of all her hopes; but, in keeping with the treatment generally accorded to women in these wars, she suffered no more direct penalty.

Marguerite's father wrote to her with his hope that God might help her with His counsels, 'For rarely is the aid of man tendered in such a reverse of fortune.' Edward IV's records show payment to one Bawder Herman 'for the expenses and daily allowances to Margaret, lately called the Queen, and to other persons attendant upon the said Queen'. After her first few months of confinement Marguerite was moved to the kindly custody of her old friend Alice Chaucer, the dowager Duchess of Suffolk, at Wallingford, who was paid five marks a week for her expenses. She was probably even freed to some degree: in 1475 she joined the London Skinners' Fraternity of the Assumption of the Virgin, on the same occasion as two of Elizabeth Woodville's ladies; the queen herself was already a member. Marguerite was, in other words, accepted back – if she had ever left them – into the networks of aristocratic women; and by men accorded the half patronising, half chivalric courtesy seen time and again in the treatment of ladies.

The Lancastrian 'Readeption', as the Lancastrians themselves called Henry VI's brief second reign, was over barely six months after it had begun. This time – for this branch of the family – there would be no coming back. As one contemporary put it: 'And so no one from that stock remained among the living who could claim the crown.' Except, posterity would add, for Margaret Beaufort and any heirs of her body . . . .

Margaret had shown all too clearly her pleasure in that brief restoration of the Lancastrian dynasty. That she did not suffer any penalty is due to the actions of her husband. When Edward re-entered London, Stafford had been there to welcome him; at Barnet, where Warwick was killed, Stafford had been badly wounded fighting for Edward's army. In the last week of March Margaret's cousin Somerset, having taken on his dead brother's role as a prominent Lancastrian leader, had visited Woking in an attempt to persuade Stafford to fight for their cause, but in vain. After Tewkesbury, this latest inheritor of the Somerset title had been dragged out of sanctuary and killed: evidence of Edward's determination and ruthlessness that Margaret would have taken seriously.

Jasper and Henry Tudor had been in Wales when they heard of the disaster that had overtaken the Lancastrians. Jasper would have had no option but to flee abroad: Bernard André says it was Margaret who begged him to take her young son Henry too. With the deaths of Henry VI and his son, Henry Tudor had suddenly assumed a dangerous importance: he was the only Lancastrian heir (even if not all his contemporaries admitted it) since his mother was simultaneously disabled and protected by her gender. It would be fourteen years before Margaret saw her son again.

PART THREE

1471–1483

ELEVEN

My Lovely Queen

Clarence and Gloucester, love my lovely queen,
And kiss your princely nephew, brothers both.
Henry VI Part 3, 5.7

As the Yorkists returned to power, the Lancastrian threat, it seemed, had finally been eliminated. From now on, the only challenge would come from within. The years ahead would prove it was indeed a serious threat – but there was little sign of that in the summer of 1471. When the infant Edward, Elizabeth Woodville's long-awaited son, was created Prince of Wales at the end of June it was a symbol that this time the Yorkists intended to stay.

Just as significant, perhaps, was the fact that Queen Elizabeth was head of the little prince's council and that all the others named – the king's brothers Clarence and Gloucester, the queen's brother Anthony Woodville, the leading bishops – were given power to advise and counsel him 'with the express consent of the Queen'. That September king and queen went on pilgrimage to Canterbury, a favourite place, and at Christmas in Westminster they took care to display themselves going to mass in the Abbey 'wearing their crowns', though for the Twelfth Night procession Elizabeth went uncrowned 'because she was great with child'. This child, Margaret, was to die before the end of the year – a year which also saw the death of Elizabeth's mother Jacquetta on 30 May. Joy, therefore, was mixed with sorrow; but in her public capacity, Elizabeth was riding high.

The *Liber Niger* or 'Black Book' of Edward IV, compiled between summer 1471 and autumn 1472, was intended to implement much-needed economies in the royal household. None the less it described an impressive edifice divided into two principal departments, the *domus providencie* (kitchens, buttery, laundry and so on) and the *domus magnificencie* (chapel, signet office, wardrobes, and knights and esquires of the body). The queen's household was on a smaller scale and would have included far more women. Even so, Elizabeth too had grooms and kitchen staff, clerks, auditors, carvers, almoners, attorneys who served on her council, butlers, bakers, pages and pursuivants, surgeons and squires. Her offices – of course she had offices – at Westminster were in the New Tower, next to the king's exchequer.

There is a good description, written in 1472, of the pleasure and state in which the royal family lived in their great palaces close to the Thames: Greenwich, Eltham, Westminster, Windsor (so extensively remodelled by Edward III a century before) and Sheen. While Edward had been in exile in Burgundy he had been entertained by Lord Gruuthuyse, whose palace survives in Bruges today. Now it was the restored king's chance to reciprocate, and the details of the visit the Burgundian nobleman made to the court at Windsor are preserved in the account by a herald, Bluemantle Pursuivant.

After being greeted by the royal couple, and escorted to their chambers, the visiting party were served dinner there, in the company of a number of English officers. Then 'the King had him to the queen's chamber, where she had there her ladies playing at the marteaux [a game like bowls], and some of her ladies and gentlewomen at the Closheys [ninepins] of ivory, and Dancing. And some at divers other games, according. The which sight was full pleasant to them. Also the King danced with my lady Elizabeth, his eldest daughter' – and so they parted for the night.

The next morning came matins and mass in the king's own chapel, after which Edward gave Lord Gruuthuyse a gold cup embellished with pearls, a huge sapphire and a 'great piece of a Unicorn's horn'. After breakfast came hunting; dinner in the lodge; then more hunting, with half a dozen bucks run to death by the castle hounds. 'By that time it was near night, yet the King showed him his garden, and Vineyard of Pleasure, and so turned into the Castle again, where they heard evensong in their chambers.'

Elizabeth did her part in honouring Gruuthuyse:

The Queen did cause to be ordained a great Banquet in her own chamber. At which Banquet were the King, the Queen, my lady Elizabeth, the King's eldest daughter, the Duchess of Exeter [the king's sister Anne], the Lady Rivers, and the Lord Gruthuyse [sic], sitting at one mess, and at the same table sat the Duke of Buckingham [and] my lady his wife [Elizabeth Woodville's sister] with divers other Ladies . . . . And when they had supped, my lady Elizabeth, the King's eldest daughter, danced with the Duke of Buckingham, and divers other ladies also. Then about nine of the clock, the King and the Queen, with her ladies and gentlewomen, brought the said Lord Gruthuyse to three chambers of Pleasure, all hanged with white silk and linen cloth, and all the floors covered with carpets. There was ordained a bed for himself, of as good down as could be gotten, the sheets of Reynes, also fine fustians, the counterpoint cloth of gold, furred with ermine, the Tester and the Ceiler also shining cloth of gold, the curtains white sarsenet; as for his head Suit and Pillows, [they] were of the queen's own ordinance.

127

The attention that both herald and queen paid to the furnish-ings is notable (along with the charming description of Lord Gruuthuyse ending a wearing day by lingering in the bath, in company with the lord chamberlain). So too is the way that access to the queen's chambers was regarded as a privilege in the chivalric style, the chambers themselves presented as a place where monarchy could be seen – or displayed – in its most accessible and human guise.

This was an age when greater privacy was in demand. Great builders such as Edward III, John of Gaunt at Kenilworth and Lord Scrope at Bolton Hall had already started to limit the use of the great hall, once the all-purpose centre of the house, to big public functions. Royalty and noblemen had looked to their peers on the continent for inspiration, daring to require more rooms (even if still multi-functional), privies, fireplaces and chimneys, more painted walls and tiled floors. But what survives now not in buildings but only in illuminated manuscripts is the sheer riot of colour that would have greeted the visitor: on textiles, painted glass, tiles, bright wooden roofs and corbels, to say nothing of clothes and livery.

Wood panelling instead of wall hangings was just coming in, as was translucent glass: a new spirit of luxury and comfort was in the air. Sir John Fastolf's fifty-room brick castle at Caister could boast feather beds, collections of jewels and plate, an astrolabe in the owner's bedroom and books in the bathing chamber. Back in 1456, so the Paston letters recorded, Cecily Neville had 'sore moved' Sir John to sell her the place, so impressed was she.[1]

The great houses also had their gardens; formally enclosed plots with herb beds and rose bowers, lavender and lilies; and half-wild meadows with the sweet scent of elderflower in spring and the soapy smell of may. Smell was important in the medieval world: a sweet odour was one of the signs by which a saint could be identified. Sight, too, was perceived as a way to God. While in winter the occupants of these residences had to make do with images in the chapel (Edward bought a fabulous gold statue of the Virgin, for instance, for the chapel at Windsor), in spring and summer, as they walked on the grass, the blue of columbine might remind them of the Virgin's robe, the golden heart of a honey-scented oxslip the promise of her heavenly crown. In one work introduced into England around this time the paths through an orchard became an allegorical rendition of a saint's mystical dialogue with God. At the time of Gruuthuyse's visit, in autumn, the swelling of fruit on trees and grapes on vines brought its own message of God's favour, of promise and prosperity.

But there were other, darker symbols too. That same year as Gruuthuyse's visit, 1472, saw a comet that blazed across the sky for almost two months; no one knew what the portent signified. The next year brought fevers and a bloody diarrhoea, and it was through a troubled landscape that in the spring of 1473 the two-and-a-half-year-old Edward was sent to Ludlow, on the borders of his Welsh principality, with Elizabeth's brother Anthony destined to be his governor. Anthony was, in Mancini's words, 'a kindly, serious and just' man, both educated and gifted as a military commander; one whose spiritual leanings reputedly led him to wear a hair shirt underneath his courtly garments; and undoubtedly well suited to his task.

Two of Elizabeth's other brothers were the young prince's counsellors and another his chaplain, while her son by her first marriage – assisted by her cousin – became his comptroller and her brother-in-law by her first marriage his master of the horse. Abbot Mylling, who had been so kind to Elizabeth in sanctuary, became his chancellor. In the years ahead such a comprehensive placing of Woodville connections about the boy would prove a vulnerable point, giving rise to mistrust among the nobility, but at the time it must have made Elizabeth feel safe. When her son set out for Ludlow she went with him, despite being once again pregnant, and stayed until the autumn.

The instructions his father sent for the rearing of the little prince sound a caring domestic note. He was to rise 'at a convenient hour according to his age'; hear matins in his chamber and mass in the chapel; then after breakfast 'to be occupied in such virtuous learning as his age shall suffer to receive'. Every care was to be taken as to his companions and his conversation at dinner, 'so that the communication at all times in his presence be of virtue, honour, cunning, wisdom, and deed of worship, and of nothing that shall stir him to vice'. No 'swearer, brawler, backbiter, common hazarder or adulterer' was even to be admitted to the household. After two more hours of lessons he might 'be shewed such convenient disports and exercises as belong to his estate to have experience in'; then after evensong those about him were 'to enforce themselves to make him merry towards his bed'.

But Elizabeth's role on this journey was not purely domestic and maternal: at Hereford, for example, she and the prince presided over the trials of those responsible for the recent disorder. Again, when the little Prince of Wales was sent to visit Coventry Elizabeth could be found making friendly overtures to the city officers. Her letter assured them that a servant of her husband's who had made an affray there would receive no special treatment: 'for as much as you shall now certainly understand that we do not intend in any way to maintain, support, or favour any of my said lord's servants or ours in any of their riots or unfitting behaviour . . .'. Gifts were offered, too: 'Memorandum that our sovereign lady, the queen, has given to the mayor and his worshipful brethren and to the mayoress and her sisters twelve bucks . . . six of the said bucks to the said mayor and his brethren, and the other six of them to their said wives . . .' Elizabeth and her husband had always been mindful of the usefulness of women. The *Great Chronicle of London* relates how Edward, raising money for his wars, kissed an old lady to such effect that she upped her £10 donation to £20; and his welcome into London after the Readeption was said by Commynes to be in part due to the 'ladies of quality and rich citizens' wives with whom he had formerly intrigued', and who persuaded their husbands to declare for his side.

Mindfulness, of course, could go too far – from a wife's viewpoint, anyway. Edward was happy to take the freedoms the age accorded to any wealthy husband, never mind a king, and avail himself of the services of mistresses. Elizabeth, especially given the frequency of her pregnancies and retreats into confinement, must up to a point have accepted this situation. But around this time Edward began a liaison that would become a matter of comment in the next reigns for its personal qualities, as well as its capacity for use in political propaganda – his affair with 'Jane' Shore, as the 'goldsmith's wife' is usually known. (Her real name was Elizabeth.) And yet these might be called the golden years for the Yorkist monarchy – for the queen as much as for Edward. Their second son, Richard, was born on 17 August 1473 at the Dominican Friary in Shrewsbury.

Nevertheless, the rifts that had caused the Readeption were still evident. There had been rumours of troubles ahead. In February 1472, soon after Edward's resumption of the throne, Sir John Paston had written that the king and queen, with Clarence and Gloucester, had gone to Elizabeth's own palace of Sheen: 'men say not all in charity; what will fall men cannot say'.

George of Clarence and Richard of Gloucester had recently been on different sides of a deadly dispute, but now they had a new cause of enmity. The death of Edward of Lancaster, Marguerite's son, had left his young wife Anne Neville a widow – and potentially a hugely wealthy one. Warwick's treason and death meant that his estates reverted to the crown; it seemed likely (though illegal) that his wife's huge Beauchamp and Despenser inheritance would also be taken from her. Clarence's wife Isabel was to be the first beneficiary. Her sister Anne might also benefit – and, coincidentally or not, Richard now desired to marry her.

Clarence had no wish to see his brother share the bounty. The Crowland chronicler claimed that Clarence spirited Anne away to a house in London, disguised as a kitchen maid.[2] Richard, discovering her whereabouts, moved her to sanctuary at the College of St Martin-le-Grand while a deal was thrashed out. In April 1472 papal dispensation was granted for two such close connections to marry; Richard had already had a clause put into the contracts assuring him of Anne's inheritance even if the dispensation failed to arrive.[3] It is not known exactly when or where the ceremony took place, but marry they did and with the support of Edward. After Clarence's recent treachery the king can have had no desire to see so much wealth and power concentrated in that brother's hands. It seems that the queen approved too, for in the preceding months she had made a point of renewing a grant Richard held from her.

None of the reports hint at Anne's feelings, unless it is that of the Milanese ambassador in France. Some time later, in February 1474, he sent a patchily erroneous account of enmity between Richard, who 'by force has taken to wife a daughter of the late Earl of Warwick', and Clarence, who feared this might deprive him of 'Warwick's county'. The 'force', of course, may mean that it was against Clarence's will rather than against Anne's. Indeed, she may not have wanted any other choices.[4] Anne and Richard had known each other as children:

between 1465 and 1468 Richard had received part of his upbringing in Warwick's castle at Middleham in Yorkshire, so it is conceivable there was an element of affection involved. The early seventeenth-century antiquary George Buck,[5] indeed, has Richard desisting from taking any part in the killing of Anne's first husband, Edward, 'in regard of this prince's wife, who . . . was akin to the Duchess of York his mother, and whom also he loved very affectionately, though secretly'. Richard's later demonisation owes much to his enemies' propaganda, perpetuated by Shakespeare. Nothing for which evidence exists – his prowess in battle, for example – suggests that there was anything about Richard that would have turned a prospective bride away.

But even if there were affection between Richard and Anne, it would not have been considered important. This was a matter of property. John Paston reported that Clarence told Richard 'he may well have my lady his sister-in-law, but they shall divide no livelihood'. If so, Richard was clearly uninterested in the lady without her lands.

With the royal brothers squabbling over the Neville estates, one woman was certainly robbed – Anne's and Isabel's mother the Countess of Warwick, who after her husband's death had fled to Beaulieu Abbey, only to find that on the king's orders she was not permitted to leave. The appalled widow wrote pleading letters (in her own hand . . . 'in the absence of clerks') not only to the king and to her sons-in-law themselves but to 'the Queen's good Grace, to my right redoubted Lady the King's mother, to my Lady the King's eldest daughter [the six-year-old Elizabeth] . . . to my Ladies the King's sisters, to my Lady of Bedford mother to the Queen, and to other Ladies noble of the realm'. But on this occasion, the female network was powerless. In June 1473 the countess was taken north to Middleham, now the property of her new son-in-law. Rous[6] describes her as being 'locked up', and by Anne as much as by Richard. Her lands were to be shared out, in the chilling words of an Act of Parliament of May 1474, as though 'she were naturally dead'.

Middleham was a Norman keep, substantially modernised and now impressive enough to earn the sobriquet the 'Windsor of the North'. The medieval age did not distinguish between castles and houses – by this point houses were often being built with purely decorative crenellation, and moats were being converted into lakes. But Middleham was still a fully functional fortress. Northern houses were more likely to be used for genuine defence, close as they were to Scotland and England's only land frontier.

Anne's only child, Edward 'of Middleham', was born there in 1473, some accounts suggest, or possibly in 1476 or 1477, just before the first definite record of his existence – cited as to be prayed for, along with his parents, in a chantry. A huge number of question marks also hang over Anne – more than over any other woman in this story. Rous says she and Richard were 'unhappily married', but there is little other evidence and 'unhappily' here may simply mean that it ended unfortunately. Still, to modern eyes there is something worrying in Anne's absence from the records, even by the standards of a fifteenth-century wife. In order to create a power base for himself, Richard needed to make use of his wife's heritage and lineage – to present himself as the legitimate inheritor of Neville authority in the north. But perhaps that need made him all the more determined to limit her autonomy.

While Anne, and her fortune, were thus absorbed into the Yorkist structure, Margaret Beaufort had been working towards her own rehabilitation. Her husband Stafford had died in October 1471 of wounds he received at the battle of Barnet some months earlier, and within eight months she had married again.

She had, it seems, been fond of Stafford – they celebrated their wedding anniversaries, feasting on plovers and larks, sharing pleasures as well as property. If Edmund Tudor had been the father of her child, it was Stafford whose favourite house, in later years, she would painstakingly rebuild. But after his death she had for a short time moved out of Woking into the London home owned by her mother – perhaps because she needed to put herself visibly in the marketplace again.

With her absent son's interests to protect, her Beaufort relatives dead or disgraced, her own reputation lately tarnished with disloyalty, Margaret could not afford to remain unprotected. We cannot know for sure at what point Margaret Beaufort really did start to shape her own destiny – the records of her business affairs do not distinguish between her own decisions and those of a husband until much later in her life – but surely we may speculate that it was now. The leading Beauforts had all been executed – so there was only the king who might be expected to exercise direct control over her affairs; and Edward must have been only too glad to see her married to a man who seemed wholly reconciled to the Yorkist monarchy. Margaret's third (or, technically, fourth) marriage would be a matter of business sealed by elaborate contracts that would later be to some degree dissolved, by mutual consent, when need no longer required and opportunity offered. None the less in its own terms it was a success story, with every sign that this husband respected his wife's abilities.

Thomas, Lord Stanley, a hard-headed man of property, was distinguished chiefly for having avoided firm commitment to either side. He was therefore not wholly trusted; all the same, at this juncture he had achieved the position of lord steward of Edward IV's household, and had moreover forged connections through marriage with the Woodville family. A widower, already with children, he was content with the fact that no children would come from his marriage with Margaret. She, however, increased his status, while his position within the Yorkist regime fostered her security and that of her son Henry.

When they had fled England Jasper and Henry's ship, steering for France, had been forced by storms to make instead for the duchy of Brittany, further west. There Duke Francis received them courteously as guests, but in reality they were bargaining counters and were not permitted to leave. Both the French king and Edward in England had tried to negotiate them out of Breton hands, Edward being convinced (Polydore Vergil says) that with the two Tudors on the continent he could never live 'in perfect security'. But Duke Francis had refused and there, for the moment, the matter rested, while Margaret went on consolidating her policy of reconciliation.

When Edward invaded France in 1475, in pursuance of England's long-standing claim to the French crown, Margaret Beaufort's husband Stanley was one of the accompanying lords selected to negotiate the resulting treaty. But the French expedition marked a significant point for another woman too. Before he left for France Edward brought his young heir back from Ludlow as nominal ruler with the title Keeper of the Realm, under his mother's charge. The will the king made before his campaign acknowledged Elizabeth's importance. His two eldest daughters were to have 10,000 marks each as a marriage dowry so long as 'they be governed and ruled in their marriages by our dearest wife the Queen and by our said son the Prince, if God fortune him to come to age of discretion'; if they should marry themselves 'so as they be thereby disparaged, as God forbid', the dowry was forfeit. His third daughter, Cecily, was to receive 18,000 marks (on top of 2000 already paid), but then her marriage to the heir of the king of Scots had already been arranged so as to secure the Scottish border before the army went to combat the French. The York lands were to go to his younger son, Richard; the queen herself was to have the revenues of all the lands she already possessed for her lifetime, and her personal property to dispose of as she would: 'all her own goods, chattels, stuff, bedding, arrases, tapestries, verdours, stuff of household plate and jewels, and all other things which she now hath and occupieth'. She was named first of his ten executors: 'our said dearest and most entirely beloved wife Elizabeth the Queen . . . our said dearest Wife in whom we most singularly put our trust in this party'.

Elizabeth was granted £4400 a year for the maintenance of the king's household that she and her son would now occupy. She was not in any sense given a regency of the kind that was well known in France, the kind Marguerite had sought. This was probably partly down to the memory of Marguerite, partly to the lack of recent precedent, and perhaps partly also to personality. Perhaps Edward felt that Elizabeth's talents were more suited to protecting the interests of her children, and to handling her and their property, than to ruling a country. All the same, it was a declaration of trust.[7]

The invasion of France had been planned in alliance with its neighbour and traditional rival Burgundy, and Margaret of Burgundy had rushed to see her brothers Edward and Richard as they landed. In the event – to the annoyance of the more militant Richard – Edward was easily persuaded to accept a peace treaty and a pension from the French, rather than pursue his claims to their throne. Margaret now had to mediate between her brother and her husband, the duke having been deprived of England's aid against their common enemy.

Commynes described the rulers of England and France meeting on a bridge and embracing through a grating. Louis joked that if Edward wanted to come and meet the French ladies he would lend him the Cardinal of Bourbon for his confessor 'who he knew would willingly absolve him, if he should commit any sin by way of love and gallantry'. The peace was cemented not only by that pension for Edward, but by the promise of a marriage between young Princess Elizabeth and the Dauphin. 'Also for the inviolate observation of the friendship, it is promised, settled, agreed, and concluded that a marriage shall be contracted between the most illustrious Prince Charles, son of the most powerful prince of France, and the most serene lady Elizabeth, daughter of the most invincible king of England, when they shall reach marriageable years. . . .' Edward returned to his delighted capital calling his eldest daughter 'Dauphiness' and declaring that she must have a new wardrobe in the French style. And as one daughter prepared to depart, another arrived: a fifth girl, Anne (probably named for Anne Mortimer, through whom came Edward's best claim to the throne), was born to the royal couple on 2 November that year.

As part of the peace deal the French king had offered Edward 50,000 crowns (£10,000) in exchange for Marguerite of Anjou signing over to him all rights of inheritance in her parents' lands. The wording of the documents denies she had ever been a queen of England, let alone one of the most active in that country's history. Louis signed an agreement concerning 'the daughter of the King of Sicily'; and it was as 'I, Margaret, formerly married in the Kingdom of England' that Marguerite herself was forced to renounce 'all that I could pretend to in England by the articles of my marriage'.

An entry in the roll of accounts reads: 'To Richard Haute, esquire, paid as a reward for the costs and expenses incurred by him for conducting Margaret, lately called the Queen, from London to the town of Sandwich . . .' From here, early in 1476, Marguerite was returned across the Channel to live as Louis' pensioner; and there is no record of how she – who in the past had made her feelings so plain – felt about the decision. For a short while she may have enjoyed the company of her father, but René of Anjou died in 1479. Holinshed in his sixteenth-century chronicles would moralise on the subject, describing how 'this queen' was 'sent home again with as much misery and sorrow as she was received with pomp and triumph. Such is the instability of worldly felicity, and so wavering is false flattering fortune. Which mutation and change of the better for the worse could not but nettle and sting her with pensiveness, yea and any other person whatsoever that, having been in good estate, falleth into the contrary.'

Hall describes an equally gloomy scenario. 'And where in the beginning of her time, she lived like a Queen, in the middle she ruled like an empress, towards the end she was vexed with trouble, never quiet nor in peace, and in her very extreme age she passed her days in France, more like a death than a life, languishing and mourning in continual sorrow, not so much for herself and her husband, whose ages were almost consumed and worn, but for the loss of prince Edward her son.'

TWELVE

Fortune's Womb

Some unborn sorrow, ripe in fortune's womb,
Is coming towards me, and my inward soul
With nothing trembles.

Richard II, 2.2

These were the mature years of Edward IV's kingship. Time would prove that fractures within the Yorkist dynasty had never entirely healed – but for the moment they were concealed.

In 1476 came a chance for the celebration of the dynasty. An illustration probably made around that time shows the royal family and court in an earthly equivalent of the sacred Trinity they reverenced. The king and his men kneel on one side, the queen and her ladies on the other, with Elizabeth's mother-in-law Cecily behind her wearing as a cloak the royal arms of England. Everything was set for an extraordinary scene – the reburial of Richard, Duke of York, Edward's father.

It had been more than fifteen years since the duke and his son Edmund had perished at the battle of Wakefield and been buried there in the north with the scant ceremony accorded to those on the losing side of any war. It was time for them to be reburied in an appropriately splendid tomb, in the church attached to the Midlands castle of Fotheringhay. The ten-day procession south was intended to show the people that the Yorkist regime was here to stay; besides fulfilling filial piety, naturally.

The trailing black draperies must have turned brown with dust as the days went by. They had chosen high summer for the journey to avoid the winter mud that might make the horses slip and fall – it would have been unthinkable for the hearse to tilt and upset its precious cargo. The country people, too, would be out in the fields at this season and would see the procession pass by. The black clothes of the noble mourners, the black velvet stretched on hoops over the vehicle that bore the coffins, would have stood out like a stab of darkness against the blue and gold of the countryside. And in the towns, every trade guild could send its own little train of riders and banners to pay their respects, proudly carrying with them their crosses, their holy water and their holy relics, without too much fear that rain would spoil the local officials' best clothes or tarnish the gold embroidery.

It had been on or shortly before Sunday, 21 July, that the bodies had been exhumed, probably from the priory of St John the Evangelist near Pontefract Castle. Central to the ceremonials was a life-size effigy of the duke. This was an honour normally permitted only to kings, queens and bishops – so a point was being made in relation to the legitimisation of the current monarchy. The effigy used at a king's funeral represented the public, symbolic body of the monarch, still present and active even when the physical body had died. This duke's effigy was clad in dark blue, the colour of a king's mourning, and an angel held a crown over his head to signify the same assumption of royal dignity that had led his widow Cecily to call herself 'queen by right'.

As chief mourner, Richard, Duke of Gloucester rode directly behind the coffins. His habitual residence in the north made him the natural choice to escort his father's body south. Behind him rode the nobles and officers, then four hundred poor men on foot, each carrying a taper. The choir of the Chapel Royal sang at each church where the bodies rested overnight. This extraordinary cortège travelled about 13 miles a day.

The church of Fotheringhay still stands, its three-storey tower and belfry odder-looking, if less impressive, today since the chancel and cloisters were destroyed after the Reformation. But of the castle, only a grassy mound remains. Yet nothing can destroy the grandeur of the setting, looking south over the once-great river Nene, surrounded by the hunting forest of Rockingham. Besides the castle complex, the church and the market town there was formerly a collegiate establishment large enough to boast twelve fellows or chaplains – a centre of learning and piety. In 1476 Fotheringhay had only recently been relinquished, at his insistence, by Edward's mother Cecily. But whether or not she had gone willingly she would have approved her son's intention for Fotheringhay – to make it into a mausoleum for the York family. The installation of magnificent stained-glass windows in the chapel, begun by Cecily, was now complete: hence the timing of this ceremony.*

The king, according to a herald's account, met his father's body at the entrance to the churchyard and 'very humbly did his obeisance to the said body and laid his hand on the body and kissed it, weeping'. During the service he 'had his chamberlain offer to the body seven pieces of cloth of gold and each piece was five yards long, and the queen had five yards offered

---

* Elizabeth of York would own Fotheringhay eventually, and her death would mark an end to its warm association with the royal family. Elizabeth of York's granddaughter Elizabeth I would have another of her descendants beheaded there, and now the name of Fotheringhay will for ever be associated with that of the Scots queen Mary.

by her chamberlain and they were laid in the shape of a cross on the said body'.[8]

Cloth of gold was not necessarily gold in colour, more an indication of status. A sumptuary law of 1483 would state that no one 'except the king, the queen, the king's mother, the king's children, his brothers and sister' should wear it. Its mention during the Fotheringhay ceremonies is significant for another reason: it is the first time any woman has been referred to – even acting by proxy, and offering through her chamberlain – in the course of the obsequies.

The next day a horse was led to the church door, part of the traditional offering of the dead man's knightly trappings: his coat of arms, shield, sword and helmet, each brought in by a different nobleman. 'Then the king came to offer the mass penny, and in passing did his obeisance before the said body. Next the queen came to offer, dressed all in blue without a high headdress, and there she made a great obeisance and reverence to the said body, and next two of the king's daughters came to offer in the same way.' The daughters are not named but would surely have been the eldest – ten-year-old Elizabeth, recently betrothed to the French Dauphin, and Mary. That the queen came without a hennin – the tall pointed cone from which floated a flattering veil, or the veiled, backward-pointing 'butterfly' headdress – was presumably a conventional token of grief.

Another, French, account includes a fourth woman: 'the king offered for the said prince his father and the queen and her two daughters and the countess of Richmond offered next.' Since this account survives as a medley of late fifteenth- and sixteenth-century documents it is always possible that a later hand added the name of Margaret Beaufort, Countess of Richmond – later, when her son Henry VII was on the throne, when she had become 'My Lady the King's Mother', when her presence at any gathering would have become worthy of record and indeed tactful to do so. This could account for the fact that, apart from queen and her two daughters, she is the only woman mentioned specifically. But the blandly undescriptive words do infer just how well Margaret Beaufort was doing in trying to placate the ruling Yorkist family.

It is not recorded whether Anne, Duchess of Gloucester was at Fotheringhay, despite the conspicuous part played by her husband Richard. Her presence may have gone unremarked, as Anne Neville's doings so often did; though surely, had she been there, she would have offered before Margaret Beaufort. Her absence may simply have been due to a pregnancy. If it were around now that Anne's single child was born, after several years of marriage, it might have been good reason not to risk an arduous journey. In any case, there would have been no role for her in that stylised procession from the north.

There are, however, mentions of Anne in other records around this time. In 1475/6 she sent a message to the city of York, conveyed by one of her husband's councillors, suggesting that she was able to deputise for him in his absence. In 1476 she was admitted to the sisterhood of Durham Cathedral priory. In December that year some of Richard's payment warrants, issued from London, show purchases of furs and silk for 'the most dear consort of the lord duke'. The following year she and Richard joined the guild of Corpus Christi at York and funded a chantry at Queens' College, Cambridge. So there is probably no reason to read anything sinister into Anne's absence – but one omission from the list of those present at the Fotheringhay ceremony does look more pointed.

It is hard not to read something into the apparent absence of the woman with most reason of all to be there – Cecily, Duchess of York, the dead man's widow. It is true that royalty did not customarily attend funerals, and that a woman might in any case have no place at the actual funeral ceremony of a man. But this was not a funeral as such, and neither the king nor queen stayed away. A later account affirms Cecily's continued affection for Fotheringhay: 'Memorandum that the Lady Cicelye, Duchess of York mother to King Edward the iiijth, died at her castle of Berkhamstead, and was buried by [beside] her husband in the College of Fotheringhay.' She may just have been ill – she was, after all, past sixty which was old for those times.

Maybe Cecily simply watched the ceremony,[9] instead of taking part. But when Margaret Beaufort, for example, was an observer during her son's reign, her presence would be recorded. If Cecily had indeed been absent entirely, the question has to be why.

Cecily and Elizabeth Woodville were not, in this story, the only mother and daughter-in-law who did not always agree. Perhaps Cecily did not care to take a subordinate role to the daughter-in-law she despised as a low-born interloper – not at this, of all ceremonies.

It is tempting to read between the lines of a letter written in October 1476 by a member of the Stonor family. Elizabeth Stonor writes[10] to her husband of how she had attended the Duchess of Suffolk – the king's sister Elizabeth – on a visit to Cecily Neville.

'And also on Saturday last was I waited upon [the Duchess] again, and also from thence she waited upon my lady her Mother, and brought her to Greenwich to the King's good grace and the queen's: and there I saw the meeting between the King and my lady his Mother. And truly me thought it was a very good sight.' It sounds almost as though Cecily failed to meet her daughter-in-law, even though Elizabeth Woodville was obviously at Greenwich. Worse, it sounds as though Edward's sister had to 'bring' Cecily to see her son, and that the fact of her meeting her son was thought worth commenting on.

One letter perhaps written in 1474[11] had been to her son Richard, about a servant and whether Richard had yet fulfilled 'your promise made unto us at Syon . . . praying you that no man intromitt with our said servant's matter, saving only our counsel learned and yours, as our faithful trust is in you.' There is the sound of a mother's finger wagging, and more specifically in the next lines: 'Son, we trusted you should have been at Berkhamsted with my lord my son [Edward] at his last being there with us, and if it had pleased you to come at that time, you should have been right heartily welcome. And so you shall be whensoever you shall do the same, as God knoweth, whom we beseech to have you in governance.' Though we need read no more into it than a mother's natural desire to see as much as possible of her son, one could also perceive a desire to bind ties in what had already long been shown up as a dangerously fractured family.

The ranks of Cecily's children had been diminished, at the start of 1476, by the death of her eldest daughter Anne in child-birth. Four years earlier Anne had obtained what the sixteenth-century chronicler John Stow called a divorce (probably an annulment) from her estranged husband the Duke of Exeter, and married her long-standing lover, the Kentish gentleman Thomas St Leger. By contrast Cecily's second daughter Elizabeth,[12] Duchess of Suffolk, was enjoying an access of independence and influence after the death of her own formidable mother-in-law Alice Chaucer in 1475. But this particular scion of the York family seems, none the less, to have taken little personal part in political affairs. They were, on the other hand, the daily concern of Cecily's youngest and grandest daughter, Margaret of Burgundy. And as 1477 dawned Cecily must have been worried also about her daughter across the Channel.

When she had married Duke Charles in 1468 Margaret had entered a court, and a political system, where the duchess was expected to play a comparatively active role; this despite the fact that her new husband was more than a decade older than she, strongly committed to his own rule, ferocious in war and frequently absent. Attention at first was likely to have focused on her prime duty: the provision of heirs. This Margaret would, for unknown reasons, never manage, and Charles's existing daughter Mary remained his sole heiress. But although before Margaret's arrival he had told his subjects that his bride was 'ideally shaped to bear a prince', there is no sign of the frantic and reproachful flailings after a male heir in which Margaret's great-nephew Henry VIII of England would indulge.

Only a few years into the marriage, records of their movements show that the couple were rarely together, though relations seem to have been amicable. With Charles at the wars Margaret none the less retained enough hope to make offerings to those saints associated with childbirth and fertility: St Waudru, St Margaret of Antioch, St Colette and St Anne. In 1473 she made an unusual two-month trip to a palace designated as a place of cure and recovery; her trouble may possibly have been the loss of a child.

Alone or in company with her stepdaughter (with whom, as with her mother-in-law, she seems to have got on well), Margaret travelled indefatigably, raising men and money for her husband's campaigns, and receiving petitions and ambassadors in his frequent absences. Her secure position survived not only the child-lessness which would destroy Henry VIII's queens, but the polit-ical turmoils in England which cast into doubt her other prime function, as living guarantor of the Anglo–Burgundian alliance.

Duke Charles, having made his own truce with the French, had been fighting on his other frontiers throughout 1476. In the frozen January of 1477 came news – filtering only slowly through to his womenfolk, and to his foreign allies – that he was dead. Immediately, Louis of France laid claim to a significant part of his lands. It was lucky that Margaret at thirty-one already had considerable experience of the swift reverses of fortune. She and her stepdaughter (Mary as the new ruling duchess, and Margaret under the title of *Duchesse Mère*) acted together to summon the Burgundian parliament, the

Estates General, and negotiate arrangements to satisfy the complaints they had had against the rule of Duke Charles; to urge the individual cities and provinces of Burgundy to resist the French invaders; and to buy diplomatic time by sending a letter pleading for the protection due to 'widows and orphans'. (Louis' first response was to suggest a marriage between the twenty-year-old Duchess Mary and his seven-year-old son the Dauphin – who, of course, had two years earlier been betrothed to Elizabeth of York as part of another peace treaty.)

In the course of a fraught spring and summer the two women would achieve what they had set out to do; but things got worse before they got better. Margaret and Mary had to cope with the arrest and execution, by the Estates, of their most trusted advisers. Margaret had also, like so many widows, to battle for her dower rights, withheld on the grounds that her brother had never paid all the dowry he had promised; eventually Mary intervened on behalf of a woman who, she said, had always held 'our person and our lands and lordships in such complete and perfect love and goodwill that we can never sufficiently repay and recompense her'.

Nor were these Margaret's only problems. First there was a whispering campaign against her, sponsored by the French king. Before her marriage he had spread rumours about her chastity. Now he was about to spread a different story, which would have repercussions in England. Secondly, her brother Edward would not send military support and risk his own rapport with (and pension from) the French, even though Louis was attacking her dower lands.

Margaret wrote to Edward in the strongest terms, protesting that he had once made her 'one of the most important ladies in the world' but she was now 'one of the poorest widows deserted by everyone, especially by you'. She implored him to send a thousand or more English archers 'to rescue me from the King of France who does his best to reduce me to a state of beggary for the rest of my days'. Margaret was deeply dissatisfied with her brother, who did no more than write to Louis on her behalf. As events would prove, she was not a woman to take dissatisfaction lightly.

She was not the only York sibling to feel aggrieved. Just two years after the triumphant symbolism of the Fotheringhay ceremony, the Yorkist dynasty and its matriarch Cecily were racked by the fate of her second surviving son.

THIRTEEN

Mother of Griefs

Alas, I am the mother of these griefs;
Their woes are parcelled, mine is general.
Richard III, 2.2

George, Duke of Clarence, had been a disaffected troublemaker for much of his brother's reign. For ten years he had been Edward's heir, which had given him an exaggerated sense of entitlement. He has gone down in history as, in Shakespeare's words, 'false, fleeting, perjured Clarence'; and this reputation is bound up with the story of the women around him.

Clarence's wife Isabel Neville had died at the end of 1476, less than three months after giving birth to a son. This baby, Isabel's third living child, very shortly followed her, and (though the Tewkesbury chronicler definitely links the sad event to childbirth) rumours would soon accrue about the deaths of both mother and child.

The first effect of Isabel's departure was to make Clarence an available widower. The Crowland chronicler reports that Margaret of Burgundy, 'whose affections were fixed on her brother Clarence beyond any of the rest of her kindred', now devoted her energies to reviving the old idea of a match between him and Mary of Burgundy. But, just as when the idea had first been mooted almost a decade earlier, King Edward refused his permission.

All the royal siblings may to some degree have been victims of the French king Louis, who was still trying to break up the anti-French alliance established between England and Burgundy. Now French envoys spread the story that Margaret and certain English lords were planning to have Mary kidnapped and taken to England to marry Clarence; and whispered into Edward's ear the poisonous suggestion that Margaret and Clarence would then use Burgundian troops to seize the English throne. (Burgundy itself, in the person of Mary, had a claim to that crown – she was descended through her grandmother from John of Gaunt.) But within a couple of months of Duke Charles's death Margaret and Mary were actively seeking the long-planned marriage between Mary and Maximilian, the Archduke of Austria and son of the Holy Roman Emperor, which finally took place in summer 1477 to the satisfaction of all parties immediately concerned.

But Clarence's history must have made these malicious tales all too credible. Any suggestion of a stronger Anglo–Burgundian link could – assuming the stories had not been instituted by the French king himself – have broken the fragile peace with France and thrown that country back on its old alliance with the ever-troublesome Scots.[13] But whatever the rumours, no intervention by either Louis or Margaret may have been necessary: Clarence had an almost unparalleled capacity for making trouble on his own.

In the spring of 1477 he was involved in two bizarre trials. At the first, one Ankarette Twynho, formerly a servant of Clarence's wife but now perhaps in the Woodvilles' sphere, was accused of having given Isabel poisoned ale – given, it was claimed, on 10 October, though improbably not causing death until 22 December. Two others were accused of having conspired with her to poison also Isabel's baby, who died ten days later. Ankarette was snatched from her home by Clarence's men and taken across three counties to Warwick, where he held sway. There, despite the absurdity of the charges, she was found guilty by a jury who later pleaded that Clarence had left them no choice, and executed on the spot.

A few weeks later, in an apparently unrelated case, three men were tried and convicted in London for 'seeking the destruction of the King and Prince', as Crowland reported, by seditious means but also by necromancy – witchcraft. At least one of the men was a close associate of Clarence's, who later, in May, stormed out of the king's council after having the men's declarations of their innocence read. He was displaying a flagrant lack of respect for the due process of law, and also for the king's authority. Crowland relates how Edward summoned the duke to Westminster and inveighed against his behaviour 'as derogatory to the laws of the realm and most dangerous to judges and jurors throughout the kingdom'. The two had, as Crowland writes, come to look upon each other with 'unbrotherly' looks. In June, Clarence himself was arrested and sent to the Tower.

At the beginning of 1478 Clarence was attainted on a rhetorically elaborate charge of treasons past and present, and the parliamentary sessions in which he was tried began on 16 January. The date reflects the complicated life of the York family, for the previous day had seen, by contrast, a resplendent wedding ceremony. Early in 1476 the last Mowbray Duke of Norfolk had died, leaving only an infant daughter, Anne, and Edward had immediately seized on the heiress for betrothal to his younger son, Richard. Now, two years later, he had a good opportunity to have the marriage formally celebrated – despite the youth of the participants – in the presence of many of his nobles who had assembled for a very different purpose.

Elizabeth Woodville's brother Anthony, Earl Rivers, led the

little girl into the king's Great Chamber where the whole court was gathered to receive her – a daunting experience for a five- or six-year-old. The next day, followed by a retinue of ladies and gentlewomen, she was led by Earl Rivers again, and the 'Count of Lincoln', son to Edward's sister Elizabeth, in procession through the Queen's Chamber, the king's Great Chamber and the White Hall into St Stephen's Chapel, hung with blue tapestry decorated with gold fleurs de lys, where the royal family waited under a canopy to receive her.

The king gave the bride away, largesse was flung to the crowd from gold and silver bowls brought in by the Duke of Gloucester, and a banquet, with Anne Mowbray honoured as Princess of the Feast, completed that day's celebrations. A few days later there was a great tournament, at which the queen's brother appeared as St Anthony the hermit, with a hermit's house of black velvet – complete with a belltower and a bell that rang – built into his horse's trappings. The little duchess had to award the prizes – assisted, in the interests of practicality, by the princess Elizabeth and a council of ladies.

But beneath all this ceremony the Mowbray marriage is noteworthy for the way it demonstrated Edward's own sometimes cavalier attitude to the law. The king's son had already been created Duke of Norfolk, anticipating presumably that it would be in the right of his tiny wife, and two Acts of Parliament were now passed to ensure that if she died before bearing children her lands would pass to her 'husband' rather than to her heirs-at-law. Anne Mowbray's mother the Duchess of Norfolk, Elizabeth Talbot, urged or forced out of much to which she was entitled, seems barely to have figured in the wedding ceremony. Neither, of course, did the bridegroom's uncle Clarence, imprisoned in the Tower only a few miles away. Convicted by parliament, Clarence was sentenced to death in the early days of February; and when Edward hesitated for ten days the Speaker of the Commons asked the House of Lords to impose the penalty. He was executed on 18 February – famously drowned in a butt of Malmsey wine. Mancini wrote that 'The mode of execution preferred in this case was, that he should die by being plunged into a jar of sweet wine', and the story was considered plausible enough to be repeated all over Europe, by de Commynes and the *Great Chronicle* among others. Clarence's daughter would be painted with a wine cask as an emblem on her bracelet. The wine has served to lend a note of comic horror to Clarence's death – but the bare facts of the case open the door to a wealth of speculation, not least as to where the responsibility should lie.

Thomas More – writing in the next century, and always a detractor of Richard III (then still Duke of Gloucester) – claimed that some 'wise men also ween that his drift, covertly conveyed, lacked not in helping forth his brother of Clarence to his death: which he resisted openly, howbeit somewhat (as men deemed) more faintly than he that were heartily minded to his wealth'. It is true that several of Richard's men were in the parliament that nodded through the attainder (as well, of course, as many of the Woodvilles' adherents); true too that, inheriting some of Clarence's titles and offices as well as his place in the succession, he greatly benefited from Clarence's fall. But so too did Edward, who got Clarence's great estates and needed the money; Margaret Beaufort must have noted with interest that the Richmond earldom – which in 1471 had been granted to Clarence for his lifetime – was once again vacant. Almost everybody stood to gain from Clarence's death.

Mancini placed the blame very differently, as a grievance that would fester and burst forth in 1483. Visiting England in Richard's reign and perhaps susceptible to his propaganda, Mancini wrote that at this time 'Richard Duke of Gloucester was so overcome with grief for his brother, that he could not dissimulate so well, but that he was overheard to say that he would one day avenge his brother's death.' He clearly blames the queen who had 'concluded that her offspring by the king would never come to the throne, unless the duke of Clarence were removed; and of this she easily persuaded the king.' Indeed, More too would postulate as another possible cause of Clarence's fall 'the Queen and the lords of her blood, which highly maligned the king's kindred (as women commonly not of malice but of nature hate them whom their husbands love)'.

Elizabeth Woodville and her kin were, of course, always blamed for greed; and certainly the Woodvilles were not only prominent in the councils leading up to Clarence's trial but joined in the general harvest of Clarence's goods and offices. Mancini says it was now, with Clarence dead and Richard lying low on his own lands, that Elizabeth really started to ennoble her relatives. 'Besides, she attracted to her party many strangers and introduced them to court, so that they alone should manage the public and private businesses of the crown, surround the king, and have bands of retainers, give or sell offices, and finally rule the very king himself.' But as Mancini was also suggesting, there could have been another reason for her particular animosity towards Clarence at this time. His suggestion of 'calumnies' against her – 'namely that according to established usage she was not the legitimate wife of the king' – may have been just another rehashing of the old outcry against the secrecy of her marriage, her position as a widow. But it is also possible that Clarence was holding dangerous knowledge over his brother's and sister-in-law's heads.

One theory is that Clarence had been dropping hints about a lady called Eleanor Butler to whom, it was alleged, Edward had been pre-contracted or indeed actually married in the early 1460s – making his subsequent marriage to Elizabeth Woodville invalid. Eleanor, daughter of the great Earl of Shrewsbury,[14] was a widow of rank and notable piety who had died in 1468; Edward would have met her at the very beginning of his reign. (More says that Edward boasted of having three concubines: the merriest, the holiest and the wisest harlot in the kingdom. If Jane Shore was the merriest, Eleanor might have been the holiest.) Commynes says that Edward 'promised to marry her, provided that he could sleep with her first, and she consented' – the same technique he practised on Elizabeth Woodville. Commynes says also that Robert Stillington (later Bishop of Bath and Wells) 'had married them', though his involvement would hardly have been necessary: witnessed consent and consummation alone would have sufficed. Mancini and Vergil too make reference to the story. The implication is that Stillington (who seems now to have been cast briefly into prison, possibly for something to do with the Clarence affair) had passed this lethal information either directly to Clarence or to Eleanor's sister the Duchess of Norfolk and her husband, friends of his – the same duchess whose little daughter Anne Mowbray had just been snapped up as a royal bride.

But evidence for all this is circumstantial: Eleanor's arranging for the disposition of her property in the form open to a married woman, rather than that possible only for a widow; and the coincidence of Stillington's career now and later. Against that, there are no signs that, after Eleanor's death, Edward and Elizabeth attempted to regularise their liaison. Thomas More, after all, muddied the waters considerably by saying that Edward was pre-contracted not to Eleanor but to another of his mistresses by whom he had had a child, a married woman of lower rank called Elizabeth Lucy.[15] The question is whether he did so from ignorance, or in order to discredit a story so potentially damaging to the Tudor dynasty.

Probably the most that can be said is that Edward's pattern of behaviour with his women makes it impossible simply to dismiss the tale. But whether the allegation is true or false, if Clarence were indeed spreading this rumour it lends weight to the idea that Elizabeth Woodville believed him a threat to her children. The story would certainly reappear, greatly to her sons' detriment, a few years down the line.

Where did the other women in the family stand – and what, more particularly, was Cecily Neville's attitude, faced with this lethal rift among her children? The short answer is that we do not know. Crowland relates that in parliament 'not a single person uttered a word against the duke, except the king; not one individual made answer to the king except the duke'. It is said that Edward later lamented that 'not one creature' interceded for Clarence. But women, of course, would not be speaking in a parliament anyway: whatever was said by them, was said behind closed doors and was not recorded. At any rate, she made no cries of protest loud enough to catch the ear of any contemporary observer. It is often said that it was Cecily's pleading which won Clarence the right to choose his own manner of death, but evidence is hard to find. (The contemporary chronicler Jean de Roye wrote in his journal, the *Chronique scandaleuse*, that the dreadful sentence of hanging, drawing and quartering had been commuted 'by the great prayer and request of the mother', but his nineteenth-century editor Bernard de Mondrot pointed out that the words 'of the mother' were added between the lines, and in a later hand.)

Certainly Cecily had been present when, the day before the parliament began that was to try Clarence, the little Duke of York was married to Anne Mowbray. Perhaps she had at last given up on this particular branch of the Yorkist tree. It was, after all, Clarence who had impugned her chastity. One of the grounds on which he was accused was that he had 'upon one of the falsest and most unnatural coloured pretences that man might imagine, falsely and untruly noised, published and said, that the King our Sovereign Lord was a Bastard, and not begotten to reign upon us'.

Others have seen this very differently. One theory is that it was Cecily who offered Clarence the idea of her adultery, in pursuit of the family good. This was a world where, as one author puts it,[16] other loyalties might sometimes have to take precedence over 'the sacredness of each individual life'; and that conflict would be even more crucial for the York family in the years ahead. These were the stark choices Cecily would have to contemplate – not once, but repeatedly. It would seem she accepted Clarence's death. But it may have significantly altered her life.

From this point there are fewer mentions of Cecily taking part in court rituals. Naturally, the business of running her estates continued. Besides her main residence, 'our Castle of Berkhamsted', letters are signed from 'our place at Baynard's Castle' and from the priory at Merton. She never ceased to exercise her good ladyship[17] – to administer her lands and insist on her dignities. One letter from her begins: 'By the rightful inheritor's wife of the realm of England and of France, and lordship of Ireland, the king's mother, Duchess of York.' Another sent a stinging reproof to an officer she felt had fallen down over the administration of her East Anglian lands. He should amend on his 'faithful and true devoir [duty]', and 'fail not hereof as you will avoid the awful peril that may ensue with our great displeasure and heavy ladyship'.

She can be glimpsed[18] licensing seven men in Thaxted to form a fraternity in 1481; joining in Edward's petition on behalf of a Carthusian monastery to which, the letter urged, the king's mother 'has a singular devotion'; requesting absolution for a clerk of the diocese of York notwithstanding his 'bigamy and irregularity'. But at Berkhamsted she seems to have adopted a life of increasing piety. A few years later[19] Cecily's daily regime was recorded at length for posterity.

> She is accustomed to arise at seven o'clock and has ready her chaplain to say with her matins of the day, and matins of Our Lady; and when she is full ready she has a low mass in her chamber, and after mass she takes something to recreate [recruit, restore] nature; and so goes to the chapel, hearing the divine service and two low masses; thence to dinner, during the time thereof she has a reading of holy matter . . . .
>
> After dinner she gives audience to all such as has any matter to show to her by the space of one hour; and then she sleeps one quarter of an hour, and after she has slept she continues in prayer to the first peal of evensong; then she drinks wine or ale at her pleasure. Forthwith her chaplain is ready to say with her both evensongs; and after the last peal she goes to the chapel and hears evensong by note; from thence to supper, and in the time of supper she recites the reading that was had at dinner to those that be in her presence.
>
> After supper she disposes herself to be familiar with her gentlewomen, to the following of honest mirth; and one hour before her going to bed, she takes a cup of wine, and after that goes to her private closet, and takes her leave of God for all night, making end of her prayers for that day; and by eight of the clock she is in bed. I trust to Our Lord's mercy that this noble princess thus divides her hours to His high pleasure.

Cecily had chosen what the age called the mixed life:[20] the 'medled [*sic*] life that is to say sometime active sometime contemplative', as it was described by the late fourteenth-century northern cleric and author Nicholas Love, whose translation of the *Life of Christ* was in Cecily's library alongside numerous other devotional works. So too was the *Letter on the Mixed Life* written by Love's associate Walter Hilton, while *The Abbey of the Holy Ghost* (of which Cecily's daughter Margaret of Burgundy owned a copy) was written to teach those 'unable to leave the world how they might build an abbey in their soul and keep the rules of an order in their heart'. Cecily's was an English, a less intellectual, version of the *devotio moderna* which her daughter espoused in its full reforming fervour.

Cecily also owned copies of *De Infantia Salvatoris* (apocryphal stories of the miracles of Christ's infancy) and of the ever-popular *Legenda Aurea*, the Golden Legend. But she also owned copies of the lives and visions of the great female mystics like Matilda of Hackenborn, Saint Bridget of Sweden and Saint Catherine of Siena. It was St Catherine who advised those who wished to follow her example, but were still constrained by the demands of the world: 'Build a cell inside your mind, from which you can never flee.'

Cecily's piety has traditionally been seen almost as a psychological alibi that allowed her to sail tranquilly above the turmoils of her family. She must often have needed the sense of a special relationship with God, and might have reflected on the biblical stories of brothers' struggles: Esau and Jacob, whose mother Rebecca showed him how to snatch his elder brother's birthright; Joseph, whose brothers conspired to kill him; David, chosen to be the king of the Jews above his elder brother Elijah.

It is conceivable that Cecily found in her faith an angry affirmation of, and vindication for, the vicissitudes imposed upon her family and those they had imposed upon themselves. In the years of Cecily's childhood, Thomas à Kempis had written in his *Imitation of Christ* of the rashness of relying on anyone but God, of the triumph in the Last Judgement of the oppressed over the oppressor: 'Then shall rightwise men stand in great [constaunce] against them that have anguished them and oppressed them.' At the very least Cecily must have needed the power of prayer to clear and focus the mind; to achieve that state of integration and acceptance that in the Middle Ages could only be couched in spiritual terms.

Like many devout women, Cecily probably made a particular identification with the Virgin Mary: relevant for a mother who lost two sons to political strife. St Bridget's prayer of the *Fifteen Oes* specifically encourages the devout to share the pain of Christ and of the Virgin; a few years later, Margaret Beaufort would collaborate with Elizabeth of York to commission a printed version from Caxton. Religious enthusiasm was a powerful link between almost all these women: a socially and morally acceptable way, perhaps, of evading or triumphing over other divides.

FOURTEEN

A Golden Sorrow

I swear, 'tis better to be lowly born,
And range with humble livers in content,
Than to be perked up in a glist'ring grief,
And wear a golden sorrow.

Henry VIII, 2.3

The saga of Clarence's death had demonstrated the divisions in the ruling York family, and at the same time had drawn attention to the important and at times divisive role played in English affairs by Margaret, Duchess of Burgundy.

The life she had been leading in her widowhood was, on a day-to-day level, a good one, despite the turmoils that had followed Duke Charles's death in 1477. Burgundy was replete with the profits of trade: Margaret's new home would be rich in tapestries, a single example of which could cost a wealthy landowner a whole year's income, and in books. In tapestries and other depictions Margaret is seen at falconry and the hunt; one, entitled *The Bear Hunt*, shows her riding side-saddle on a horse led by a groom.

As her stepdaughter Mary's marriage to Archduke Maximilian bore fruit, Margaret stood godmother to her children. Her dower lands included a prosperous and well-maintained collection of villages and towns. She chose to make her main residence at Malines in Brabant, purchasing a number of adjoining houses which she extended and rebuilt in red brick decorated with white stripes, with a balcony on which she could display herself to the people. She commissioned gardens designed to be seen from her palace windows, as well as a tennis court, a shooting gallery and hot baths. She had a chair of state, in the vast council chamber, upholstered in fine black velvet; and a study hung with violet taffeta, its beautiful books and manuscripts protected by a wrought-iron grille. She had her volumes on chess, her knives with handles of ebony and ivory, her knight of honour and her doctors, her dogs, her horses and her maker of preserves.

All the same, it seems likely she had an abiding sense of grievance – not least about her brother's failure ever fully to pay her dowry. And there was a hint of mysticism about her religious feeling, despite the crusading practicality with which she tackled the reform of religious orders in her domain. In an odd echo of the dream that Margaret Beaufort once claimed to have had, Margaret of Burgundy figured herself as visited in her chamber by the risen Jesus. The scene is described in a book written at her request soon after her marriage; she had it painted, too.[21] In the vaulted bedchamber, by her blue and scarlet bed, Margaret kneels fully dressed on a carpet, waiting to kiss the bleeding hand extended to her.

A 'beatific and uncovered vision', He was, naked under His crimson cloak, displaying His wounds, instructing her to make ready the bed of her heart in which she was to lie with Him 'in purest chastity and pure charity', ready to receive His instruction that she should look well upon the fires of hell and the glory of God. Christ had entered her bedchamber so quietly that even her greyhound did not wake; but she was so wholly convinced of His coming that she kissed the covers of her bed His body had touched until the colour was worn away. The same fanaticism could also surface in her secular affairs, skilled and competent though she might usually be.

Now, in 1480, Margaret returned to England to encourage her brother in his goodwill towards Burgundy, to turn him away from the French, and to negotiate a match between Edward's daughter Anne and Mary of Burgundy's little son. The magnificence of the visit can be summed up in the lavish clothes and other textiles that were ordered; two pieces of arras [tapestry] 'of the story of Paris and Elyn [Helen]' to help furnish a house for the visitor's use; 47 yards of 'green sarsenet' garnished with green ribbon for curtains; and 'great large feather beds'. A hundred servants were given new 'jackets of woollen cloth of murrey [purple-red] and blue;' the Yorkist colours. Edward Woodville, sailing across the Channel to escort Margaret back home, was given a yard of blue velvet and a yard of purple for a jacket; the twenty-four men who rowed her up the Thames in the king's barge after she disembarked from the *Falcon* at Gravesend sported jackets trimmed with white roses; an embroiderer called Peter Lambard was paid a penny for each small rose. The horses Edward gave her were harnessed in green velvet, embellished with gold and silver, and the reins were of crimson velvet.

Few princesses returned to their native land unless, like Marguerite of Anjou, disgraced and desperate or, in their widowhood, returned as surplus to the requirements of their marital country. This was different; whatever her brother may have thought, as he contemplated arranging for her a fresh match in Scotland, Margaret was here to carry out the agenda of her adopted land. As she was rowed upstream and into London, past Greenwich, round the great loop of the river, the city itself began to come into view.

Streets where the shopkeepers sold everything from silks to strawberries; hot sheep's feet to Paris thread; peascods and pie; where an Italian visitor two decades later would write that in the fifty-two goldsmith's shops in one road alone there was such a magnificence of silver vessels that in Rome, Venice and Florence together you might not find its equivalent. The Tower, London Bridge with its tall rows of houses, Baynard's Castle came into view, and further ahead, past another green burst of country, the spires and turrets of Westminster: this was her own old home city.

A house had been prepared for her near her mother's residence of Baynard's Castle, as well as an apartment in the palace at Greenwich, her home in the first few years of her brother's reign. Edward gave a banquet at Greenwich in honour of her and their mother; Richard even came down from the battles with Scotland to see her. Margaret's older sister Elizabeth visited, too. Perhaps their presence made the absence of Clarence the more poignant; perhaps, too, there was some awkwardness in the adjustment of positions and protocols now that the youngest daughter of the house of York had become the dowager duchess of a foreign power. But the reforging of relationships would be important in the next reigns.

The celebrations went well; the diplomacy was more edgy. If he yielded to Margaret's persuasions, Edward stood to lose his French pension and that flattering match between the five-year-old Princess Elizabeth and the Dauphin. As far back as August 1478 Edward had been pushing for Elizabeth's French marriage to go ahead, but at that time Louis was less than keen; a son and heir's marriage was too important a tool of diplomacy to be squandered lightly. So it was surely no coincidence that Louis now chose this moment not only to send over a delegation with Edward's annuity of 50,000 crowns but to offer an additional 15,000 a year for Elizabeth until she and the Dauphin were actually wed.

The match that Margaret was offering may have been all in the family, but the bargaining was nevertheless keen. Edward asked whether Burgundy would compensate him, if promising his daughter Anne cost him his French pension; he also proposed that Anne should come without a dowry. Margaret had to send home for Maximilian and Mary's opinion, and the result was a compromise. Edward would allow English archers to reinforce the Burgundian troops, and would declare war on France if Louis did not restore Margaret's lands by Easter the following year. Burgundy would pay his pension if the French withdrew it. Anne would bring a dowry, albeit only half the one hoped for, but Burgundy would pay her an annuity until the marriage could be finalised. Margaret, meanwhile, gave her four-year-old niece a wedding ring ('in the style of a circlet with eight fine diamonds and a central rose of three hanging pearls') and a chain on which – until her fingers grew – it could be hung.

But no sooner had Margaret confirmed the details than she received word that Maximilian had negotiated his own truce with the French, doubtless using the current English rapprochement as leverage. She feared that Maximilian's duplicity would anger her brother – in fact he took it with the calm of one who would have done exactly the same thing. Back in Burgundy, she felt she would have to explain to Maximilian why she had not been able to agree better terms. One can only hope she did not take the double-dealing personally, but merely as evidence that a woman's diplomatic work is never done.

The visit ended as it had begun, however, on a note of personal happiness. Edward accompanied Margaret as she rode out of London, on her way to Canterbury to visit the shrine of St Thomas à Becket. Before sailing from Dover she spent a week at the Kent estate of Anthony Woodville, talking books and philosophy. Margaret had sent William Caxton, who had been her financial adviser in Bruges, to England a few years earlier, and in 1476 Anthony had become his patron, translating books for him to print. A stream of works emerged from Caxton's press in the yard of Westminster Abbey: Chaucer, Malory's stories of King Arthur, Boethius' *The Consolation of Philosophy*, *The Mirror of the World*, Higdon's *Polychronicon*, *The Golden Legend*, *Aesop's Fables*, *The Life of Our Lady*.

After this agreeable intellectual interlude Edward's 'well-beloved sister', as he wrote to Maximilian, went home. She would continue to look across the Channel, as one of Edward's successors would discover all too painfully. But, for the moment, England seemed established in comparative tranquillity.

The turn of the decade had seen business as usual for King Edward and his family. Elizabeth Woodville was now well established as a wielder of influence and distributor of patronage; endowing, for example, a chapel dedicated to St Erasmus in Westminster Abbey. The powerful group of traders known as the Merchant Adventurers had cause to be grateful for the 'very good effort' she put into helping them negotiate a reduction in the subsidy demanded of them by the king. Intercession had been made by several nobles, their records noted, 'but especially by the Queen'. It is a useful reminder that these women were consumers and negotiators; patrons as well as parents; readers and (on their own estates) rulers. Even the young Princess Elizabeth had long had her own lands. On 4 November 1467 the Calendar of the Patent Rolls records a 'Grant for life to the King's daughter the Princess Elizabeth of the manor of Great Lynford, county of Buckingham'.

Some time in 1477 Elizabeth Woodville had given birth to a third son, George, who died in infancy. Her sixth daughter, Katherine, was born in 1479 at Eltham, a favourite residence, and her last child, too, was born there in November 1480. This daughter was named after St Bridget, the former court lady turned religieuse who founded her own order – a path of life that would come to seem prophetic in the family. When Bridget was christened at Eltham Margaret Beaufort was asked to carry her in the formal procession – a mark of high esteem. The godmothers were the baby's grandmother Cecily Neville, and her elder sister Elizabeth of York.

Today the Great Hall at Eltham built by Edward, with its hammerbeam roof and its discreet 'archers' gallery', where a bodyguard with drawn bows would stand facing the crowd as king and queen dined, can still be seen. And though their walls are now only ruins, it is possible to trace the pattern of the surprisingly tiny rooms Elizabeth would have used when she visited her children here – for Eltham was always the first choice as a nursery palace, and would remain so when Elizabeth of York came to rear her own children. It was a fit setting for a happy family.

And such the king's family had been throughout the 1470s; Crowland described the court as filled with 'those most sweet and beautiful children'. A visitor to the court in 1482 described the young Richard, Duke of York as singing with his mother and one of his sisters, playing at sticks and with a two-handed sword. There had been sadnesses too, of course, as when in November 1481 Richard's eight-year-old bride Anne Mowbray died, followed six months later by Elizabeth Woodville's fourteen-year-old daughter Mary, recently betrothed to the king of Denmark. But by and large, even after the new decade dawned, glimpses of the family are cheerful ones. There was a visit to Oxford, where they were joined by the king's sister Elizabeth, the Duchess of Suffolk. A set of signatures in an early fourteenth-century manuscript of an Arthurian romance – 'E Wydevyll' on the back, and 'Elysabeth, the kyngs dowther' and 'Cecyl the kynges dowther' on the flyleaf – suggests that Queen Elizabeth's daughters may have been reading the book she had once owned as a girl.

A stained-glass window in Canterbury Cathedral depicts the royal family diminished slightly in number, but still in all its glory. It can be dated to 1482 or later by the fact that Cecily is shown as the king's second daughter: until her elder sister Mary died earlier that year she had been the third. The king and queen, each kneeling at a prayer desk, face each other in the two central panels, with their children, similarly posed, lined up in order and dwindling size behind them. The two surviving boys have each a panel and a desk to themselves; the five surviving girls have to cram themselves into a matching pair.

The boys, like their parents, are garbed in royal purple cloaks over robes of cloth of gold, collared in ermine. The girls wear matching purple gowns girdled in gold, with flashes of jewels and fur at neck and hem, and their long yellow hair hangs down their backs. All are crowned or coroneted, all have an open book on the prayer desk before them; this was a family who knelt only to God. The panels would once have flanked an image of the Crucifixion under a depiction of the seven holy joys of the Virgin Mary, before the window became the target of Cromwell's wreckers in 1642.

After the great reburial ceremony at Fotheringhay, it seems that the first daughter, Elizabeth of York, had been considered old enough to join her mother on other ceremonial occasions. In the Garter procession that marked the feast of St George in April 1477, the records note, the queen came to mass 'on horseback in a murrey gown of Garters. Item: the lady Elizabeth, the King's eldest daughter, in a gown of the same livery.'

Her later tastes and abilities indicate something of Elizabeth of York's education. Her Latin was not fluent – she would later request that her prospective daughter-in-law Katherine of Aragon be taught French before her arrival, since English ladies did not usually understand the other tongue – yet she did learn to write, not by any means a given even for ladies of the highest rank. But Elizabeth's was an educated family: her father collected books, and her uncle Anthony's literary interests seem to some degree to have been shared by the wider Woodville clan. Later Elizabeth would hunt and shoot, keep her own musicians, play at games of chance and sew expertly, all of which were expected of ladies. What was perhaps less common was the degree to which Edward's daughters learned to fill their imaginations with the world of written thought and story.

Of course high-born children grew up with Bible stories and the lives of saints, as well as tales from the allegories and spectacles of pageantry. In *The Treasury of the City of Ladies* Christine de Pizan had urged that: 'A young girl should also especially venerate Our Lady, St Catherine, and all virgins, and if she can read, eagerly read their biographies.' But Elizabeth and her sisters would have had an unusual opportunity to get their information and story direct. Their uncle Anthony had translated the *Dictes or Sayengis of the Philosophers* and the *Moral Proverbs* of Christine de Pizan; their mother too was a patron of Caxton's.[22] Elizabeth would have got to know the Arthurian stories, with their wildly mixed messages about a woman's love and a queen's duty, their tales of Guinevere and the other heroines maying and feasting, shamed and repenting. (Such books were dangerous, declared a contemporary at the Castilian court, 'causing weak-breasted women to fall into libidinous errors and commit sins they would not otherwise commit'.) Elizabeth and her sister Cecily also wrote their names on a French story of the world and the funeral rites of an emperor of the Turks: here are mosques and minarets, slaves and strange palaces.

But underneath these pleasures of daily life it became apparent as the 1480s moved on that Elizabeth of York's future was less secure than it had seemed; and perhaps her early experience of uncertainty influenced her sometimes controversial actions in the time ahead. For in these years King Edward's diplomatic affairs – in which the royal children were such useful pawns – were going less than smoothly.

When the Prince of Wales was betrothed to Anne of Brittany, Louis of France struck back by encouraging the Scots to attack northern England. This was what compelled Edward, in 1481, to excuse himself to the Pope for not joining a crusade against the Turks, on the grounds that 'the acts of our treacherous neighbours' kept him fully occupied during 'this tempestuous period'. But things were about to get worse: in March 1482 Mary of Burgundy died after a riding accident, an event that gave her subjects the opportunity to decide that they preferred peaceful relations with the French to Mary's husband and his English treaty.

On her deathbed Mary begged her stepmother Margaret to protect her two surviving children, which at first looked like a case of helping Mary's widower Maximilian keep them in a country he proposed to rule himself. This, however, would soon prove impossible: although the little boy Philip remained largely in Margaret's care, after Christmas that year news reached England that Mary's three-year-old daughter was to be sent to France to be married to the Dauphin, who – as had so often been threatened before – would thus be reneging on his betrothal to Elizabeth of York. At seventeen, comparatively late for a royal girl to remain unmarried, Elizabeth would have been old enough to feel both the slight and the uncertainty.

Edward's marital plans for his daughters had not been going well. In October 1482 he had had to call off Cecily's arranged marriage with the Scottish prince. The betrothal between Anne and the Burgundian heir Philip, too, would founder on

Edward's parsimony over Anne's dowry, which allowed Philip's father Maximilian to abandon it for a better match elsewhere. In this difficult diplomatic climate, Edward suggested for his eldest daughter a match that would once have seemed most unlikely – marriage to Henry Tudor, still living in exile in Brittany.

An agreement had already been drawn up to return Henry Tudor home, 'to be in the grace and favour of the king's highness', and to enjoy a portion of the lands recently left by the death of his grandmother, Margaret Beaufort's mother. And Edward mooted also the possibility of a marriage that would attach Henry to the Yorkist family.

Holinshed says that such a marriage had been suggested several years before. At that point the offer was probably only tactical; and when the ruler of Brittany was persuaded to hand over his principal pawn he may well (as Vergil would later have it) have been handing 'the sheep to the wolf'. Henry had been entrusted to the English envoys but – warned, says the Tudor poet Bernard André, by his mother, who had scented a deception – when he reached St Malo to board ship for England he feigned illness, slipped into a church and claimed sanctuary, from where he was able to slip back to a remorseful Duke Francis in Brittany.

But now times had changed. With the new alliance between France and Burgundy, with the danger that England might once again be at war with the French, King Edward may have found the thought of Henry Tudor – a potential English claimant – as a loose cannon at the French court too dangerous to contemplate. To Margaret Beaufort this new plan may well have seemed a reasonable advancement for her son. Her acquiescence may have represented an acceptance of the status quo – that Henry's Lancastrian claim had no immediate prospect of bearing fruit. But, as had happened so many times before, events were about to overthrow all plans.

Edward's way of life had long been intemperate enough to affect his health. Mancini wrote that: 'In food and drink he was most immoderate: it was his habit, so I have learned, to take an emetic for the delight of gorging his stomach once more.' He had now 'grown fat in the loins, whereas previously he had been not only tall but rather lean and very active'. What is more, the legendarily beautiful and loving Elizabeth Woodville always had to suffer her husband's flagrant infidelity: 'He pursued with no discrimination the married and unmarried, the noble and lowly: however he took none by force. He overcame all by money and promises and having conquered them, he dismissed them.' Quarrels over mistresses, Mancini added, would create a major rift between Elizabeth's eldest son Dorset and the king's great friend Lord Hastings, an admirer of the king's favourite mistress Jane Shore. The whole question of Edward's relations with women, licensed or unlicensed, would become political dynamite. But his mistresses were important in another sense as well: the toll the king's self-indulgence was taking on his health.

At Candlemas in early February 1483 the king and queen went in procession from St Stephen's Chapel to Westminster Hall. It looked – and was meant to – as if the royal family were here to stay, in prosperity and stability. But that spring Edward fell sick. Mancini said that he had been out fishing in a small boat and allowed the damp cold to strike his vitals; Commynes believed that it was apoplexy following a surfeit. Some even put it down to chagrin at the failure of his diplomacy. The English accounts are all sixteenth-century and inevitably include the suspicion of poison, but Hall says that since the French campaign of 1475 Edward had suffered from a fever 'which turned to an incurable quarten'. Whatever the cause, on 9 April he died, at the age of just forty. John Skelton wrote:

Where is now my conquest and victory?
Where is my riches and my royal array?
Where be my coursers and my horses high?
Where is my mirth, my solace, and my play?
As vanity, to naught all is wandered away.
O lady Bess, long for me may ye call!
For now we are parted until doomsday;
But love ye that Lord that is sovereign of all.

If Edward IV had lived longer, the events that followed his death would surely have unfolded differently. The young Prince Edward, his heir, might not have been perceived as so dangerously under Woodville influence. There would not have been the same shock to a country only ten years away from the last throes of civil war and still in recovery from the long-term effects of the minority rule of Henry VI. Mancini noted that Edward IV left two sons, adding: 'He also left daughters, but they do not concern us.' It was to prove a poor prophecy. Women's choices and women's alliances would play a pivotal part in the years ahead.

The woman who had done most to challenge the patriarchal assumptions of these years had however, now departed. On 25 August 1482, at the Château de Dampierre near Saumur, Marguerite of Anjou had died. She had, according to her Victorian biographer Mary Ann Hookham,[23] been visited there by Henry Tudor, whom she urged to continue his struggle against the house of York. Marguerite died poor, as her will recorded. The 'few goods' which God and King Louis had allowed her were to be used to pay for her burial: 'And should my few goods be insufficient to do this, as I believe they are [King Louis took her hunting dogs as the only goods of value], I implore the king meet and pay the outstanding debts as the sole heir of the wealth which I inherited through my father

174

and mother and my other relatives and ancestors ....'
Resentment of her poverty and pride in her lineage are evident
here. Her political life had long been over, but she had been
one of the most forceful women in a century not short of them.

At the beginning of *Richard III*, Shakespeare has Marguerite
returned from exile like a vengeful ghost to curse Elizabeth
Woodville:

> Long mayst thou live to wail thy children's death
> And see another, as I see thee now,
> Decked in thy rights, as thou art stalled in mine.
> Long die thy happy days before thy death,
> And after many lengthened hours of grief,
> Die neither mother, wife, nor England's queen.

Perhaps Marguerite's ghost lived on – in the mind of
Richard of Gloucester, for example, eyeing the accession of a
twelve-year-old to the throne with all the paranoia of one born
into the era of Marguerite's battles to rule the country for her
infant son at the time of Henry VI's insanity.

PART FOUR

1483–1485

FIFTEEN

Weeping Queens

For my daughters, Richard,
They shall be praying nuns, not weeping queens
Richard III, 4.4

The marriage of Elizabeth Woodville and Edward IV had been one of the great royal love stories, combining physical passion with warm domesticity; it rewrote the rules of royal romance, with all the implications that would have in the next century. There can be little doubt that under normal circumstances Elizabeth would have allowed herself to mourn most sincerely. But the circumstances were far from normal: she was a queen fighting for position, given her son's minority. Edward IV's death left a twelve-year-old boy as king – a difficult situation in any but the most stable country. The problem of competing factions within English court circles could only have been resolved by the accession of a strong and adult ruler.

Christine de Pizan took special pains to advise the princess in a war-torn land, widowed while her son was still a minor, that she should 'employ all her prudence and her wisdom to reconcile the antagonistic factions'. Richard of Gloucester was riding high: the parliament of January 1483 had acknowledged and rewarded his efforts against the Scots. Perhaps it had been in response to his high profile that in the same month Anthony, Elizabeth Woodville's brother, seemed to be trying to recruit the Woodville interest. In February and March he had been making sure that his appointment as Prince Edward's governor was renewed, and requesting confirmation of his right as such to raise troops in Wales. Ever since, the question of who took the aggressive initiative – or who was merely getting their retaliation in first – has been argued endlessly.

The events which followed the death of Edward IV are still controversial. The main protagonists brought with them the memory of experiences that would make anyone wary. Elizabeth's were of the downturn in fortune that had followed the death of her first, Grey, husband; and of the moment when her second husband's crown had been snatched back from him in 1470. Richard, Duke of Gloucester must have remembered that the last two dukes of Gloucester, Henry VI's uncle Humfrey and Richard II's uncle Thomas Woodstock, both holders of the reins during a royal minority, had both died imprisoned. Moreover, he would have recalled all too clearly the time of Henry VI's insanity, when Marguerite of Anjou attempted to take over in her infant son's name. With Elizabeth Woodville manoeuvring in London, it must have seemed a most alarming precedent.

Richard, as the only royal uncle of the new boy king Edward V, had recent custom on his side. It was his uncles who had governed for the infant Henry VI. What is more, Richard was aligned with the 'king's men' led by Lord Hastings, the Duke of Buckingham, the Duke of Suffolk and the Earl of Lincoln (the latter two being respectively brother-in-law and nephew of Edward IV through his sister Elizabeth). Buckingham had reputedly never forgiven Elizabeth Woodville for marrying him, as a child, to another Woodville sister whom he considered beneath him; and he may have felt that the Woodvilles had deprived him of the influence in Wales that his landholdings on the Welsh border should have allowed him to enjoy. Hastings and the queen had a different quarrel, says More: she was not only resentful of 'the great favour the King bare him [but] also for that she thought him secretly familiar with the King in wanton company'.

More describes a deathbed scene, with Hastings, like the queen and her eldest Grey son, among the leading players. He gives Edward a moving speech: 'in these last words that ever I look to speak with you: I exhort you and require you all, for the love that you have ever born to me, for the love that I have ever born to you, for the love that our lord beareth to us all, for this time forward, all griefs forgotten, each of you love other.' ('If you among your selves in a child's reign fall at debate, many a good man shall perish and haply he, too, and you, too, ere this land find peace again', More has him add prophetically.) They all agreed – but whether they would keep their agreement once Edward had died was another story.

The council met immediately, and Elizabeth Woodville met with them. There was, however, no question of her having an actual regency; nor of her having even the measure of influence she had been given when her husband went to France in 1475, or the generous measure of control handed to her when her son's council as Prince of Wales had been set up. Her husband was dead, his wishes no longer paramount.[1]

Perhaps there was never any question of a regency as such. What Henry VI's senior uncle had held in the king's infancy was a protectorate, which allowed the incumbent to 'protect' prince and state but without assuming regal powers. Some said that Edward IV had wanted his brother Richard to occupy such a position. But Richard was not in London to make any claim: he must have felt that events had overtaken him, just as Elizabeth must have felt herself cast adrift by the sudden loss of the man from whom all her influence had derived. But for the Woodvilles in general this looked like an opportunity to grasp even greater power. It was, after all, they in whose company and under whose guidance the new young king had been brought up.

In the event the council took a decision which they hoped would neatly evade these problems. Edward V could become a legal adult at his coronation – he was, after all, twelve, and Henry VI had been declared adult when not much older; this was a device which would allow the council to govern under the boy king's nominal rule. It looked like a balanced and viable decision, but it ignored one thing. A twelve-year-old was inevitably going to fall under somebody's sway, and he would have ever more opportunity to be influenced by it as he neared maturity and exercised more actual governance. That some-body was likely to come from the mother's family who had surrounded him since infancy.

Dominic Mancini, the commentator who dismissed Edward's daughters, was, ironically, the one who described how Richard (incited by Hastings) wrote to the council on hearing the news of his brother's death, emphasising his rights and his long tradition of loyalty. 'He had been loyal to his brother Edward, at home and abroad, in peace and war, and would be, if only permitted, equally loyal to his brother's issue, even female . . .[2] if perchance, which God forbid, the youth should die.'

On 14 April Prince Edward was told of his father's death; two days later a letter declares his intention of setting out from Ludlow 'in all convenient haste'. There was considerable debate as to the number of men who should accompany him on his journey: some 'suggested more, some less'. All who were present, Mancini says, keenly desired that this prince should succeed his father in all his glory; but feared if the Woodvilles were allowed to escort young Edward to his coronation 'with an immoderate number of horse' it would be impossible subsequently to get rid of them. Hastings in particular (between whom and the Woodvilles there was 'much ill-will') warned that an army would send the wrong signal; and Elizabeth took the point. Indeed, Crowland describes how 'The Queen most beneficently tried to extinguish every spark of murmuring and disturbance, and wrote to her son, requesting him on his road to London, not to exceed an escort of two thousand men.'

It was 24 April before the king, his escort headed by his uncle Anthony Woodville and his half-brother Richard Grey, finally left Ludlow. Richard of Gloucester was also on the move, leaving his wife Anne Neville behind in the north. It may seem strange – or significant – that Anne herself was not on the way down to take part in her nephew's coronation, scheduled for less than a week away. But it is unknown how far, at this stage, Richard's own plans went – let alone how much he had confided to his wife.[3]

When the young king and his entourage diverted to meet his uncle Richard on the 29th at Stony Stratford in Northamptonshire, there was no apparent reason to fear. Richard, after all, had already 'wrote unto the King [Edward V] so reverently, and to the Queen's friends, there so lovingly', says More, that they 'nothing earthly' mistrusted. He had moreover himself sworn, and required all northerners to swear likewise, an oath to Edward V.

While the king remained at Stony Stratford for the evening Richard, and Buckingham who had joined him, invited Anthony Woodville (Lord Rivers) to dine where they were staying at Northampton, some 11 miles away. The party made 'much friendly cheer', and parted for the night with 'great courtesy'. But next morning when Woodville came to leave he found he was locked in, arrested by Richard's men. Meanwhile

Buckingham rode to Stony Stratford to inform Edward that his uncle Anthony and both his half-brothers, among others, stood accused of attempting to rule the king and to cause dissension in the realm. Edward, if Mancini is to be believed, answered courageously and to the point: that these were the ministers his father had given him, and he trusted his father's judgement; that concerning the government of the kingdom 'he had complete confidence in the peers of the realm and the queen'. Then, 'On hearing the queen's name, the duke of Buckingham, who loathed her race . . . answered, "It was not the business of women but of men to govern kingdoms, and so if he cherished any confidence in her he had better relinquish it."' Anthony Woodville and Richard Grey were sent north, to be held in one of Richard's castles.

On hearing what had taken place, Elizabeth's first reaction was to strike back. 'When this news was announced in London the unexpectedness of the event horrified every one,' Mancini reported. Elizabeth and her elder Grey son, Dorset, 'began collecting an army, to defend themselves, and to set free the young king from the clutches of the dukes. But when they had exhorted certain nobles who had come to the city, and other, to take up arms, they perceived that men's minds were not only irresolute, but altogether hostile to themselves. Some even said openly that it was more just and profitable that the youthful sovereign should be with his paternal uncle than with his maternal uncles and uterine brothers.' Other sources suggest that Elizabeth fled with her children into sanctuary the minute she heard the news; whatever the order of events, flee she certainly did.

Elizabeth surely cannot be blamed for fleeing into sanctuary; though it has often been seen as hysterical and unnecessary, a move designed to wrongfoot Richard, the man she saw as her enemy. More describes how 'the Queen in great flight and heaviness, bewailing her child's ruin, her friends' mischance, and her own infortune, damning the time that ever she dissuaded the gathering of power about the king, got herself in all the haste possible with her younger son and her daughters out of the Palace of Westminster in which she then lay, into the Sanctuary'. Dorset and her brother Lionel, the bishop, were to join her there. Thomas Rotherham, Archbishop of York and Lord Chancellor of England, went to see Elizabeth in the midst of the crisis and described a scene of chaos: 'much heaviness, rumble, haste and business, carriage and conveyance of her stuff into sanctuary, chests, coffers, packs, fardels, trusses, all on men's backs, no man unoccupied, some loading, some going, some discharging, some coming for more, some breaking down the walls to bring in the next way . . .'. The queen herself, as More reports Rotherham's finding, 'sat alone low on the rushes all desolate and dismayed'.

He comforted her in the best manner he could and gave into her custody the Privy Seal, of which he was keeper. It showed there was still a game to play. But the archbishop regretted his impetuous move and next day sent to ask for his seal back. After all, Richard had not moved against the crown as such. Hastings (who, in Crowland's words, was congratulating himself that the whole affair had been accomplished with no more bloodshed than 'might have come from a cut finger') was reassuring those in London that Richard was still faithful to Edward's wishes and that nothing whatsoever had been done save a transfer of power from one to another side of the new king's family.

On 4 May the young Edward entered London, riding in blue in a splendid procession, obsequiously attended by Richard who had technically done nothing to breach his oath of loyalty. This should have been the day of Edward's coronation, which was now postponed to the end of June. On the 7th a meeting was held at Baynard's Castle, Cecily Neville's London residence, at which the most powerful lords of the country, spiritual and temporal – Richard among them – officially took possession of Edward IV's goods, seals and jewels on the grounds that they were executors of his will. In the will of 1475, of course, Elizabeth had been among the executors. Richard, says Mancini, had arrived in London preceded by four wagons bearing the Woodville emblems and loaded with arms, which he claimed were designed to be used against him. The excuse was obviously trumped up – Mancini says everyone knew the weapons had really been collected to use against the Scots – but Richard's move must have seemed another ominous sign to Elizabeth in sanctuary.

At a council meeting on 27 May Richard was declared the man 'thought most meet to be the Protector of the King and his realm'. He would hold the post, however, only until Edward was crowned and declared of age just four weeks later, which opened up the prospect of fresh dispute and may have helped push Richard to seek a more definitive solution.

Some time in the first few weeks after his arrival the young king was moved, at Buckingham's suggestion, from the Bishop of London's palace (too small for a full royal retinue) to the Tower. There was nothing sinister in that, necessarily – the Tower was a conventional royal residence, traditionally used by monarchs preceding their coronation. Moreover, it is hard to think where better Edward could have gone: the out-of-town palaces like Sheen and Eltham were too distant, and the nearer Westminster was ineligible because his mother was self-immured close by.

There seems to have been a tentative plan for Richard to continue his role at head of government beyond the coronation – there must also have been a fear that the king, once declared of age, would recall his mother and her family to his side.

Elizabeth's brother Edward had been commanding a fleet in the Channel to guard against the French, but now his soldiers were ordered to desert while he himself was to be seized; in fact, he escaped with two ships and made his way to Henry Tudor in Brittany.

Richard was possibly already taking steps towards claiming the throne for himself. It has been suggested that, in the early days of June, Bishop Stillington (who some sources said had married Edward IV to Eleanor Butler before he married Elizabeth Woodville) told the council what he knew. One chronicle describes doctors, proctors and depositions being brought in to the lords. A case was being prepared.

A letter from Simon Stallworthe to Sir William Stonor on 9 June reports that the Queen 'keeps still at Westminster'. 'My Lord Protector, My Lord of Buckingham with all other lords as well temporal as spiritual were at Westminster in the Council Chamber from 10 to 2, but there was none that spoke with the Queen.' There was, he says, 'great business' about the young king's coronation which was due to take place just a fortnight later; and when he adds that 'My Lady of Gloucester' – Anne Neville – came to London 'on Thursday last', the assumption must still have been that it was to attend this function. The parliament which always followed a coronation had been called; government was working normally. But there is a hint that even outside the Protector's rooms other possibilities were being mooted, when Stallworthe urges Stonor to come to town 'and then shall you know all the world'.

On the 10th and 11th June Richard wrote respectively to the city of York and to Lord Neville of Raby (his mother's family, whatever divisions there had been in it), asking them to bring troops from the north with all diligence 'to aid and assist us against the Queen, her bloody adherents and affinity; which have intended and daily doth intend to murder and utterly destroy us and our cousin the Duke of Buckingham and the old royal blood of the realm'. It is a reasonable assumption that Elizabeth was still hoping – plotting – to overthrow him, although her Grey son and her brother, hostages in Richard's custody, may have given her pause. But it is hard to believe Richard really feared she still had the means to put her hopes into effect; the more so because of what happened on 13 June.

The exact circumstances of the story, as described by Thomas More, have reinforced the legend of Richard's villainy. He arrived smiling at a council meeting, praising the strawberries from the Bishop of Ely's garden. This was Bishop Morton, Margaret Beaufort's ally.[4] But after Richard left the room, he returned with a frowning face and accusation on his lips. More's account has Richard pulling up his sleeve to show a withered arm. 'See in what wise that sorceress [Queen Elizabeth] and others of her counsel, as Shore's wife with her affinity, have by their sorcery and witchcraft thus washed my body', Richard said. 'Jane' Shore, once Edward IV's 'merriest harlot', was now the lover of Lord Hastings; and More shows his scepticism about that part of the story in particular. 'The Queen was too wise to go about any such folly. And also if she would, yet would she of all folk least make Shore's wife of counsel, whom of all women she most hated, as that concubine whom the King her husband had most loved.' But Hastings and Morton were both arrested, also on the charge of having plotted to destroy Richard, and Hastings, hitherto Richard's ally, was (so the dramatic tale goes) unceremoniously beheaded the same day.

This looks like the first indisputable evidence that Richard now sought the crown. Hastings, Edward IV's loyal friend, may well have believed the country would be better governed in Edward V's minority by his father's loyal and able brother than by the queen and her family, but he would surely have baulked at what was to follow.

After this, events moved swiftly. At the next meeting of the council Richard insisted that his namesake, Elizabeth Woodville's second son, be brought out of sanctuary – nominally, to attend his brother's coronation. On 16 June a delegation was sent,[5] and More details their arguments at length. Some were technical: that an innocent child could have no reason to claim – could have no reason to be given – sanctuary, which was for those who had done wrong or who had reason to hide; that it was as reasonable for the council to fear to leave the prince in the queen's hands as for her to fear to hand him over, since he might be spirited away. Other arguments were political: that the queen's evident refusal to trust the council was causing division in the realm and distrust outside it. One objection was directly gender-related: that her refusal sprang from what the senior cleric present charitably called 'womanish fear' but the Duke of Buckingham called 'womanish frowardness [perversity]'.*

Other points were designed to appeal directly to a mother's heart. Elizabeth was, the delegation accused her in a shrewd blow, like Medea avenging herself at the expense of her own children by keeping her son mewed up in sanctuary. The lords asserted it was no place for a child, being full of 'a rabble of thieves, murderers, and malicious heinous traitors'. Young Edward V needed his brother's company, they insisted, and a life without play was unsuited to 'their both ages and estates'. The saga of argument and counter-argument runs on for pages.

More has Elizabeth answering fluently and bravely. If the young King Edward needed company, why should not both her

---

* Elizabeth had, he said, no need to fear since there was 'no man here that will be at war with women' . . . and as for the rights of sanctuary: 'What if a man's wife will take sanctuary because she list to run away from her husband? I would ween if she can allege no other cause, he may lawfully, without any displeasure to St Peter, take her out of St Peter's church by the arm.'

royal sons be placed in her care – the more so since the younger boy had been ill and needed his mother's attention? It was, of course, the last thing to which the councillors were likely to agree. Why not find other peers' sons for him to play with, rather than his still ailing brother? She replied that the law made her as his mother his guardian ('as my learned counsel shows me') in the absence of any other knightly ties. 'You may not take hence my horse from me; and may you take my child from me?' she asked. It was another telling point. She added that the imprisonment of her brother and Grey son Richard hardly inspired confidence; that protection for herself or her other children could not be assured in a time of 'greedy' men; and that yes, her son did have the right to claim sanctuary: Richard had come up with 'a goodly glose' – a clever misinterpretation – to claim that 'a place that may defend a thief may not save an innocent'.

But the real point, of course, was the unspoken one: the fear that if Elizabeth refused to hand over her boy he would simply be snatched away. Sanctuary was a moral rather than a physical concept; this was the middle of Westminster, with the Protector himself waiting in another part of the palace only a few hundred yards away; and Mancini says that 'with the consent of the council [Richard] surrounded the sanctuary with troops'.

As More tells it, the question of taking the boy by force was a matter of some dissent among the lords themselves, some of the lords spiritual holding back, but the majority agreeing to do whatever was necessary. In the end it was Thomas Bourchier, the Archbishop of Canterbury (and a relative of the York brothers through their father's sister), who broke the deadlock, telling Elizabeth that if she sent the boy now he himself would guarantee the prince's safety, but that if she refused he would have nothing more to do with a woman who seemed to think that 'all others save herself lacked either wit or truth'. More adds: 'The Queen with these words stood a good while in a great study.'

More's pages need some decoding,[6] for Elizabeth's words were surely polished afterwards: 'And at the last she took the young duke by the hand, and said to the lords, "my Lord", quod she, "and all my lords, I am neither so unwise [as] to mistrust your wits, nor so suspicious to mistrust your troths."' It may have been More's hindsight that makes her add: 'We have also had experience that the desire of a kingdom knows no kindred. The brother has been the brother's bane. And may the nephews be sure of their uncle?' But these are considerations of which everyone must, in any case, have been aware.

As her son prepared to depart, 'And therewithal she said to the child, "Farewell my own sweet son, God send you good keeping. Let me kiss you once yet before you go, for God knows when we shall kiss together again." And therewith she kissed him, and blessed him, turned her back and wept and went her way, leaving the child weeping as fast.' When the lords brought the little boy through the palace to his uncle, waiting in Star Chamber, Richard received him kindly, welcoming him 'with all my very heart'. The Stonor letters report confidently that the child had gone with the archbishop to the Tower 'where he is blessed be Jesu merry'. But his uncle's hands were now free. Immediately, both coronation and parliament were deferred until November.

On 21 June Simon Stallworthe, who had previously urged Sir William Stonor to come to London, was writing: 'I hold you happy that you are out of the press, for with us is much trouble and every man doubts other.' The Archbishop of York and Morton, the Bishop of Ely, were in the Tower but he hoped 'they shall come out nevertheless'; Mistress Shore was in prison and 'what shall happen her I know not'; twenty thousand of Richard's and Buckingham's men were expected in the city, 'to what intent I know not but to keep the peace'. Crowland too wrote of armed men 'in frightening and unheard of numbers'. The detention of Edward V's servants and relatives, he added, had been causing widespread concern, 'besides the fact that the Protector did not, with a sufficient degree of considerateness, take measure for the preservation of the dignity and safety of the Queen'.

The dignity of Elizabeth Woodville was about to suffer a far worse insult. On Sunday, 22 June a Dr Ralph Shaa delivered at St Paul's Cross a sermon to the effect that 'Bastard Slips Shall Never Take Deep Root'. Other sermons on the same theme were preached around the city that day. The most serious – because more plausible – of the various allegations made was the spectre raised by Clarence during his rebellion: that Edward IV's marriage to Elizabeth Woodville had been invalid, because he was already contracted to another lady. The debate still runs today as to whether there was any truth in the accusation; or, indeed, whether invalidity in his parents' marriage would necessarily have debarred Edward V from the throne.

On the 24th the Duke of Buckingham addressed a Guildhall convocation with a secular version of the story: the tale of a prior contract, along with the old slur that Edward's marriage to Elizabeth Woodville was in any case 'not well made' since her blood 'was full unmeetly to be match with his' and a general deprecation of Edward's sexual appetite. There was, More represents him as saying, no woman who caught Edward's eye 'but without fear of God, or respect of his honour, murmur or grudge of the world, he would importunately pursue his appetite' so that 'more suit was in his days to Shore's wife, a vile and abominable strumpet, than to all the Lords in England'. Commynes declares it was Bishop Stillington who told Richard the truth about his brother's marriage; it has been suggested, by those who believe the allegation, that he now displayed his proof.

There was another allegation in the air, too; one on which (More said) Buckingham touched only lightly, since Richard had asked him to avoid it because 'nature requireth a filial reverence to the Duchess his mother'. The allegation was that other spectre Clarence had once raised: that Edward (and indeed, it was now hinted, also Clarence himself) were the bastard fruits of Cecily's adultery.

More has the preacher Shaa declaring that neither Edward IV nor Clarence was 'reckoned very surely' as the Duke of York's children, since they more closely resembled other men. Vergil says Shaa simply stated that their bastardy 'was manifest enough, and that by apparent argument'. Both More and Vergil were writing some years later; and it has been suggested that the whole notion of Richard's having raised the issue – of, as Vergil puts it, the 'madness' of his 'wicked mind' – was simply a Tudor slander. The Tudors, of course, did need to find alternative grounds for Richard's complaint, since the allegation about Edward's own marriage touched Elizabeth of York too nearly. But Mancini does say that 'corrupted preachers' declared Edward 'was conceived in adultery', no way resembling his supposed father, and Mancini was writing within months of the event.

On the question of the adultery itself, there is no real evidence from Cecily's time at Rouen on which to judge. But a decade later, on the edge of eternity, she would declare herself in her will 'wife unto the right noble prince Richard late Duke of York, father unto the most Christian prince my Lord and son King Edward the iiiith'. Cecily did not so boast of Richard of Gloucester; but then to do so in Henry VII's reign would have lacked tact. But she made no bequests to Clarence's children as she did to her other grandchildren, which possibly militates against the idea that she herself had originated the claim he had made.

Vergil states that Cecily, 'being falsely accused of adultery, complained afterwards in sundry places to right many noble men, whereof some yet live, of that great injury which her son Richard had done her'. Another view,[7] however, holds that she

193

was entirely supportive of Richard's takeover, if not actually the orchestrator of it – even to the extent of letting her reputation be sullied. But evidence is wanting.

Richard based himself at Baynard's Castle, his mother's house, for some of this time, but it is not known whether she was actually there. The Archbishop of Canterbury recorded that the first, early May, meeting, at which it was agreed to take possession of Edward's seals, was held at the '*solite*' (accustomed, wonted) residence of the duchess. But the London house was not Cecily's only regular residence, and the list of those present at the meeting – senior clerics and officials, all male – does not mention her name.

It is conceivable that Cecily's animosity towards Elizabeth Woodville extended to her sons – but there is no reason to assume that at the time it would have been clear beforehand that the deposition of the boys would be followed by their deaths. Arguably, the simple substitution of an adult for an under-aged male to ensure the York family maintained the power it had only recently attained might not have seemed so outrageous in an earlier era. The right of inheritance to the throne[8] was not too clearly defined in the fifteenth century – witness the comparative flexibility in the matter of choice that had allowed one ruler to depose another with comparative impunity. In such a climate, to replace a juvenile member of the family by a more viable candidate from the same house might seem a simple matter of practicality when its status was seen as dependent not on the safety and welfare of its individual members but on the progress of the family as an entity. Moreover, if Cecily did indeed collaborate with Richard to any degree she may have seen her function as that of a mediator or intercessionary, since part of the duties of a medieval lady was to prevent the men in her family going far too far.

Cecily must have given a measure of acquiescence, since she did not cut off contact with Richard (the next spring, the grant of her manors and lands,[9] and of Berkhamsted, were confirmed); but possibly no more than that. If she were indeed by now living largely retired from the world, she may have taken refuge in her solitude and distance. And if she were anything less than totally committed to Richard's plan, then Vergil's report that she 'complained afterwards' about the slur on her virtue has a certain ring of probability. It would surely have been easier for Shaa to preach that sermon if Cecily and Cecily's servants weren't in London to hear it? By the time report of it spread it could be softened or explained slightly . . . And on one significant occasion at the end of these few weeks, we do have at least negative evidence as to Cecily's movements. When her son Richard was crowned king Cecily would not be there. That is far from conclusive: the widow of a deceased monarch did not normally attend the coronation of his successor, and some such prohibition may have inhibited Cecily.* Margaret Beaufort would be recorded as observing, rather than playing an active part in, her son's coronation ceremony. But Cecily is not mentioned at any point during the extensive records of Richard's lengthy festivities.

Whatever Cecily's role, on 25 June in the north of England, Anthony Woodville was executed, as was Elizabeth Woodville's son Richard Grey. On the same day Buckingham, with a deputation of London officials, went to Baynard's Castle to beg Richard to assume the throne.

---

* When the rule was finally broken by Queen Mary in 1937, her attendance at the coronation of George VI was taken as evidence of her strong views on his brother's Abdication.

SIXTEEN

Innocent Blood

Rest thy unrest on England's lawful earth,
Unlawfully made drunk with innocent blood.
Richard III, 4.4

On 26 June Richard proceeded to Westminster Hall to take the royal seat in the court of the King's Bench. It was from this day that he dated his accession. On 6 July he was crowned and Anne Neville, with whatever different expectation she may have arrived in London, was crowned as his queen in the first double coronation of an already-married king for almost two centuries.

There must have been a particular concern that in these most unusual circumstances everything should be done by the book – literally. A special document, the *Little Device*, laying down the formalities was drawn up in addition to the more generally applicable *Liber Regalis*. The list of accounts for, and goods provided by, the Great Wardrobe is in itself an extra-ordinary document:[10] page after page records everything from the commissioning of silk fringe and buttons of Venice gold from two silkwomen, Alice Claver and Cecily Walcote, to 'slops' of Spanish leather, banners and saddlery.

Anne first takes centre stage in these records on 3 July, when she and Richard exchanged formal gifts. He gave her 24 yards of purple cloth of gold and seven of purple velvet; in return she offered 20 yards of purple velvet decorated with garters and roses. Next day they travelled to spend a night in the royal apartments at the Tower, as tradition dictated. The hurried nature of the proceedings, the briefness of the journey from Baynard's Castle and the fact that Anne was not being crowned in a separate ceremony meant that she did not receive the usual pageants not only to honour her queenship and lay down her specific role but to acknowledge her ancestry and her own identity.

Richard, Mancini says, had summoned six thousand men from his estates and Buckingham's, and now stationed them 'at suitable points' in case of 'any uproar'. When they set out for the Abbey the new queen wore her hair loose under a jewelled circlet in the symbol of virginity which had become linked to the coronation ritual – however inappropriate it might be for the long-married Anne, as it had been for Elizabeth Woodville before her. Seated in a canopied litter of white damask and white cloth of gold, fringed and decorated with ribbon and bells, Anne and her procession followed Richard's. She was dressed, too, in white cloth of gold, tasselled and furred (in July!) with ermine and miniver. Two of her gentleman ushers and her chamberlain preceded her; her henchmen, her horse of state and three carriages bearing twelve noblewomen came behind.

Despite her royal surcoat and train of crimson velvet, it would have been shoeless that Anne followed the king into the Abbey, flanked by two bishops and followed by two duchesses, her ladies, knights and esquires. Prostrating herself on ground carefully carpeted and cushioned, she was anointed after her husband (the *Little Device* specified that her surcoat should be made 'opened before unto her waist fastened with a lace for the holy unction'), ringed, crowned and invested with a sceptre and rod. Her ceremony, however, deliberately fell slightly short of Richard's. The couple then celebrated mass and drank from the same chalice in 'a sign of unity', says the *Liber Regalis* which had made provision for this rare event, because in Christ they were one flesh by bond of marriage. Anne was now consecrated to her country's service and must surely have felt a dizzying, almost terrifying mix of grandeur, responsibility and sheer fatigue.

By St Edward's shrine king and queen were taken to separate closets and allowed to break their fast, and there the queen 'shall be changed by her gentlewomen of her Chamber into new garments' – a surcoat and long-trained mantle of purple velvet this time – before resuming their thrones and their regalia; and thence back to Westminster Hall and to their chambers.

The menu for the banquet that afternoon in Westminster Hall included pheasant in train (with its tail feathers); roasted cygnet, egrets and green geese; roe deer 'reversed in purple' (literally turned inside out and the meat dyed); glazed kid; baked oranges; fresh sturgeon with fennel; and fritters flavoured with rose and jasmine. As many as three thousand guests may have been fed, and the proceedings lasted so long that the third course could not be served. Everyone who was anyone was in town for the parliament that had been summoned to greet not this king but Edward V.

Almost everyone, anyway. Not only was Cecily Neville not there, nor was the Duke of Buckingham's Woodville-born wife – despite his own prominence in the ceremony. Richard's sister Elizabeth, Duchess of Suffolk, however, walked behind the queen leading Anne's ladies. Archbishop Bourchier, who had promised Elizabeth Woodville her younger son's safety, had officiated but, says Mancini, unwillingly – and apparently he abstained from the banquet. Margaret Beaufort, by contrast, carried the new queen's crimson train.

Before the coronation, Margaret's husband Stanley had been in trouble with the new regime: Thomas More describes him as having been attacked by the same men who arrested Hastings at the council meeting, and Vergil has him being placed under arrest. But Richard quickly changed tactics with the great land-owner: when Richard arrived at the Tower before his coronation, he appointed Stanley steward of his household. Margaret's own intentions at this point seem to have been merely to come to an accord with Richard and get her son Henry Tudor home from Brittany, on the terms agreed with Edward IV the previous year. She had opened negotiations in June through Buckingham; again the possibility of a marriage between Henry and one of Edward IV's daughters had been mooted; this was, however, to be subject entirely to Richard, 'without any thing to be taken or demanded for the same espousals but only the king's favour'.

On 5 July she and her husband met Richard and his chief justice at Westminster. Margaret might even then have been two-faced in her approach – just as Richard was simultaneously conducting his own less well-intentioned negotiations with Brittany to get Henry handed back to him. The events of the next few months would force these players to reveal their hand.

A month before Richard and Anne's coronation, that of Edward V was still assumed a certainty; three months earlier Edward IV had still been alive, the future of his dynasty appar-ently assured. All the same, Richard's speedy takeover seemed to be accepted not only by Margaret Beaufort but also by Margaret of Burgundy – who probably saw this as a simple transfer of power without contemplating any fatal con-sequences. In any case, the Burgundian Margaret had matters of her own to attend to. By the terms of the treaty of Arras of December 1482 the Dauphin was to marry the deceased Mary of Burgundy's daughter in place of Elizabeth of York: the infant had been handed over to the French on the same day,

24 April, as the putative Edward V left Ludlow. Mary's young son and heir Philip was in Ghent, whose authorities refused to give him up. As his father Maximilian struggled to regain control of the duchy and the motherless child, Margaret was preoccupied by the need to help and then to care for the little boy. She appealed to her brother for aid.

Richard, however, was more concerned with establishing himself in his own kingdom. Soon after the coronation, the new king and queen set out on progress. On 19 July they travelled from Greenwich to Windsor, where Anne stayed while Richard made a diversion westwards, to meet up with the queen again in Warwick in the second week of August. Anne seems not to have taken part in the whole of Richard's exhausting programme. But on 15 August she joined him for the rest of the progress north to York, where they stayed for three weeks.

The highlight of their visit to York was to be the investiture of their son Edward as Prince of Wales. Young as he was – perhaps no more than seven – he would still be the figurehead representing his father's rule in the north. Such ceremonies were all the more important for a regime still trying to demonstrate its legitimacy – and besides, the city had always been faithful to Richard. The citizens of York deserved to see their new, their own, king and queen, wearing their crowns and walking through the streets, holding the hands of their newly honoured son.

On their arrival in York from Pontefract the city dignitaries escorted them past a series of pageants to the archbishop's palace. On 8 September, a celebratory mass, at which the Minster's relics were displayed, was followed by the knighting of the prince, along with Richard's nephew Warwick and his own bastard son, and Edward's investiture. In due course the couple escorted their son back to Pontefract before moving on to Lincoln on 11 October. At Lincoln, however, news of a fresh crisis greeted them.

As Richard (and Anne) consolidated his rule, Elizabeth Woodville's young sons had presumably remained in the Tower. Mancini wrote that 'after Hastings was removed' – in the second half of June – 'all the attendants who had waited upon the king [Edward V] were debarred access to him. He and his brother were withdrawn in the inner apartments of the Tower proper, and day by day began to be seen more rarely behind the bars and windows, till at length they ceased to appear altogether.' He adds that 'the physician Argentine, the last of his attendants whose services the king enjoyed, reported that the twelve year old king, like a victim prepared for sacrifice, sought remission of his sins by daily confession and penance, because he believed that death was facing him'. Fabian's report of the boys seen 'shooting and playing in the gardens of the Tower by sundry times' might seem to run on into late summer or early autumn; but More embroiders Mancini's story and relates how after some time in captivity the elder boy 'never tied his points, nor ought wrought of himself' – which sounds very much like a state of depression. The continental chronicler Jean Molinet who had replaced Georges Chastellain at the Burgundian court gives a dramatic description of the younger boy urging his brother to learn how to dance, and the elder replying that they should rather learn how to die 'because I believe I know well that we will not be in this world much longer'.

Polydore Vergil – that unabashed Tudor apologist, writing well after the event – was very sure he knew just what had happened since the first days of August. He has Richard arriving in Gloucester on progress, and there 'the heinous guilt of wicked conscience' so tormented him that he decided to free himself of his anxieties once and for all. It was from there, Vergil says, that he sent word the princes were to be killed. But the

Lieutenant of the Tower, Robert Brackenbury, refused to obey such wicked instructions, so Richard was forced to find another instrument.

Vergil's timing cannot be presumed accurate. Crowland suggests only that, while Richard was on his progress, rumours began to spread – adding that in those same months it was advised 'that some of the king's daughters should leave Westminster in disguise and go in disguise to the parts beyond sea; in order that, if any fatal mishap should befall the said male children of the late king in the Tower, the kingdom might still, in consequence of the safety of the daughters, one day fall again into the hands of the rightful heirs'. Richard responded by ordering a blockade of the Tower. All the same, there is a reason Richard's attitudes towards the princes might indeed have been hardening in late July. There had been a rescue attempt.

Around that time a number of men were arrested because 'they were purposed to have set on fire diverse parts of London, which fire, while men had been staunching, they would have stole out of the Tower, the prince Edward, & his brother the Duke of York'. The report comes from the antiquarian John Stow a century later, but the contemporary Thomas Basin confirms it. Interestingly, the men also 'should have sent writings to the earls of Richmond and Pembroke' – Henry and Jasper Tudor. In early August Margaret Beaufort's half-brother John Welles led a rising at her childhood home of Maxey. From this, many commentators have deduced that Margaret Beaufort gave her support to the plot: the seventeenth-century antiquary George Buck believed the negotiations with Richard had been a feint on the part of the 'cunning countess' – though it is not easy to see just where her advantage lay in freeing the princes. It is easier to imagine Richard – when the news had reached him, in the west – deciding that the boys were not, as he had hoped, altogether neutralised by the declaration of bastardy.

Vergil's account, written in the sixteenth century, can no longer be distinguished from information or disinformation put out in the interim: it is likely he had been fed a version of events that suited the Tudors. But as Vergil points out, it is interesting that at York Richard founded a college of a hundred priests, which might have been a huge gesture of expiation or reparation. Vergil says also that Richard purposely let it slip out that the boys were dead, '[so] that after the people understood no issue male of king Edward to be now left alive, they might with better mind and good will bear and sustain his government'. He describes, moreover, the reception of the news by 'the unfortunate mother' Elizabeth Woodville, to whom it was 'the very stroke of death':

> for as soon as she had intelligence how her sons were bereft this life, at the very first motion thereof, the outrageousness of the thing drove her into such passion as for fear forthwith she fell into a swoon, and lay lifeless a good while; after coming to her self, she weepeth, she cryeth out aloud, and with lamentable shrieks made all the house ring, she struck her breast, tore and cut her hair, and, overcome in fine with dolour, prayeth also her own death, calling by name now and then among her most dear children, and condemning herself for a mad woman, for that (being deceived by false promises) she had delivered her younger son out of sanctuary, to be murdered of his enemy.

Her only resource was to beg God for revenge.

It may have been now that Margaret Beaufort recast her hopes for her son Henry. (In 1483 she purchased from William Caxton a copy of a French romance called *Blanchardin and Eglantine*, about a lover exiled from his intended bride, who was herself shut up in a citadel, surrounded by her enemies.) And if it were now that Elizabeth Woodville

– possibly influenced by Margaret's agents – became convinced her sons were dead, it is no wonder she gave her consent to a joint conspiracy.

The go-between keeping the two ladies in touch was Margaret Beaufort's physician, the Welshman Lewis Caerleon – 'a grave man and of no small experience', says Vergil, with whom 'she was wont oftentimes to confer freely'. Cambridge-educated, also an astronomer and mathematician, he would still be in the records as employed by Elizabeth of York a decade later.

> And she [Margaret], being a wise woman, after the slaughter of king Edward's children was known, began to hope well of her son's fortune . . . Wherefor forthwith not neglecting so great an opportunity, as they were consulting together, she uttered to Lewis that the time was now come when as king Edward's eldest daughter might be given in marriage to her son Henry . . . and therefore prayed him to deal secretly with the queen of such affair; for the queen also used his head, because he was a very learned physician.

Vergil says Lewis, presumably on Margaret's instruction, pretended this idea was 'devised of his own head'.

Elizabeth Woodville, Vergil reports, was 'so well pleased with this device'[11] that she sent Caerleon back to Margaret promising to recruit all Edward IV's supporters, if Henry would be sworn to take Elizabeth of York in marriage as soon as he had the realm (or else Cecily, the younger daughter, 'if th'other should die before he enjoyed the same'). Margaret sent out her man Reginald Bray to gather her friends; Elizabeth Woodville sent word to hers. Margaret was on the point of sending a protégé of Caerleon's, a young priest called Christopher Urswick[12] whom she had taken into her household, to her son Henry in Brittany when she had news that halted her in her tracks. Hers was not the only conspiracy afoot.

The Duke of Buckingham had played a leading part in placing Richard on the throne but had since become disaffected. When Buckingham left Richard at Gloucester in early August, and returned to his own home of Brecon Castle, that discontent had been purposefully fostered by the man he had been asked to hold in custody there: Margaret's old associate John Morton, Bishop of Ely. Morton urged Buckingham to take the crown 'if you love God, your lineage, or your native country'.

Buckingham responded that only recently he had indeed 'suddenly remembered' his own lineage through the Beaufort line: on his way home to Brecon, however, he had happened to meet Margaret Beaufort on the road, which reminded him of her superior claim (superior if the legitimacy question is ignored). This image of a chance meeting is likely to be disingenuous; but at some stage the conspirators must have decided to pool their resources. In the seventeenth century George Buck declared that Margaret's was the brain behind the final plans 'for she was entered far into them, and none better plunged in them and deeply acquainted with them. And she was a politic and subtle lady.'

Of the three main conspirators it was inevitably Buckingham, the man, who took charge of the armed rebellion launched on 18 October. Leading his men from Wales, he was to have joined up with the other military leaders – Elizabeth Woodville's son Dorset among them – but freak weather conditions made it impossible for his forces to cross the swollen river Severn. His men began to desert and – probably contrary to expectations – Margaret Beaufort's husband Stanley remained loyal to the king.

Henry Tudor's attempts to sail from Brittany with a fleet

provided by the Breton duke had likewise repeatedly been thwarted by the weather; and by the time he saw the English coast, it was evident that his only option was to sail back across the Channel. Buckingham was captured – betrayed by his servant for the reward – and summarily executed. Others, including Elizabeth Woodville's son Dorset, fled abroad to join Henry. But as so often with women's stories, that clear and simply told version is not the whole tale. Each conspirator had different aims.

It is often said that Elizabeth Woodville must have known the princes were dead or she would never have gone along with this plan. But against that is the fact that her late husband Edward IV had, at the end of his life, promoted the idea of bringing Henry Tudor safely into the fold. It is, moreover, possible that she had originally agreed to throw her weight behind the rebellion in the belief that it would place her living son on the throne. Crowland certainly suggests that the rebels first contemplated arms in the prince's name and then, after 'a rumour arose that King Edward's sons, by some unknown manner of violent destruction, had met their fate', turned to Henry Tudor in their need for 'someone new at their head'.

It is Margaret Beaufort's position that is more equivocal. If her sole aim were to bring her son safely home she might simply have continued negotiating with Richard – unless she mistrusted him and feared treachery. If, however, by the time she committed herself to the rebellion she knew or believed the princes were dead, the situation would have changed significantly. Henry Tudor's chances were better; and Elizabeth of York more important. If she did believe this, she must have considered whether to share that belief with Elizabeth Woodville or to conceal it.

Buckingham's position is yet more puzzling. Most commentators now dismiss Vergil's idea that he had quarrelled with Richard over lands promised but not granted. He may have been belatedly defending the rights of princes he believed to be still living. No manifesto for the rebels survives, but it seems that the rebellion (or, at least some of the minor risings) were indeed popular ventures aimed at freeing the princes. Crowland reports that 'in order to deliver them from this captivity, the people of the southern and western parts of the kingdom began to murmur greatly, and to form meetings and confederacies'. But as word of the princes' deaths filtered out, Buckingham's involvement became anomalous. He may have been genuinely disinterested enough to wish, while avenging the princes, to elevate Henry Tudor to the crown. But from everything that is known of him it seems unlikely.

Buckingham may well have been an opportunist, taking advantage of the princes' deaths to promote his own claim. If so, he probably hoped to dupe Margaret Beaufort into believing he supported her son's claim – striking a deal with her to get the Tudor and Woodville supporters as allies, while planning to take Henry Tudor's place himself. But it is just conceivable that he was himself the dupe – that Margaret (his aunt, through her marriage to Stafford) invited him to join a rebellion nominally in support of the princes, while actually interested only in her own son.

There is yet another possibility – that Buckingham had the best of all reasons to know that a rebellion could safely be raised in the princes' name, without in the end placing an Edward V on the throne. He was to some contemporaries, and remains today, an outside candidate for villain of the story[13] – the murderer of the princes. On the failure of his rebellion, Buckingham was executed by Richard on 2 November. But that, perhaps, just makes him even more convenient a scapegoat.

The majority of historians from Vergil and More onwards[14]

have believed that Richard III murdered his nephews; and thanks largely to Shakespeare, it has become the accepted view among many who care nothing for history. A vocal minority are utterly convinced he was not guilty, while propounding various alternative versions of the boys' fate. Others again believe it is virtually impossible to be certain, which makes it wrong to declare Richard guilty. In that uncertainty the writer's most honourable option is simply to present both the few known facts, and the relevant theories.

If Richard did not kill the boys, we have to ask why he did not simply produce them when rumours of their murder began to spread. One conceivable reason he did not is that he knew they had died – by someone else's hand, or indeed from natural causes – and that he would be blamed for their deaths anyway.

While both Richard and Buckingham certainly had both motive and opportunity, so too did others – such as the adherents of the man who would become Henry VII. Candidates suggested include Margaret Beaufort's ally Bishop Morton; her husband Lord Stanley; and Margaret Beaufort herself.[15] Assumptions about her gender may have insulated Margaret from suspicion, but the early seventeenth-century antiquary George Buck claimed to have read 'in an old manuscript book' that it 'was held for certain that Dr Morton and a certain countess, [conspirin]g the deaths of the sons of King Edward and some others, resolved that these treacheries should be executed by poison and by sorcery'.

Henry Tudor, of course, was out of the country; some dismiss him for that reason, but he had a highly able and totally committed representative in the person of his mother. None of the leading candidates was in London for the whole of the relevant period, but it is unreasonable to claim that any grandee would necessarily have done the deed themselves. The Tudor party had plenty of motive. For Richard to rule, it was technically necessary only that the boys should be declared illegitimate, and this he had arranged soon after his brother's death. If Henry were to bolster his own genealogically weak claim with that of Elizabeth of York, he needed the princes dead. If the whole family were declared illegitimate, then Elizabeth had no claim. If they were legitimate, her brothers' claim would take precedence over hers for as long as they lived. What is more, while the assumption of Richard's guilt depends on a posthumous reputation for savagery it was Henry VII (and later Henry VIII) who would, one by one, eliminate all the rival Yorkist line with chilling efficiency.

If track record is anything to go by, practically any ruler of the era could have done the deed. Edward IV, after all, had had his own brother Clarence executed, and had possibly had Henry VI and Henry's son murdered. The fact that the princes were under age makes all the difference to modern minds, but it may not have done so in the fifteenth century. Childhood ended early in those days: if Edward V did die soon after his uncle's accession, he was not much younger than Margaret Beaufort had been at the time of her pregnancy. The twenty-first-century image of the boys is much influenced by Victorian painting, showing them in flaxen-haired innocence.

There was certainly a mounting body of rumour. Weinreich's *Danzig Chronicle* of 1483 claimed that 'Later this summer Richard the king's brother seized power and had his brother's children killed, and the queen secretly put away'. The French chancellor Guillaume de Rochefort warned the States General in a speech on 15 January the following year: 'Look what has happened in [England] since the death of King Edward: how his children, already big and courageous, have been put to death with impunity, and the royal crown transferred to their murderer by the favour of the people.' Not every accusatory finger, however, was pointed at Richard. The *Historical notes of a London citizen* declared that: 'King Edward the Vth, late called Prince of Wales and Richard Duke of York, his brother . . . were put to death in the Tower of London by the vise [advice] of the Duke of Buckingham.'[16]

Other contemporaries heard different stories that did not speak of murder at all. The Silesian visitor Nicolaus von Popplau reported hearing the rumours in 1484 but added: 'Many people say – and I agree with them – that they are still alive and kept in a very dark cellar.' Even Vergil reported whisperings that they had been sent to 'some secret land'. The usually reliable Crowland does not actually say Richard killed the boys, mentioning only the rumour.

What everyone thought, of course, is not evidence, which is in short supply.[17] Over the centuries many have taken as conclusive the dubious confession to the murders supposedly made in 1502 by Sir James Tyrell – but that is something that could not have been known in 1483. The princes' mother and sisters may not have known what to believe; they may have had to persuade themselves to believe what was necessary.

SEVENTEEN

Letters to Richmond

Stanley, look to your wife. If she convey
Letters to Richmond, you shall answer it.
Richard III, 4.2

When, following the October rebellion, Richard III called a parliament, Henry Tudor was inevitably among those attainted but was beyond reach of punishment, back in Brittany. His connections in England, however, were in less safe a position.

Margaret Beaufort was attainted at the end of 1483: 'Forasmuch as Margaret Countess of Richmond, Mother to the king's great Rebel and Traitor, Henry Earl of Richmond, hath of late conspired, "confedered", and committed high Treason against our sovereign lord the king Richard the Third, in diverse and sundry wises.' But in the end, as so often with women, the full lethal penalties were not enacted. 'Yet nevertheless, our said Sovereign lord, of his grace especial, remembering the good and faithful service that Thomas lord Stanley hath done . . . and for his sake, remitteth and will forbear the great punishment of attainder of the said countess, that she or any other so doing hath deserved.'

Her goods were to be taken away from her, but given over to her husband for the term of his life. Richard, like Edward

211

before him, hesitated altogether to alienate such a powerful and chancy magnate as Stanley. Margaret had chosen her latest husband well. She was, however, to be held in Stanley's charge and deprived of 'any servant or company'. The instructions made it clear that this was less a punitive measure, more a means of preventing her from taking further action: Vergil reports that 'she should not be able from thenceforth to send any messages neither to her son, nor friends, nor practise anything at all against the king'. Her immediate future lay in the north, probably (since it was there that Stanley later asked leave to retire) in his residences of Lathom and Knowsley.

Henry Parker, a member of Margaret's household towards the end of her life, wrote that 'neither prosperity made her proud, nor adversity overthrew her constant mind, for albeit that in king Richard's days, she was often in jeopardy of her life, yet she bare patiently all trouble in such wise, that it is wonder to think it'. That is later hagiography: at the time even she must have been in a tumult of regret and fear. But the very fact of an uprising in her son's name must have underlined his present closeness to the throne, and she continued to exert herself on his behalf. There is some evidence, too, that Stanley secretly but actively continued to support her in this.

On Christmas Day 1483, in Rennes Cathedral in Brittany, Henry Tudor made a public declaration of his intention to marry Princess Elizabeth, now nearing her eighteenth birthday. He was aiming to catch the disaffected elements from the now-divided Yorkist party, and his existing supporters swore homage to him as if he were already king. Elizabeth of York, however, was still with her mother, increasingly isolated in sanctuary where Buckingham's widow, Elizabeth Woodville's sister, had now joined the family of women.

On 23 January 1484 Richard's parliament enacted the bill of Titulus Regius, starting that 'the said pretended marriage betwixt the above named King Edward and Elizabeth Grey, was made of great presumption, without the knowing and assent of the Lords of this Land'. More to the point, it declared also that at the time of that marriage 'and before and long time after, the said King Edward was and stood troth plighted to one Dame Eleanor Butler'; and that because of this Edward and Elizabeth had 'lived together sinfully and damnably in adultery'. It went on to assert that, because their children were thus bastards, they were 'unable to inherit or to claim anything by inheritance, by the Law and Custom of England'.

The marriage, according to the bill, had been made 'by Sorcery and Witchcraft, committed by the said Elizabeth, and her Mother Jacquetta, Duchess of Bedford'. Jacquetta of course was dead, as were her accusers at that time too, so the sorcery allegation was credited as 'the common opinion of the people and the publique voice and fame is through all this land'. Any allegations of the living Cecily's adultery were not repeated, unless something is implied in Richard's description of himself as 'the undoubted son' of York. But the allegation against Elizabeth Woodville stood, apparently uncontested; and if her brothers were by now dead, the real point of Titulus Regius must have been the political disabling of Elizabeth of York. Crowland wrote simply that parliament 'confirmed the title, by which the king had in the preceding summer, ascended the throne' – even though, as the clerical author sniffily pointed out, the lay court was hardly empowered to determine the validity of a marriage (a matter for ecclesiastical jurisdiction) and only reluctantly 'presumed' to do so.

It was, says Crowland also, in February that 'nearly all the lords of the realm, both spiritual and temporal, together with the higher knights and esquires of the king's household . . . met together at the special command of the king' in certain lower rooms near the passage which leads to the queen's apartments; and here, 'each subscribed his name to a kind of new oath . . . of adherence to Edward, the king's only son, as their supreme lord, in case anything should happen to his father' – never mind that this was yet another heir who had still not reached his teens.

With the turn of the year, in other words, the pressure was being piled on Elizabeth Woodville. Stripped of the dower rights she would have enjoyed as former queen, she would be without income if she and her daughters stayed in sanctuary.

On 1 March, in the presence of lords spiritual and temporal and the mayor and aldermen of London, Richard swore

> upon these holy Evangels of God [relics of the Evangelists] by me personally touched, that if the daughters of dame Elizabeth Grey, late calling herself Queen of England, that is to wit Elizabeth, Cecily, Anne, Katherine and Bridget, will come unto me out of the Sanctuary of Westminster, and be guided, ruled and demeaned after me, then I shall see that they be in surety of their lives, and also not suffer any manner hurt by any manner person . . . to be done by way of ravishment or defiling contrary their wills, nor them or any of them imprison within the Tower of London or other prison.

The mention of the Tower may imply that, as Richard was well aware, Elizabeth was still suspicious of him. Instead, he would 'put them in honest places of good name and fame, and them honestly and courteously shall see to be found and entreated, and to have all things requisite and necessary for their exhibition and findings as my kinswomen; and that I shall marry such of them as now be marriageable to gentlemen born'. The prospect of a mere 'gentleman' was not exciting for the former princesses, but expectations had sunk and it was better than no marriage at all.

The declaration was firstly about the daughters, not about Elizabeth Woodville herself. But it went on: 'I shall yearly from henceforth content and pay, or cause to be contented or paid, for the exhibition and finding of the said dame Elizabeth Grey during her natural life, at four terms of the year, that is to wit at Pasche [Easter], Midsummer, Michaelmas, and Christmas, to John Nesfield, one of the squires for my body, for his finding to attend upon her, the sum of seven hundred marks of lawful money of England.'

Elizabeth relented. Vergil wrote of how Richard 'often' sent messengers to her in sanctuary, 'promising mountains'. 'The messengers being grave men, though at the first by reducing to memory the slaughter of her sons they somewhat wounded the queen's mind, and that her grief seemed scarce able to be comforted, yet they assayed her by so many means, and so many fair promises, that without much ado they began to mollify her (for so mutable is that sex), in so much that the woman heard them willingly, and finally said she would yield herself unto the king.'

Some time that month Elizabeth's daughters left sanctuary.[18] It is not known where they went, or in what company. The younger ones at least may have been moved to the country for some time – they may even have been among the unnamed royal children at Sheriff Hutton in Yorkshire about whose maintenance instructions were given in July. Psychologically speaking, it would surely have been better if they had all gone to the country rather than face those at court who had known them in their glory. But it is also possible that the girls went straight to court, and it is this picture – of their blithely enjoying the gaieties provided by the man who may have killed their brothers – that has done much to damage the reputation of the women of Edward IV's family.

Even if Elizabeth Woodville believed her sons to be dead

by Richard's hand, she may have felt for a variety of reasons that she had no option but to leave sanctuary and come to some sort of terms with him. She may have been afraid that, by this late point in the Middle Ages, the laws of sanctuary might not be respected; she had no means of financial support there; and her clerical hosts must have been growing desperate for her to leave. She may have been enough of a pragmatist to accept that her boys were gone, and her responsibility now was to make the best deal for her girls – though, if she believed Richard had killed her sons, then surely she was sending those daughters into the lion's den. She may have been such a venal woman she could not resist the chance of better living conditions, even if the donor were her sons' murderer. But there are several other more intriguing possibilities.

It seems possible (given her earlier plots, and her imminent conversion to Henry's cause) that her compliance was only on the surface, and that she was secretly working against Richard. Even more interestingly, when Elizabeth herself left sanctuary in 1484, possibly rather later than her daughters, she may have had reason to know that Richard was *not* guilty of her sons' deaths.

For the rest of Richard's reign, Elizabeth Woodville simply disappears. One suggestion which has been made would explain this completely: either or both princes left the Tower alive, and when Elizabeth emerged from sanctuary it was because she had been promised that her sons, or at least the younger of them, would be quietly allowed to join her.[19] The elder boy is supposed to have been ill in the summer of 1483, and it is possible he had died from natural causes.[20] None of the later pretenders to Henry VII's throne claimed to be the elder prince, suggesting that he, unlike his brother, was known by then to be dead. They were, in any case, no longer princes but officially royal bastards – of whom there were several already. But the boys' ultimate fate remains a mystery.

The possibility cannot wholly be ruled out that the younger boy at least may – with or without Richard's connivance – eventually have been sent abroad (just as Cecily sent her sons abroad in time of danger), and/or given a new identity. Francis Bacon,[21] writing a century later, has Perkin Warbeck, the pretender who claimed to be Elizabeth Woodville's younger son, saying that he would not reveal details of his escape from the Tower. 'Let it suffice to think I had a mother living, a Queen, and one that expected daily such a commandment from the tyrant for the murdering of her children.' The clear implication is that Elizabeth Woodville smuggled her younger son away; and though the words of a pretender must lack credibility, it shows the idea was in currency.

If this were done with Richard's connivance, the intention might have been to get the boy out of the way of Henry, to whom he could have figured as either a tool or a threat. If so, it would not only explain Elizabeth Woodville's sudden accord with Richard, but help to clear up one minor mystery: why Elizabeth was lying so low during these months that her whereabouts are uncertain, from the time she left Westminster Abbey right up to the time she starts appearing in documents, after Richard's death, as one of the new king's beneficiaries.

The real mystery about the Princes in the Tower concerns the behaviour of their family's women. That the princes' mother and sisters could, within months of their deaths, come to terms with their murderer has been put down to fear and pragmatism in a brutal age. Of course if Richard gave assurances of his innocence the women might have been eager to be convinced: they had, after all, few options other than compliance. But if Elizabeth Woodville believed her boys had not been murdered – or not murdered by Richard – it would explain everything even more simply.

For a few weeks the kingdom seemed to settle down. Richard in many ways was proving himself an admirable ruler: his parliament had enacted a considerable amount of socially beneficial law making, for example, the legal system more accessible to the poor. But once again unforeseen events were to change the situation completely, and once again it was the fate of a son which determined that of a dynasty.

On 9 April 1484 young Edward of Middleham, the only child of Richard and Anne, died after what Crowland calls 'an illness of but short duration'. It took some days for the news to reach the court but then, says Crowland, 'you might have seen his father and mother in a state almost bordering on madness, by reason of their sudden grief'. Anne's state must have been truly pitiable. Looking at the extremely limited records of her short life as queen, it is striking just how isolated she seems. In-fighting over her parents' estates had left her alienated from those powerful relations who survived; while Richard had taken to himself the interests of those northerners once regarded as her family's allies and was giving away some of her family lands[22] to bolster his network of support. The death of Richard and Anne's son may have struck a fatal blow to their relationship. Vergil suggests that it was now Richard began to complain of Anne: she had given him an heir, but that heir was gone and there was no spare. Judging by her mother and sister, low fertility seems to have run in Anne's family.

Richard, as the Crowland chronicler points out, had at least the concerns of the kingdom to distract him. The death of his only heir made the political situation more dangerous: the succession was again in doubt. There was of course Warwick, Clarence's son, who had been brought to London and, for a time at least, placed in Anne's charge. Clarence's attainder theoretically removed all rights of inheritance from his son;

attainders, however, could be reversed or ignored. But if that were done Warwick, as the son of Richard's elder brother, would have a stronger claim to the throne than Richard himself.

Warwick, however, passed into manhood apparently placidly, in a kind of genteel captivity; Vergil later spoke of his simplicity, and there is a received impression, so widespread it may suggest a grain of truth, that there was something wrong with him. It cannot have been an obvious disability – but while his name served for pretenders, no one ever seems to have considered placing Warwick himself on the throne.

Warwick apart, it has even been suggested that Richard planned eventually to rehabilitate the princes as his heirs. Another good candidate for heir apparent was his sister's son John, Earl of Lincoln – a grown man able enough for Richard to entrust him with the task of controlling the north. But certainly Henry Tudor gained in importance by Anne's son's death; and so, naturally, did Elizabeth of York.

That summer Richard was in the north, once Anne's own family turf. In addition to the usual business of kingship, there was other trouble there. In the summer of 1484 Richard wrote a letter to his mother Cecily: 'Madam I recommend me to you as heartily as is to me possible, Beseeching you in my most humble and effectuous wise of your daily blessing to my Singular comfort & defence in my need. And madam I heartily beseech you that I may often hear from you to my Comfort.'

He offers, through the mouth of his servant, 'such News as been here'; recommends a man of his own to be her officer for her Wiltshire lands, trusting he should do her good service, 'And I pray god send you the accomplishment of your most noble desires.' All allowances made for the style of the times, surely this letter from Cecily's 'most humble Son' shows a real degree of warmth? – or, alternatively, an eagerness to placate.

In the summer of 1484, an unflattering ditty was posted up

around London: 'The cat, the rat, and Lovell our dog, rulen all England, under an hog' – Catesby, Ratclyff, Lord Lovell and Richard himself, whose emblem was a white boar. Things were going sour. The rebellion of the past autumn and its suppression had in some ways lanced a boil, but it had also made clear that Henry Tudor was a significant threat, especially if he could be coupled with Elizabeth of York; and it had shown Margaret Beaufort in her true colours as a continuing source of danger. Richard, so Vergil says, 'yet more doubting than trusting in his own cause' was so 'vexed, wrested, and tormented in mind' with fear of Henry's threat that he had 'a miserable life'. That is why he decided to 'pull up by the roots' the source of his trouble and sent messages to the Breton court.

Duke Francis was at that time suffering from some kind of mental illness. This left negotiations in the hands of his treasurer, who was less honourable and more amenable. By June Richard had been able to announce a treaty of cooperation with Brittany: Margaret must have feared that its terms included handing back Henry. In September those fears were realised: her son would be exchanged for England's backing in Brittany's quarrels.

That month, however, the deal was thwarted. Vergil describes how John Morton in his Flanders exile sent word to Henry 'by Christopher Urswycke, who was come to him out of England about the same time . . .' This emissary, like Morton, had been a member of Margaret Beaufort's household. There was an urgent message to France to confirm that the exiles would be welcome there; a dramatic escape; and a chivalrous finale when Duke Francis, recovering his health and sanity, paid the expenses for Henry's fellow exiles, under Edward Woodville, to join him in France.

Fresh impetus had now been given to any attempt to promote Henry's claim. The French were bound to seize on him as a pawn both in their ongoing negotiations with Richard, and in their own power struggles which had followed the death of King Louis in the summer of 1483 and the accession of the thirteen-year-old Charles VIII. The tussle for control of the young king resulted in victory for Charles's elder sister Anne of Beaujeu – which meant, ironically, that yet another woman would play a significant part in English political affairs. From the time Charles was informed on 11 October that Henry had crossed his border, the Tudor claimant was treated with a sympathy that gave him every hope the French would fund another invasion attempt.

It was probably November 1484 when Henry began sending letters to England, trying to garner support. Their style suggested he was already king: 'Being given to understand your good devoir and entreaty to advance me to the furtherance of my rightful claim, due and lineal inheritance of that crown, and for the just depriving of that homicide and unnatural tyrant, which now unjustly bears dominion over you . . .' The letters were signed 'H.R.' – Henricus Rex.

In retaliation, on 7 December Richard issued a proclamation against Henry which poured scorn on his rival's pretensions to a royal estate 'whereunto he hath no manner interest, right, or colour', and warning of 'the most cruel murders, slaughters, robberies and disinheritances that were ever seen in any Christian Realm'. It must have felt like an insult also to Margaret Beaufort in isolation in the north. Richard was trying to chip away at her alliances and accessories: her useful tool Reginald Bray had been given a pardon at the beginning of the year: now pardons were extended also to Morton and, the following spring, to Elizabeth Woodville's brother Richard.

On the other hand, Henry's band in exile had for some time now included a number of Stanley affiliates. And when, towards the end of 1484, they were joined by the dedicated and militarily experienced Lancastrian Earl of Oxford, who for some years had been a high-profile prisoner of the Yorkist regime, Molinet claimed that the advice of Lord Stanley had been key to his custodian's decision to let him escape. There must, indeed, have been a perverse, edgy reassurance for the Lancastrians in the very importance Richard had come to attach to the Tudor threat. Step by step, Henry was gaining ground. He now instructed Bishop Morton to seek the papal dispensation necessary for him to marry Elizabeth of York. The kingdom still held quiet under Richard's rule, but it was becoming increasingly clear that something had to break.

EIGHTEEN

Anne My Wife

The sons of Edward sleep in Abraham's bosom,
And Anne my wife hath bid this world good night.
Richard III, 4.3

On 6 January 1485, the English court celebrated the festival of Epiphany with particular splendour. There would have been seasonal rituals such as the burning of an oak log to draw heat back into the earth, together with the licensed revelry of the fools and the more malicious clowning of whichever young courtier had been appointed Lord of Misrule for the day. The king made a point of appearing 'with his crown'. But it is easy to surmise that Richard was not naturally lively that day.

Crowland wrote that 'while [Richard] was keeping this festival with remarkable splendour in the great hall . . . news was brought to him on that very day, from his spies beyond sea, that, notwithstanding the potency and splendour of his royal state, his adversaries would, without question, invade the kingdom during the following summer'. The king's reaction to certain news at last was to declare that 'there was nothing that could befall him more desirable, in as much as he imagined that it would put an end to all his doubts and troubles'. But among the other courtiers, the news must have sent a ripple of unease through the party mood.

Perhaps the women of the royal household were trying to keep things merry. Not that Richard's queen, Anne Neville, can have found it any easier than he. Anne had been in poor health for months, and in the hothouse atmosphere of a palace she could hardly fail to have known that courtiers and diplomats were speculating on what would happen if, as looked increasingly likely, she were to die. She had the company of her elder nieces, who were spending Christmas at court. Buck says that Elizabeth Woodville sent her four younger daughters along to 'colour' the appearance of the eldest, Elizabeth of York: '[And t]he queen regnant entertained also the young ladies with all her courtesies and gracious caresses, and especially the Lady Elizabeth, whom she used with so much family[arity] and kindness as if she had been her own sister.' They were, after all, hardly a decade apart in age. 'But the queen had small joy and little pleasure in the festi[val and] pompous time, because she was sick and was much in languor and [sorrow] for the death of the prince, her dear and only son, and the which grieved her sorely.'

Indeed, Elizabeth's company must have represented a very mixed pleasure for Anne. At the festivities (where, as the Crowland chronicler disapprovingly relates, 'far too much attention was given to dancing and gaiety') 'vain exchanges of clothing' took place between Anne and Elizabeth, 'being of similar colour and shape;[23] a thing that caused the people to murmur and the nobles and prelates greatly to wonder thereat'.

All the same, Crowland seems to suggest some point was being made. Despite that official declaration of bastardy, many still regarded Edward IV's children as the natural inheritors of the throne. It was already being whispered that, if anything were to happen to Anne, a marriage between Richard and

Elizabeth would square the circle of inheritance nicely. She was his niece, to be sure, but was there anything a papal dispensation could not legitimise? (And if there were any question over the papal dispensation that had allowed Anne and Richard's marriage to go ahead, that could provide grounds for an annulment.) It 'was said by many that the king was bent, either on the anticipated death of the queen taking place, or else, by means of a divorce, for which he supposed he had quite sufficient grounds, on contracting a marriage with the said Elizabeth'. Vergil described it as a plan 'the most wicked to be spoken of, and the foulest to be committed that ever was heard of'.

At that Epiphany party, it is unlikely that anyone spoke openly of the possibility of such an alliance between Richard and his niece – but rumours were already flying. The marriage would be a severe blow to Henry Tudor. And Richard might have had other incentives, as Anne must miserably have realised. Elizabeth was a buxom eighteen; later in her life the Portuguese ambassador noticed her 'large breasts', while a Venetian diplomat called her 'very handsome'.

'In the course of a few days after this', Crowland wrote, 'the queen fell extremely sick, and her illness was supposed to have increased still more and more, because the king entirely shunned her bed, declaring that it was by the advice of his physicians that he did so. Why enlarge?' the chronicler asks, maddeningly. But perhaps he trusted his readers to understand the coded message of 'declaring that . . .'. It may be that Anne's illness was infectious – or that Richard wished further to distance himself from her.

Elizabeth's own supposed feelings were related by the seventeenth-century antiquary George Buck. In 1619, in his *History of King Richard the Third*, he set down a précis of a letter in which, he said, Elizabeth expressed her passionate longing to marry her uncle. She was, said Buck, writing towards the end of February to John Howard, Duke of Norfolk, an influential magnate and once her father's friend:

> First she thanked him for his many courtesies and friendly offices, and then she prayed him as before to be a mediator for her in the cause of the marriage to the king, who, as she writes, was her only joy and maker in this world, and that she was his in heart and in thoughts, in body, and in all. And then she intimated that the better half of February was past, and that she feared the queen would never die. And all these be her own words, written with her own hand, and this is the sum of her letter, whereof I have seen the autograph or original draft under her own hand.

Not only surprising, but damning in several ways:[24] the callousness of the fear that Anne would never die, the possible sexual implications of that 'his . . . in body, and in all'. But there have long been doubts over Buck. Some have suggested that he could simply (especially when blinded by his prejudices) have misinterpreted a letter that he did indeed see; others that it was not written by Elizabeth, or not written at this juncture and in relation to this match. Indeed, a far less controversial marriage was proposed for Elizabeth very soon afterwards, and the words could be made to fit. At the most extreme, it has even been claimed that the letter was a total invention.[25]

Buck himself may be the victim of an inadvertent injustice here. Several decades after he wrote his manuscript, his great-nephew (confusingly, also called George Buck) published a version of it. Buck's modern editor, Arthur Kincaid, has discovered that this branch of the family had a track record of forgery. The surviving manuscript versions of Buck's original show revisions not only by Buck himself but by his great-nephew:

even more importantly, the earliest of them has been very considerably damaged by fire. In an article for the *Ricardian* journal Kincaid transcribed precisely what was (and was not) left:[26]

< st she thanked him for his many Curtesies and friendly>
              as before   in the cause of<
>d then she prayed him ^ to bee a mediator for her to the K<
>ge
whoe (as she wrote) was her onely ioye and her maker in<
                  in
Worlde, and that she was [in] his, harte, in thoughts in<
and \ in / all, and then she intimated that the better halfe of
Ffe<
was paste, and that she feared the Queene would neu<

In other words, the choice of the words 'body' and 'never die' were inserted by the younger George Buck in the gaps left on the paper, with the goal of producing a sensational and saleable text rather than one of historical accuracy. The gaps mean that the cause in which the recipient was to intercede with the king is unclear – the writer's marriage to the king, or her marriage to someone else? Kincaid's own conclusion was that 'Elizabeth in her letter was referring to a hoped-for marriage – though not necessarily with the king'.

It does not seem wholly impossible that Elizabeth of York should have wanted to marry Richard. There was enough uncertainty in the air for her to be open to conviction that he was not responsible for her brothers' deaths. Power is an aphrodisiac and this was the destiny for which she had been reared – a chance to come back from the wilderness. There may be a clue in the inscription she wrote on a copy of Boethius' *The Consolation of Philosophy* – '*Loyalte mellye*' or 'Loyalty binds me.' It was Richard's favourite motto. She also wrote, on a copy of the French prose *Tristan*, '*sans re[mo]vyr*', 'without changing' above her signature, 'elyzabeth'.* She wrote on the page with the mark that showed it was Richard's property – but is that enough to show the unchanging loyalty she was expressing was loyalty to Richard? Not really.

Polydore Vergil sees it differently, of course. 'Richard had kept [Elizabeth] unharmed with a view to marriage. To such a marriage the girl had a singular aversion. Weighed down for this reason by her great grief she would repeatedly exclaim, saying, "I will not thus be married, but, unhappy creature that I am, will rather suffer all the torments which St Catherine is said to have endured for the love of Christ than be united with a man who is the enemy of my family."' But Vergil would say that – a quarter of a century later, when he was writing, it was a Tudor age. The words 'the enemy of my family' might have applied to Henry as easily as to Richard; and Richard kept Elizabeth's sisters 'unharmed' too, even those who were nearing maturity. What is more, if he wished to keep her away from Henry Tudor all he had to do was marry her to somebody else – not necessarily to himself.

Whatever the truth about Richard's plans, there were certainly rumours of the possible marriage, if not necessarily of Elizabeth's complicity. Across the Channel Henry heard them and feared loss of Yorkist support if the two York factions could thus be reunited. Vergil wrote that the stories 'pinched Henry by the very stomach', so much so that he began to seek an alternative match. He may have thought first of Elizabeth's sister Cecily but, hearing tales that Richard had married her off, turned instead to a daughter of William Herbert, Earl of Pembroke,

---

* In Malory, Tristan is an Arthurian knight fatally in love with a lady, whose mother's brother he has unfortunately killed.

the loyally Yorkist supporter of Edward IV who had cared for him when he was a child. But the message he sent proposing the match, says Vergil, never reached its destination; and in any case he must soon have heard that a marriage between Richard and his niece was no longer a possibility . . . . Unless, of course, the rumours of the marriage – rumours so discreditable to Richard – had all along been spread by Henry Tudor's own party.

Anne almost certainly heard the rumours. Over the next few weeks her condition worsened; and the suggestion is that Richard hoped it would do so – even helped the process along. The king, said Hall, 'complained to divers noble men of the realm, of the unfortunate sterility and barrenness of his wife'; he did so especially to the Archbishop of York upon whom he relied to spread the word to Anne, 'trusting the sequel hereof to take his effect, that she hearing this grudge of her husband, and taking therefore an inward thought, would not long live in this world'. Vergil even says that Anne, hearing the rumours, went to her husband 'very pensive and sad, and with many tears demanded of him what cause there was why he should determine her death. Hereunto the king, lest that he might seem hard hearted if he should show unto his wife no sign of love, kissing her, made answer lovingly, and comforting her, bade her be of good cheer.'

The reassurance did her little good. On 16 March, during a great eclipse of the sun, Anne died. Since her illness was lingering and possibly infectious, the best modern guess is tuberculosis. But there would be other suspicions, and her death would be linked to that of the princes. Vergil wrote that she died 'whether she was despatched by sorrowfulness or poison'; Rous that 'Lady Anne, his queen, he poisoned.' Commynes wrote that 'some say he had her killed', and Hall said: 'Some think she went her own pace to the grave, while others suspect a grain was given her to quicken her in her journey to her long home.'

Anne was buried on the ninth day after her death – the 25th, the Feast of the Annunciation. She was interred, says Crowland, 'at Westminster, with no less honours than befitted the interment of a queen'. The absence of a tomb – which conveys, now, an impression of lack of care or lack of ceremony – was almost certainly the result of Richard's reign having ended before he had had time to commission one. Some six weeks later, after the news had spread across Europe, the Doge of Venice assured Richard that 'your consort led so religious and catholic a life and was so adorned with goodness, prudence, and excellent morality, as to leave a name immortal'. But it is difficult not to feel that Anne's life had been a hard one, even by the harsh standards of the fifteenth century.

On 20 March, only four days after Anne's death, Sir Edward Brampton was sent to Portugal to negotiate a marriage between Richard and the Portuguese king's sister, the Infanta Joana. The Infanta was not only determinedly religious and averse to marriage, but thirty-three and, for those times, old for childbearing. It is likely therefore that her appeal was her descent from John of Gaunt – a descent that made her the senior representative of the legitimate Lancastrian line.

The Portuguese council urged Joana that it was her duty to agree, 'for the concord in the same kingdom of England that will follow from her marriage and union with the king's party, greatly serving God and bringing honour to herself by uniting as one the party of Lancaster, and York'. It was conscious that, if she refused, Richard might look instead to the next most senior marriageable representative of the Lancastrian line, the Spanish Infanta Isabel, another great-great-granddaughter of John of Gaunt.

The idea must have maddened Margaret Beaufort if she heard of it – it neatly cut out her (and her son's) Lancastrian claim. Both Joana and Isabel were descended from John of

Gaunt's earlier, uncontroversial marriages to foreign princesses, while the Beaufort line came from his liaison with Katherine Swynford, only later regularised by marriage. But Sir Edward was to negotiate a double marriage – an alliance also between a daughter of Edward IV (presumably Elizabeth) and the king's cousin, the Duke of Beja. This, it is suggested, may have been the marriage Elizabeth was discussing in the Buck letter. The speed with which the embassy set out shows that in a pragmatic age the matter must surely have been under discussion before Anne's death. Since the marriage proposed for Elizabeth[27] was dependent on the one proposed for Richard, this would explain, if not excuse, any fear that Queen Anne would never die.

The prospect of a foreign royal marriage for Elizabeth of York may, like the pardons granted to various Woodvilles, have been part of the general sweetening that persuaded Elizabeth Woodville to write summoning her son Dorset home. That spring he tried to escape from the exiled Tudor 'court'; he was making for Flanders and the coast when Henry's represent-atives, with French connivance, caught up with him and persuaded him to return. Perhaps Elizabeth Woodville had been rattled by Henry's declaring himself king before he had married her daughter. Or, of course, she may have been coerced – though it has been taken as yet more evidence of her gullible venality. Shakespeare has Elizabeth, asked by Richard how he should woo her daughter, sarcastically advising him to send her a token 'by the man that slew her brothers'. She counters each promise he makes for the future with some wrong from the past. But in the course of some 150 lines she also changes her mind – 'Relenting fool, and shallow, changing woman!', as Richard apostrophises her.

But whoever else may have been complicit, it was Richard who attracted most opprobrium for the reputed plan of marriage with his niece. The king's closest advisers, Ratclyff and Catesby, felt obliged to warn him of the unpopularity of such a union. In Crowland's words: 'For by these persons the king was told to his face that if he did not abandon his intended purpose, and that, too, before the mayor and commons of the City of London . . . all the people of the north, in whom he placed the greatest reliance, would rise in rebellion against him and impute to him the death of the queen, the daughter and one of the heirs of the Earl of Warwick, through whom he had first gained his present high position' – in order that he might, says the chronicler disapprovingly, 'to the extreme abhorrence of the Almighty, gratify an incestuous passion for his said niece'.

Besides this, certain of Richard's advisers wheeled in a dozen or so doctors of divinity 'who asserted that the Pope could grant no dispensation in the case of such a degree of consanguinity'. 'It was supposed by many, that these men, together with others like them, threw so many impediments in the way, for fear lest, if the said Elizabeth should attain the rank of queen, it might at some time be in her power to avenge upon them the death of her uncle, Earl Anthony, and her brother Richard [Grey].' It sounds as if the girl later generations assume to be placid and gentle was believed by those closer to her to be her mother's daughter.

Only a fortnight after Anne's death, just before Easter, in the great hall of the Hospital of St John, Richard was forced to take the extraordinary step of making a public repudiation of any desire to wed his niece. He spoke, says Crowland, 'in a loud and distinct voice; more, however, as many supposed, to suit the wishes of those who advised him to that effect, than in conformity with his own'.

The records of the Mercers' Company describe how, 'to the very great displeasure of the king', the 'long saying and much simple communication among the people by evil disposed persons' seemed to show 'that the queen as by consent and will of the king was poisoned for and th'intent that he might then marry and have to wife Lady Elizabeth, eldest daughter of his brother . . .'. In the presence of many of his lords, and of the city hierarchy, he 'said it never came into his thought or mind to marry in such manner wise nor [was he] willing or glad of the death of his queen but as sorry and in heart as heavy as man might be . . .'.

But the *Great Chronicle* recorded[28] 'much whispering among the people that the king had poisoned the Queen his wife, and intended with a license purchased [a dispensation] to have married the elder daughter of King Edward. Which rumours and sayings with other things before done caused him to fall in great hatred of his subjects. . . .' The stage, as Margaret Beaufort must have realised, was set for her son Henry.

NINETEEN

In Bosworth Field

> Here pitch our tent, even here in Bosworth field.
> *Richard III,* 5.1

Henry Tudor in France now had every hope of support from the teenage Charles VIII – or rather from his sister and regent Anne of Beaujeu. As the spring of 1485 grew warmer, Margaret Beaufort's servant Reginald Bray was collecting money to fund mercenaries and sending messages across the Channel. Even her cautious husband Stanley, the ultimate political weather-cock, was beginning to rate her son's chances more highly now that Richard had become so unpopular. If this were down to Margaret's influence it would soon prove to be the most important thing she could possibly have done, for all that she was in theory debarred from political activity.

Throughout the spring Richard continued to hear rumours of an impending rebellion. Perhaps he heard, too, that in France Henry Tudor was being misdescribed as a younger son of Henry VI, suggesting that the French were seriously promoting him as a royal heir.

Elizabeth of York may have been sent straight to Sheriff Hutton after the scandal of the spring; but one source has her for a few weeks at least in Lord Stanley's London house, where her furious resentment against her uncle swung her to the opposite political side. The long early sixteenth-century verse narrative the *Ballad of Lady Bessy*,[29] which chronicles the events that led up to the battle at Bosworth, survives in several different versions. On one thing, however, they all agree: Elizabeth of York played an extraordinarily active role in this story.

The *Ballad* describes how as the spring began to ripen, she waylaid Lord Stanley in the palace corridors and asked him to send a message to his stepson Henry Tudor, promising to marry him and thus greatly strengthen his cause:

> For and he were King, I should be Queen;
> I do him love, & never him see

She tears her hair in fury when Stanley refuses to commit, sinking into a swoon and lamenting that she will never be queen. But her determination has a more practical aspect too: the ballad has her raising money, rallying supporters and detailing the Stanley military strength with considerable precision. Lady Bessy volunteers to write letters to Stanley's adherents, which she boasts she can do as well as the scrivener who taught her. Presented as a 'lady bright', as spirited and beautiful as she is able, Bessy successfully brokers a contact with Henry, and he responds with his own verse:

> Commend me to Bessy, that Countess cheer [or, 'clere'], –
> & yet I did never her see, –
> I trust in god she shall be my Queen,
> For her I will travel the sea.

Did Elizabeth in truth hate Richard – and if she did, was it for trying to seduce her, or for repudiating her? It depends on what we think were or had been her feelings for her uncle. But it is certain she must have awaited events with more than uncommon tension: once more, you might say, she had been cheated of a royal match. Maybe she feared losing another, if she had heard Henry was now pursuing a Herbert heiress – or, as Francis Bacon would suggest, that he contemplated marriage to the heiress of Brittany. We cannot be sure, at this juncture, what were the relations between Margaret Beaufort, still held under house arrest, and the Woodville clan.

After having had to make that embarrassing declaration repudiating his marital intentions Richard had left London first for Windsor and then, on 17 May, to spend a few days at his mother Cecily Neville's residence at Berkhamsted,[30] possibly to update her on his European marriage plans or to explain the other marriage stories as best he might.

But war was now coming. As spring edged towards summer Richard must have heard that Charles in France was openly raising money for Henry. In the second week of June the king set out for Nottingham Castle, a military power base strategically placed in the heart of England. From there he began to raise his army and to prepare for the invasion that everyone knew would soon be on the way.

In late June Richard's proclamation against Henry was reissued, with two important changes. The first omitted the name of the Marquess of Dorset, Elizabeth Woodville's eldest son, from the list of rebels and traitors: Richard was trying to placate her and her family. The second laid out Henry Tudor's – Margaret Beaufort's – bloodline, 'descended of bastard blood, both of father's side, and of mother's side . . . [John of Gaunt's and Katherine Swynford's children being] in double avoutry [adultery] gotten'.

That week Thomas Stanley requested leave to withdraw from court and return to his estates 'in order to rest and refresh himself'. His estates in Lancashire were the site of Margaret

Beaufort's enforced residency. Richard agreed, on condition that Stanley left his son behind, as a guarantor of the magnate's continued loyalty, and the same day sent for the Great Seal, a sure sign he expected urgent business of great importance.

On 1 August Henry Tudor set sail from France. The French had wobbled in their support, granting money as a loan only. Henry was forced to pawn his household possessions and leave behind as security two Yorkist lords, including Dorset. Elizabeth Woodville's brother, however, would ride with Henry's army. With him were a hired band of expert French pikemen, and the two supporters – the Earl of Oxford, a powerful nobleman and experienced commander, and Henry's equally battle-hardened uncle Jasper Tudor – whose presence compensated for his own lack of military knowledge. Henry landed six days later at Milford Haven in Wales, where he fell to his knees and kissed the soil of a country he had not seen for fourteen years. He is said to have recited the psalm 'Judge me, O Lord, and defend my cause'.

Then the fortnight-long march eastwards began along, as Crowland described it, 'rugged and indirect tracks'. It would have taken several days for galloping messengers to bring Richard the news, but on the 11th the summons to his supporters went out: 'orders of the greatest severity' threatening reprisals on all who refused. Crowland declares that on hearing of Henry's landing Richard 'rejoiced, or at least seemed to rejoice, writing to his adherents in every quarter that now the long wished-for day had arrived, for him to triumph with ease over so contemptible a faction'.

All through Wales Henry was rallying his supporters, with more flocking to his cause. But in England he was a virtual stranger. Vergil reports that along the way he wrote to his mother. It was Margaret Beaufort on whom, directly or indirectly, he had had to rely to raise support in the country.

Margaret had presumably been left behind at Lathom in Lancashire, some hundred miles from the eventual conflict point. Her husband Stanley had been summoned back to the king's side for fear, says Crowland, that she 'might induce her husband to go over to the party of her son'. But Stanley still seems to have been refusing to commit to either side. Richard was holding Stanley's son hostage for his good behaviour; none the less, when the summons from Richard came Stanley had sent word that he was ill and unable to travel. He took his forces south but by an independent route, there to wait until the eve of battle, unattached to either party. His brother Sir William Stanley, on the other hand, took his three thousand or so men to meet up with Henry just north of Stafford. But he too refused to commit directly, pending further consultation with his brother. As the opposing armies drew closer to each other, Henry still had fewer than five thousand men under his command – only half the size of the forces his adversary had assembled, says Polydore Vergil.

Richard left Nottingham for Leicester around 19 August; on the 21st, with all pomp and wearing his crown, he rode with his forces from Leicester towards the place where Henry was camped near Bosworth. Here, so some of the often contradictory reports have it, Henry Tudor at last met his stepfather Lord Stanley, as well as Sir William. In *Richard III* Shakespeare pays brief tribute to Margaret as the link between them, an unspoken presence of which they must both have been aware.

Polydore Vergil would later report that Henry's battle plan the next day was the one agreed 'in counsel' with Lord Stanley – which suggests at the least that Henry thought he came away from the meeting with the promise of Stanley support. Certainly the Stanleys sent away with Henry two of their kinsmen backed by a force of their retainers – but they themselves remained in their own, detached, camp.

The fields around Bosworth are disputed now as thoroughly as they were trampled then. Recent archaeological work has relocated the scene of the battle* and cast a different light on its strategies – and, as a sideline, perhaps given a fresh glimpse of the women's background role in the men's story. Found in the ground where Richard's army may have camped the night before the battle were two Burgundian coins. They were legal currency in England, so it is certainly going too far to trace a link from Richard's camp back to Duchess Margaret's home of Burgundy – Burgundian mercenaries had fought in other battles of the wars. But it is a useful reminder that people and places far from the action might yet influence the progress of events.

Polydore Vergil – and, before him, the Crowland chronicler – reported that the Yorkist king slept badly on the eve of battle. Crowland says that in the morning he complained of 'a multitude of demons' surrounding him, and that although his face was always drawn it 'was then even more pale and deathly'. Vergil says he 'thought in his sleep that he saw horrible images as it were of evil spirits haunting evidently about him . . . and that they would not let him rest'. Later, of course, his unease would be put down to guilt over his reputed crimes, but at the time Richard himself told his men about it in the morning, to explain away his evident 'heaviness'.

He could not manage to 'buckle himself to the conflict with such liveliness of courage and countenance as before'. It did not help that – so Crowland reported – he awoke so early that his chaplains could not be found to celebrate a propitiatory mass, nor did the servants have his breakfast ready. Richard, he said, had had a presentiment that, whoever won the day, the outcome of this battle 'would prove the utter destruction of the kingdom

---

* Cannonballs have been found more than a mile from what was originally believed to be the site.

of England'. In this he was no prophet. But when a Spaniard called Salazar, a mercenary commander, warned him that those he trusted would betray him that day, he knew the man could be speaking the truth. He answered (or so it was later reported to the Spanish sovereigns): 'God forbid that I yield one step. This day I will die as a king or win.' He chose to wear the royal diadem above his helmet: an encouraging sight for his soldiers, but one that would mark him out as a target for the enemy.

As Polydore Vergil tells it, Richard managed to pull himself together and 'drew his whole host out of their tents, and arrayeth his vanward, stretching it forth of a wonderful length, so full replenished both with footmen and horsemen that to the beholders far off it gave a terror for the multitude, and in the front were placed his archers'. After that long vanguard came the king himself, with a 'choice' force of cavalry.

In Henry Tudor's camp, meanwhile, a few grassy fields away, the mood was hardly more cheerful. Even on the morning of the battle, his nerves had been kept on edge by the fickle Stanleys. When he sent word to Lord Stanley to get his troops ready, word was sent back that Henry should look to his own men: he would do what he had to do, when he was ready. Henry could not but notice that the Stanley force was now drawn up exactly halfway between the two opposing armies.

Though Henry was 'no little vexed, and begun to be somewhat appalled', he put his troops in order. A slender vanguard with the archers came first, making the best of the 'small numbers' of his people. When they were assembled, 'they put on their head pieces and prepared to the fight, expecting th'alarm with intentive ear'. It was perhaps eight in the morning. The fighting would be over by ten.

The traditional view is that Richard's troops were drawn up on higher ground. Henry, learning there was a marsh between the two armies, determined to keep it on his right as he

John Talbot, in his Garter robes, presents a copy of the beautifully illustrated Shrewsbury Book to Marguerite of Anjou, shown hand in hand with her new husband Henry VI. Daisies – Marguerite's personal emblem – decorate the lavish borders.

The stained-glass Royal Window in Canterbury Cathedral shows the figures of
Edward IV and Elizabeth Woodville, with their sons and daughters to either side,
kneeling at prayer desks. The royal figures originally flanked an image of the
Crucifixion, but the window was damaged by Puritan iconoclasts in 1642.

Believed to have been painted by Rowland
Lockey in the last years of the sixteenth
century, this image of the ageing Margaret
Beaufort reflects her reputation for piety.
Margaret's emblems – the mythological
beast called a Yale, the portcullis and
the red rose – adorn several Cambridge
colleges of which she was patron.

Cecily Neville's father, the Earl of Westmorland, flanked by the many children of his second marriage, in a French illustration from the fifteenth century.

Portraits of Elizabeth Woodville – mostly sixteenth- or early seventeenth-century copies of one original portrait type – show the high forehead and elaborate headdress that were a fashion of the day.

Anne Neville, depicted here in the Rous Roll, is shown in her coronation robes with orb and sceptre.

Portraits of Richard III often show a more personable figure than his later reputation might suggest.

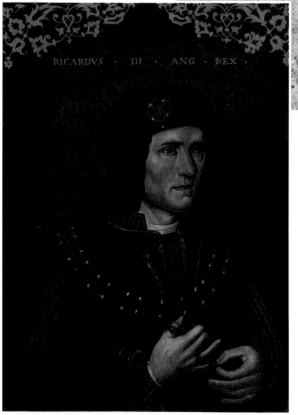

RICARDVS · III · ANG · REX ·

Opposite: This lovely miniature shows a vision in which the risen Christ appeared to Margaret of Burgundy in her bedroom, so silently that even her sleeping dog was not aroused.

ELIZABETHA · VXOR
HENRICI · VII ·

Like that of her mother Elizabeth Woodville, this
portrait of Elizabeth of York is a later version of a
single earlier painted portrait type. She holds the
white rose symbol of York in her hand.

Opposite: This depiction of the birth
of Julius Caesar reflects not only the
childbirth customs of the late fifteenth
century but also the high quality of
illumination found in Burgundian
books and manuscripts at the time.

Chascun hõme
a qui dieu a
donne raison
et entendemēt
se doibt pener
quil ne gaste
le temps en oisuete et quil ne vi
ue comme beste qui est encline et
obeissante a son ventre tant seu
lement. ¶ La vertu et la force
de lhomme est en lame et ou corps

ensamble. lame doibt cõman
der et le corps seruir et obeir. car
lame a en soy lymage de dieu .
et la samblance parfaitement et
le corps est plus commun a beste
alle foiblesse. ¶ Et pour ce q̃
vault acquerre gloire il la doibt
plus conuoittee par richesse de
sens et de uertu que par richesse
de force ne dauoir . la vie de lhõ
me est brieue . mais uertu raiso

This tapestry of a hunting scene also shows the courtly pastimes of fishing and falconry. From the marguerites woven into some of the ladies' hats, it may have been a wedding present for Marguerite of Anjou.

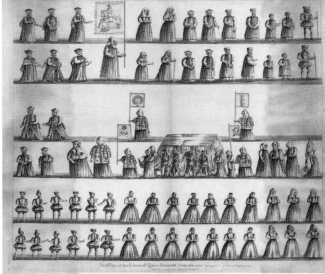

The funeral procession of
Elizabeth of York. Margaret
Beaufort's husband Lord
Stanley walks directly in
front of the bier.

The preparations for a tournament, in the *Livre des Tournois* written by Marguerite of Anjou's father René.

Margaret of Burgundy's crown may have been made for her wedding, or possibly as a votive offering. The white roses around the rim could suggest the Virgin Mary, as well as being a Yorkist emblem.

A French collection of love
songs, made with heart-shaped
pages c. 1475.

This illustration for a volume of poems by Charles, Duke of Orléans reflects his twenty-five-year imprisonment in the Tower of London. Behind the Tower itself is a panorama of the city.

Opposite: Elizabeth of York has inscribed her name – 'Elisabeth the quene' – on the lower margin of this page from a Book of Hours passed down through her family.

ꝰus in adiutoꝛium meum intende:
Domine ad adiuuandum me festi
na. Gloria patri. Sicut erat. ẏn⁹
Ueni creatoꝛ. Memento salutis.
Maria mater. Gloria tibi domine. ut supꝛa. eui.
Germinauit radix yesse. psalmus.
In conuertendo dominus captiuitate syon:
facti sumus sicut consolati. Tunc repletum e gau
dio os nostrum et lingua nostra exultacone. Tuc
dicent inter gentes magnificauit dominus facere
cum eis. Magnificauit dominus facere nobiscum

Taken from the *Troy Book* of the mid-fifteenth century, the image of the Wheel of Fortune, with a crowned king poised at its apex, would prove all too prophetic for the years ahead.

advanced, 'that it might serve his men instead of a fortress'. This also meant the sun was behind him – and in his enemies' eyes – on what promised to be a scorching day.

When Henry's troops moved out from the protection of the marsh, Richard saw his chance and gave the order to advance. As the lines drew together, and the exchange of arrows became hand blows, Henry's commander the Earl of Oxford ordered that no one should move more than ten feet from the standards in case their smaller force should be lost among the greater one. This gave rise to a pause in the fighting, and seemed also to confuse the enemy. Vergil, writing with Tudor hindsight, later suggested that Richard's men seized gladly on the break because they had no great desire for his victory.

This would explain why, when Richard caught sight of Henry surrounded by only a small guard, the king set off 'inflamed with ire' to finish the fight in single combat. Perhaps Henry's long march through Wales had been less trying on the nerves than the waiting game that had been Richard's lot – waiting, with the dawning suspicion that his support was ebbing away.

In what now seems almost a quixotic gesture, Richard had surrendered the advantage of high ground and moved beyond the protection of his forces. But it almost won the day. Richard's own horse thundered down the gentle slope with perhaps as many as a thousand knights riding behind. It would be the last time a king of England led a charge of armoured cavalry. The noise – on a battlefield already ringing with the thunder of primitive cannon, with the voices of the fighting and the dying, with the screams of horses as the foot soldiers' billhooks ripped open their bellies – must have been terrifying. The force of Richard's lance killed Henry's standard bearer and, drawing his axe, the king began to hack his way towards his adversary.

When Henry saw Richard spurring his horse towards him, he 'received him with great courage'. Vergil says that Henry 'abode the brunt longer than ever his own soldiers would have weened, who were now almost out of hope of victory'. But it was not the personal courage of either man that would decide the day. It was probably at this point – acting, crucially, for Henry's side – that Sir William Stanley threw his troops into the fray. Richard, knowing the battle was lost, resolved (as even the Tudor historian Vergil admitted) to die 'fighting manfully in the thickest press of his enemies'. His men brought him fresh horses but, in contrast to the way Shakespeare tells it, Vergil says he refused to flee, swearing again that that day he would make an end of either war or life.

As Richard fought on, his horse foundered in the marshy bog, stained red with the blood of friends and foes. It is unlikely his end was either quick or easy; but at least he could die, as even the normally unsympathetic Crowland put it, 'like a brave and most valiant prince . . . while fighting, and not in the act of flight'. At last an anonymous Welsh soldier jabbed home a final weapon – and, as generations of historians have had it, ended not just one man but a whole epoch. The Middle Ages themselves, as well as the rule of the Plantagenets, died with the unlucky Richard III.[31]

Vergil describes how Richard's body was stripped naked and slung across a horse, to be taken back to Leicester, put on public display and buried without ceremony; Crowland says many insults were offered to the corpse. If Richard's mother Cecily heard of these indignities she, and Richard's sisters, must have been hideously reminded of other deaths, other ignominies; of when Richard, Duke of York's body was decked with a paper crown.

Richard III had been not only the last English king to die in the red heat of battle, but the first since the Conquest. It is an image from those early days that comes to mind – Edith of the Swan Neck searching for her lover Harold's body on the battlefield, just as so many women must have searched here.

The battle had lasted two hours, and Vergil says that a thousand men had been killed; nine-tenths of them, it is estimated, on Richard's side. Rous has Richard's last words as 'treason – treason'. Well they might be: it was a Stanley who placed the crown on Henry's head. But the legends of Bosworth add one other telling detail – that the crown had been found on a thornbush by Reginald Bray, steward to Margaret Beaufort. The origins of the story can be traced back only to an eighteenth-century antiquary but, given the part Margaret Beaufort had played in bringing her son to this point, it has a poetic authenticity.

PART FIVE

1485–1509

TWENTY

True Succeeders

O now let Richmond and Elizabeth,
The true succeeders of each royal house,
By God's fair ordinance conjoin together.
Richard III, 5.5

The battle of Bosworth Field in 1485 is often regarded as the starting place of the early modern age,[1] but that is the result of hindsight. As Henry Tudor assumed the throne, any adult alive then would have remembered not only Richard III's overthrow of the expected order, and Edward IV's coup, but Henry VI's brief resumption of the throne. There was not necessarily any reason to think Henry VII's dynasty would be more durable.

Henry did have one important advantage. There had been a comprehensive clearing of the decks (and the Tudors would make sure it became ever more comprehensive in the years ahead). Any previous Lancastrian comeback had been shadowed by the knowledge that the sons of York were waiting, prolific and power-hungry. But now, of Cecily Neville's six adult children her three sons and one of her daughters were dead. Margaret of Burgundy would still repeatedly attempt to intervene in English affairs; and the descendants of Elizabeth, Duchess of Suffolk, would later cause problems. But for the moment, even if one or both 'Princes in the Tower' had survived, they, like their cousin Warwick, would have been still too young to have themselves mounted a credible challenge for the throne; and with Buckingham and the senior Woodvilles dead, it is hard to see who would have done it for them. What is more, it would take time for any opposition to rally after the shock of defeat: Bosworth could so easily have gone the other way.

Time is what they would not be given. Henry immediately moved to have Clarence's ten-year-old son* brought south and placed in the custody of Margaret Beaufort, for whom everything had now changed. Henry sent her from Bosworth the *Book of Hours* that had been with Richard in his tent – an appropriate tribute for one of Margaret's piety. But the book, already old when Richard began using it, had been transformed into something more personal by the addition, on blank pages, of prayers for Richard's use and mentioning his name. One prayer seeks comfort in sadness by emphasising the goodness of God; another more specifically seeks protection against enemies. Deleting Richard's name, Margaret added on the end-pages the jingle: 'For the honour of God and St Edmunde/Pray for Margaret Richmonde.' For a woman of her temperament – so prone, as her confessor would later recount, to see disaster lurking behind the greatest triumph – even so wonderful a turn of Fortune's wheel as she had just experienced could not have come altogether easily.

When she heard the news of Henry's victory Margaret would have set out south to be reunited with the son she had not seen since he was in his teens. Henry reached London by 7 September and spent two weeks at Baynard's Castle, Cecily Neville's former home. The task facing the new king was immense; to take hasty control of a country which had not only had every opportunity, in recent years, of learning to regard kings as interchangeable,

---

* It is disputed whether the boy was born in 1474 or 1475.

but one which he himself hardly knew. Even his early boyhood had been spent not in England, but in Wales, and he had had few direct opportunities of learning systems and making allies. But he did have recourse to advice.

From London Margaret and her son went for two weeks to her palace of Woking, where they could get to know each other again and Henry could receive an extended briefing. Across the Channel he would have been kept informed of events in the realm, but he was too distant to understand the competing identities and agendas. Each new recruit to his band of exiles might have brought information, but each had his own axe to grind, and his uncle Jasper had been away as long as he. As mother and son walked in the late summer orchards Henry would have been able to draw information from the one person he could trust completely; and perhaps this process gave Margaret Beaufort a role in her son's reign that would not easily be put aside.

It seems never to have occurred to Margaret to make a bid for the crown herself. She and her future daughter-in-law, Elizabeth of York, were in a different position from the other women in this story: they had their own claims to the throne. But even her son was reluctant to stake his claim principally on her blood right: he did so on the combination of marriage to Elizabeth, birth and right of battle. 'The first of these was the fairest, and most like to give contentment to the people', for whom, said Francis Bacon,[2] Edward IV's reign had made convincing 'the clearness of the title of the White Rose or house of York'.

'But then it lay plain before his eyes, that if he relied upon that title, he could be but a King at courtesy, and have rather a matrimonial than a regal power; the right remaining in his Queen, upon whose decease, either with issue, or without issue, he was to give place and be removed.' Bacon was writing in the early seventeenth century, and by then the country had known two reigning queens; at the time, the right of Elizabeth of York may not have seemed so clear. But Henry was persuaded, Bacon said, 'to rest upon the title of Lancaster as the main', and took care from the first that his prospective bride should not be given too much importance – he plastered everything with the red rose now adopted as counterpoint to the white, and with Margaret Beaufort's portcullis badge; and vaunted his God-given military victory.

But one of Henry's first actions was to see that his mother was declared a *'feme sole'*, a woman able to act independently of a husband and to own property. An Act of Parliament ordained that she 'may from henceforth [for the] term of her life sue all manner of actions . . . plea and be impleaded for . . . in as good, large and beneficial manner, as any other sole person not wife nor covert of any husband'. She could 'as well make, as take and receive, all manner of feoffments, states, leases, releases, confirmations, presentations, bargains, sales, gifts, deeds, wills and writings'. It made Margaret an independent financial entity, and potentially a real power in the land. This was unprecedented for an aristocratic woman – queens were usually allowed this privilege, and it had occasionally been used in the lower ranks of society to allow a woman to operate a business. Her husband Stanley was treated with separate generosity – created Earl of Derby, and honoured as the new king's *'beaupère'*. Over the next couple of years, elaborate arrangements would be set up to apportion Margaret's land revenues between the two of them – but her power and property were not to be at his disposal, as would be normal in the fifteenth century.

That property would be substantial. While mother and son were still at Woking, orders had gone out for repairs and improvements to the fine house of Coldharbour on the Thames for 'my lady the King's mother'. Margaret's arms were set into the windows, to be displayed to anyone passing on the water. Over the next few weeks the king's 'most dearest mother' saw the return of her own estates, now that the attainder against her was reversed; she was given power to appoint officers in the lordship of Ware, as well as effective use of the estates of the heirs of the executed Duke of Buckingham, whose son became her ward. From the 'great grant' of 22 March 1487 came the 'Exeter lands' in Devon, south Wales, Derbyshire and Northamptonshire, as well as the Richmond estates in Lincolnshire and Kendal.

Tangible benefits were given also to those close to Margaret: her trusted servants Reginald Bray, who would become Henry's great officer, and Christopher Urswick (another whom Bacon described as a man the king 'much trusted and employed'); her Stanley connections led by the new king's 'right entirely beloved father'; and Jasper Tudor, who became Duke of Bedford. Her half-brother John Welles would be allowed to marry Edward IV's second surviving daughter, Cecily, while Jasper Tudor would marry Buckingham's widow, the former Woodville girl. It was of course a favour to the men concerned – but it is also an example of how marriage could be used to bring potentially dissident bloodlines into the fold. Margaret's old associate John Morton, the Bishop of Ely, soon became her son's Archbishop of Canterbury – and later Lord Chancellor.

At the end of October 1485 Henry was crowned, under the book of rule laid down for Richard III. Powdered ermine and black furs were ordered, as well as crimson velvet and crimson cloth of gold. Margaret's confessor John Fisher later recalled that 'when the king her son was crowned in all that great triumph and glory, she wept marvellously'.

On 7 November parliament re-enacted the 1397 statute legitimating the Beauforts, without the 1407 clause barring them from the throne. The parliamentary rolls which incorporated Titulus Regius were ordered to be 'cancelled, destroyed, and . . . taken and avoided out of the roll and records of the said Parliament of the said late king, and burned, and utterly destroyed', because 'from their falseness and shamefulness, they were only deserving of utter oblivion'. Not only were the attainders against Henry VI, Margaret of Anjou and Jasper Tudor reversed, but Elizabeth Woodville was restored to her 'estate, dignity, pre-eminence and name'.

On 10 December parliament, surely at his instigation, begged Henry to 'unify two bloods' by marrying Elizabeth of York. Care, however, was taken all round to stress that Henry's rule was valid (as Crowland put it) 'not only by right of blood but of victory in battle and of conquest'. The Speaker declared that it was because the hereditary succession of the crowns of England and France 'is, remains, continues, and endures in the person of the same Lord King, & in the heirs legitimately issuing from his body' that he wished to take Elizabeth as his wife, for the 'continuation of offspring by a race of kings'.

Crowland added that marriage to Edward IV's eldest daughter merely filled in 'whatever appeared to be missing in the king's title elsewhere'; but Bacon wrote that he 'would not endure any mention of the Lady Elizabeth, no not [not even] in the nature of special entail'. There was, however, no question but that the marriage would go ahead, and on the 11th Henry gave order that preparations should begin.

The marriage plan was founded on the assumption that it was in Elizabeth of York that the best Plantagenet claims to the throne were now embodied; that Elizabeth's rights, in other words, were not superseded by those of any living brother. When Henry took control of London, he would have taken control also of the Tower; which begs the question of what – or whom – he found or failed to find there. The records are silent, which is itself suggestive.

If Henry Tudor and his adherents knew that Richard had definitely, demonstrably, had his nephews killed, it is inconceivable that he would not have declared it and made capital of the fact. If, however, he believed the boys to be dead at Richard's hands, but had no way to prove it, his silence makes perfect sense since to have declared them simply missing would have been to invite pretenders. By the same token the princes' mother and sisters must surely have felt they knew something; now would have been the moment for a hullabaloo of inquiry, and they seem to have made none. It is very possible Elizabeth Woodville and her daughters believed, like Henry, that the boys had been killed, and presumably by Richard, but that they too had no proof. That dearth of evidence might allow future doubt to creep in, but for the moment at least it could have been enough to stop them speaking out. A measure of silent uncertainty was everybody's friend.[3]

One of the new king's first acts, said Vergil, had been to send a messenger to Sheriff Hutton to summon Elizabeth of York. She progressed southwards 'attended by noble ladies' to stay with her mother, and later with Henry's. They met for what was probably the first time, and Elizabeth would have seen not the pinch-faced miser of later imagery but a man still in his twenties; already with something of his mother's hooded eyes, perhaps, but tall and slim, with blue eyes set in a cheerful face and a general appearance that Vergil could describe even some years later as 'remarkably attractive'.

Henry would have been greeted with an even more agreeable picture. Elizabeth of York really does seem to have had the blonde ('yellow') hair conventionally ascribed to queens. Later descriptions of plumpness infer that she was already buxom – certainly a comely nineteen-year-old, whether or not she were a true beauty like her mother. Vergil described her as 'intelligent above all others, and equally beautiful' – but that can probably be put down to tact.

If, when Henry looked at her, he saw the girl who had caused so much trouble with rumours of attachment to her uncle – and if she saw the man who had long been an enemy to her family

– such deals were far from rare in the marriage arrangements of royalty. The two had, after all, a shared experience of uncertainty, of the swift turns that Fortune's wheel could bring. It is likely they were both well enough pleased – and more than that. It is probable that, like Margaret Beaufort, Elizabeth had never envisaged ruling in her own right. To be a queen consort was the destiny for which she had been raised to aspire – and she had achieved it without the need to leave her own country.

Henry now applied for a second papal dispensation to allow two relatives to marry. One had already been issued, in March 1484, to cover a marriage between 'Henry Richmond, layman of the York diocese, and Elizabeth Plantagenet, woman of the London diocese'; but that might not be held to fit Henry's changed status. Margaret's husband Stanley had to swear that his wife had discussed all necessary questions of lineage before any arrangement was made between the pair. The second dispensation was issued on 16 January 1486, by which time the ring had been purchased and the wedding was only two days away. It would take place almost exactly a year after Elizabeth's name had first been coupled with that of another king of England.

Not much is known about the actual ceremonies, though Bacon wrote that 'it was celebrated with greater triumph and demonstrations (especially on the people's part) of joy and gladness than the days either of his entry or coronation, which the King rather noted than liked'.

According to the Tudor poet Bernard André: 'The people constructed bonfires far and wide to show their gladness and the City of London was filled with dancing, singing and entertainment.' Bacon summed it up by remarking that while Bosworth had given Henry the bended knee of his subjects, this marriage gave him their hearts.

Henry now ordered a third papal dispensation: one setting aside any impediment caused by the couple's relation through marriage rather than through consanguinity. Over the succeeding months the Pope was obliging enough also to threaten excommunication for anyone who challenged the right of Henry's heirs to succeed, and to issue a Papal Bull confirming the legitimacy of the union.

The couple may not have waited for the marriage ceremony before they began to live together – common enough in the fifteenth century. That third dispensation may have been requested because they knew Elizabeth was pregnant; court poets hastened to link Henry's victory at Bosworth with this speedy proof of virility. Bernard André's version has to be the most oleaginous: 'Then a new happiness took over the happiest kingdom, great enjoyment filled the queen, the church experienced perfect joy, while huge excitement gripped the court and an incredible pleasure arose over the whole country.'

Not everyone, however, had taken Bosworth as the final verdict on the future. Easter saw rebellion in Yorkshire; and for the first full year of his reign Henry rode around the country putting down local unrest and displaying himself in the guise of majesty. The women – Elizabeth of York, her sister, her mother, and her mother-in-law – summered at Winchester, in St Swithin's Priory within the Close. Elizabeth Woodville, besides being restored to her rank as queen dowager, had been awarded a grant for life of six manors in Essex and an annual income of £102. There were, however, problems, not least the jostling for place between the queen dowager and Margaret Beaufort. The former had lived through a lot but, only in her late forties, was not necessarily ready to give up; the latter, in her early forties, had only just arrived, and would surely be reluctant to see the real authority she wielded in her son's kingdom cast in the shade by the ceremonial status of a woman who technically outranked her.

But it is possible that Elizabeth Woodville had tired of court.

On 10 July she had arranged with the abbot of Westminster to take out a forty-year lease on 'a mansion within the said Abbey called Cheyne gate'. Despite possibly bringing back bad memories of her time in sanctuary, it was a practical location; though her worldly image might sometimes have masked it, her behaviour as queen had always been that of a convention-ally devout woman. Then again, her negotiations for a London home may have been her response to plans first mooted for her a few days earlier – Henry's proposal that she should marry the Scots king as part of a peace treaty.

On 20 September 1486 ('afore one o'clock after midnight', noted Margaret Beaufort in her *Book of Hours*), to widespread rejoicing, Elizabeth of York gave birth to a prince in whose veins ran the blood of both dynasties. Either the baby was a whole month early or the date is evidence that the couple had indeed cohabited before the actual marriage ceremony.

It was inevitable that Margaret would have strong views on the christening. The ordinances she set down decreed that Winchester Cathedral should be carpeted and hung with tapes-tries, that soft linen should be folded inside the font, which was placed on a stage in the middle of the church to give the crowds a better view. She and her son were both good at publicity. But Elizabeth's own maternal relations were well to the fore: her sister Cecily carried the baby to the font, with their sister-in-law the Marchioness of Dorset bearing the train. Dorset himself as well as the Earl of Lincoln, the queen's cousin, stood beside her. The queen's sister Anne carried the robe, while Elizabeth Woodville as godmother carried the little prince on to the high altar and gave him a covered cup of gold.

Margaret's ordinances also covered the rearing of her grandson, decreeing that the wet nurse should be observed by a doctor at every meal to see that the child was getting 'season-able meat and drink', and describing the leather (and presumably dribble-proof) cushion on which she should lean, and the two great basins of pewter needed for the nursery laundry. The ordinances encompass both practicality and grandeur – the pommels on the cradle, the counterpane furred with ermine and the 'head sheets' of cloth of gold – and go on for ever. Court ceremony was important, and a new dynasty had to show it could do these things magnificently. All the same, there is something a little frightening in the thoroughness with which Margaret laid down every detail. The years of her misfortune had obviously bred in her an urgent need for control. Perhaps, too, she was reaching after the kind of experience she herself had been denied when she gave birth to Henry all those years before. It is almost as if Elizabeth were her surrogate – and not the only such case in this story.

Elizabeth was ill just after the child was born; she typically suffered fevers after giving birth, and would cling to those who had seen her through one birth, like her midwife Alice Massy, to help her through the next. She would in any case have had to stay at Winchester until she was churched. The precisely ordered ceremonials for that event show Margaret once again stage-managing the scenario – a duchess or countess to assist the queen out of bed, two more to receive her at her chamber door. For Elizabeth of York her relationship with Henry's mother – like that of Cecily Neville and her daughter-in-law Elizabeth Woodville – was an issue that would never go away.

The choice of Winchester for the new prince's birth and the decision to name him Arthur were a conscious attempt to link the new Tudors with the ancient Arthurian tale. This was, as anyone who had read Caxton's newly printed edition of the *Morte d'Arthur* knew, the city that still held the Round Table. But there may have been a more serious reason for staying in a place of safety. As the court made its way back to Greenwich for the winter season, troubles were brewing.

A century later, Francis Bacon wrote that from the very start of Henry's reign there were 'secret rumours and whisperings (which afterwards gathered strength and turned to great troubles) that the two young sons of King Edward the Fourth or one of them (which were said to be destroyed in the Tower), were not indeed murdered, but conveyed secretly away, and were yet living'. In the summer of 1486 stories had begun to spread that Clarence's son Warwick had escaped from the Tower and was in the Channel Islands. The boy later identified as Lambert Simnel seemed at first to be claiming that he was Richard, Duke of York, Elizabeth Woodville's younger son; but by the time he reached Ireland by the turn of the year he had changed his story.

Henry soon brought the real Warwick briefly out of the Tower, and sent him through the London streets in a public display. But when people had claimed Simnel was Richard, the pressure on Elizabeth Woodville must have been intense. The pretender's supporters would need only a word from her to endorse his claim. The events of the next few months might suggest that, in the eyes of the authorities at least, the possibility of Elizabeth giving that word was a genuine one.

On 2 February Henry met with his council and, as Vergil reported after the fact: 'Among other matters, Elizabeth the widow of King Edward was deprived by the decree of the same council of all her possessions.' This, unconvincingly, was supposedly as punishment for the fact that, three years before, she had left sanctuary and made a deal with Richard III. Later that month parliament endorsed the alienation of Elizabeth's property. It has often been taken as evidence that the dowager queen was being held to task for having supported the pretender Simnel, with all that might imply about her beliefs as to her son's fate. Or, less drastically, it could have been a precautionary measure.

It may have been that the financial negotiations and the rebellion bore no relation to each other. This was a time of reorganisation all round: it was, indeed, the season of the 'great grant' which benefited Margaret Beaufort. A separate establishment had been set up for Prince Arthur at Farnham in Surrey; Elizabeth of York visited in January, to check on her son. And the lands lately belonging to Elizabeth Woodville were, after all, simply being transferred to her daughter, the new 'lady queen', whose position would traditionally be kept up by income from these properties. In return the older lady got an annuity of 400 marks. This, however – being less than the income Richard had allowed her – might well be called paltry. What is even more curious is the fact that it was precisely now that Elizabeth Woodville took up more or less permanent residence in Bermondsey Abbey, the great convent on the Thames already equipped with accommodation for royalty. (Katherine of Valois, Henry V's widow, had been forced to retreat there after it was discovered she had married Owen Tudor.)

There was nothing strange about the decision itself, if Elizabeth is acknowledged as not the totally worldly creature she has often been thought; many widows chose a religious retirement. And if her first choice had been the more central residence in Westminster Abbey's precincts, Bermondsey was still a convenient place – even a thrifty one, since the association with it of an ancestor of hers meant that she could board without payment. But the timing is suggestive – the more so since the lease of Cheyneygates shows she had only recently made quite different plans. It does look as though she were at the least being urged to take up a temporary retirement – if not because of anything she had done, then because of what she might do. Francis Bacon wrote that she was so deeply suspect 'it was almost thought dangerous to visit her, or see her'.

Soon after Henry had paraded the real Warwick through London, John, Earl of Lincoln made a dramatic flight from England. Lincoln was the son of Edward IV's sister Elizabeth, and Crowland says that she herself was 'longing' for Henry's overthrow. Lincoln had been received with favour at the new Tudor court and had been prominent at the christening of Prince Arthur. But now he disappeared, to turn up in the Low Countries. By Easter, it was clear that an invasion force was being assembled.

In April Lincoln took an army to Ireland, where Simnel was given an impromptu coronation ceremony and declared King Edward VI. But the involvement of this other royal line is curious: it was Lincoln, not Simnel who was later mentioned in his aunt Margaret's correspondence about the expedition. It seems possible that Simnel was just a stalking horse for Lincoln's own attempt to take over the country.[4]

In May Henry, at Kenilworth Castle in the safety of the Midlands, heard that Simnel had landed with an army. He immediately sent to the Earl of Ormond, chamberlain of the queen who was still at Greenwich: 'we pray you that, giving your due attendance upon our said dearest wife and lady mother, ye come with them unto us . . .'. Then, when Henry set out to confront the rebels, Elizabeth travelled quickly to Farnham and her baby; plans were made for them to move on, if necessary, to a house of Benedictine nuns at Romsey in Hampshire – not far from the coast, in case the worst happened and they had to flee. For the young queen it must have been a terrifying reminder of traumas past.

On 16 June at the battle of Stoke, perhaps the last familial battle of the Wars of the Roses, Lincoln was killed. The boy Simnel – in what may have been natural clemency on Henry's part, but was more certainly intended to emphasise the absurdity of his pretensions – was put to work in the royal kitchens. Lincoln's parents the Suffolks, whatever their personal loss, suffered no further penalties.

There remains the question of what, if any, role other Yorkist women might have played in the affair. Simnel's immediate sponsor, Vergil said, was an Oxford priest called Richard Simons. But there had to have been some greater personage waiting in the wings; someone better able to coach an impostor in the things he should know. Bacon believed that Lambert Simnel had been schooled, and by a Yorkist lady. 'So that it cannot be, but that some great person, that knew particularly and familiarly Edward Plantagenet [Warwick], had a hand in the business'. He was inclined to allot some of the blame to Elizabeth Woodville:

> That which is the most probable, out of precedent and subsequent acts, is, that it was the Queen Dowager, from whom this action had the principal source and motion. For certain it is, she was a busy negotiating woman, and . . . was at this time extremely discontent with the King,[5] thinking her daughter, as the King handled the matter, not advanced but depressed [lowered in status]: and none could hold the book so well to prompt and instruct this stage-play as she could.

But there was another Yorkist woman who certainly did support, and possibly coach, Lambert Simnel – Margaret of Burgundy, whom Bacon described as 'the sovereign patroness and protectress of the enterprise'. When her only remaining brother Richard was killed at Bosworth, Margaret was fully occupied with Burgundian affairs: her stepdaughter's son Philip, now returned to her care, and the Great Council which, in September 1485, had been summoned to consider the future of Burgundy. Perhaps she might have left matters alone if Henry had taken care to conciliate either Burgundy or its dowager duchess, but he failed to do so. He was, after all, a novice king and one, moreover, reared in the traditions of France and Brittany, often Burgundy's enemies.

Henry had, in 1486, been careful to renew at least some of the rights Cecily Neville had been accorded by her sons. But the trading privileges that Edward had granted his sister Margaret of Burgundy, and which her brother Richard seems to have continued, now lapsed. It is probable, therefore, that enlightened self-interest jostled emotion to govern Margaret's actions in the years ahead.

She may also have played a more fundamental role in the Lambert Simnel drama.[6] As early as the summer of 1486 a donation was made in Burgundy, for the feast of St Rombout's Day, on behalf of 'the son of Clarence from England'; while in the same year the city of Malines gave Margaret money for her 'reyse' – venture – to England. If it was Margaret who fulfilled the coach's role that Bacon ascribed to Elizabeth Woodville, she may not have been acting solely on her own behalf but also in the interests of her adopted land. After the recent rebellion Henry began to be more conciliatory towards Burgundy; the more so since he needed Burgundian aid to keep France out of his old host country, Brittany, now ruled after the death of Duke Francis by a young duchess, Anne.

Elizabeth Woodville, by contrast, had lost by the rebellion. Henry's records over the next few years do show regular, almost yearly, payments to his 'right dear' mother-in-law: 50 marks for Christmas here, the gift of a tun of wine there. But it was not the kind of wholesale funding that would allow her to play any kind of political role. Her public career was over. She would, indeed, from this point be recorded as only making occasional appearances in public while she lived a reduced life in the convent at Bermondsey.

TWENTY-ONE

Golden Sovereignty

Put in her tender heart th'aspiring flame
Of golden sovereignty; acquaint the princess
With the sweet silent hours of marriage joys.
Richard III, 4.4

This rebellion was over, though other ripples of armed discontent would plague Henry's next years. But he heeded a complaint voiced by the rebels that Elizabeth of York was being treated too casually – that, extraordinarily, she had not yet been crowned. September was full of plans for the splendid ceremony, and in October the royal couple set out from Warwick to London. Even then, the entry into the city was Henry's moment – the first time he had been there since his victory at Stoke – and the crafts guilds were out in number, lined up along the packed streets, according to a manuscript preserved by the early sixteenth-century antiquary John Leland,[7] 'hugely replenished with people'.

'And so to behold the fair and goodly sight of his coming, the Queen's Grace and my lady the King's Mother, and many other great Estates, both lords and Ladies, richly beseen, went secretly in a House beside St Mary Spittle, without Bishops Gate; and when the sight was passed, they went from thence to Greenwich to their Beds.' The ladies were withdrawing to Greenwich for the weeks before the coronation: Elizabeth was to be presented to London afresh, almost as though she were a newly arrived foreign princess.

On 'the Friday before Saint Katherine's Day' the queen (accompanied once again by 'my Lady the King's mother') set out from Greenwich in a flotilla of barges decorated with 'Banners and streamers of silk', as Leland put it. Especially fine among the accompanying vessels was the Bachelors' Barge, from which a dragon spouted flames into the Thames. Landing on Tower Wharf, Elizabeth was greeted by the king; and while he created fourteen new Knights of the Bath, she prepared for the next day.

The following morning she dressed in the traditional kirtle of white 'cloth of gold of damask' with a mantle furred with ermine and tasselled with gold. The writer noticed the 'fair yellow hair hanging down plain behind her back' – that symbol of virginity, suggesting anointed queenship as new territory. Her sister Cecily carried her train as they formed up for the procession through the city. After the horse of state and the henchmen decked with white York roses came the ladies in horse-borne litters. The first carried Katherine Woodville (Elizabeth Woodville's sister, the former Duchess of Buckingham, now Duchess of Bedford) and Cecily. The second conveyed the Duchess of Suffolk (still Elizabeth's royal aunt – never mind that her son had been Lincoln, the recent rebel), the Duchess of Norfolk and the Countess of Oxford. Behind them came their various gentlewomen.

The night was spent at Westminster and on Sunday, coronation day, Elizabeth was dressed in purple velvet furred with ermine as she walked to the Abbey over a carpet of woollen cloth which the watching crowds would traditionally be allowed to take. But: 'there was so huge a people inordinately pressing to cut the ray cloth that the Queen's Grace went ['gede'] upon, so that in the Presence certain persons were slain, and the order of the ladies following the Queen was broken and distroubled.' Then came the ceremony itself: the anointing, the crowning, the placing of a rod and sceptre into her hands. Margaret Beaufort watched with her son, from an elevated stage concealed by lattice and draperies, as another woman was transformed into a quasi-divinity. Any queen might validate and contribute to her husband's kingship, but Elizabeth's contribution was far greater than the norm. It was something that must have struck her husband and her mother-in-law as both a potential threat and an opportunity.

Next came the banquet. After grace was said, 'Dame Katherine Gray and Mistress Ditton went under the table, where they sat on either side [of] the Queen's feet all the dinner time.' She had the Duchess of Bedford and Cecily on her left, the Archbishop of Canterbury on her right, while the Countess of Oxford and the Countess of Rivers (Anthony Woodville's widow) knelt on either side of her and held up a cloth as she ate. It was the parade of homage that Elizabeth Woodville had received and, remembering the royally born Jacquetta on her knees before her daughter, it is easy to guess why Margaret Beaufort was not there. Again, 'the high and mighty princess his mother' watched with her son from a window at the side.

The banquet was two courses only – perhaps they remembered that at the coronation of Richard and Anne no one had had time to eat three. But each contained a plethora of dishes: game birds and fatted rabbits, swan 'in chawdron' and peacock in its feathers, even a whole seal 'richly served'. After alms were given and the queen was 'cried' around the hall – *'De la tres haut, tres puissant, tres excellent Princesse, la tres noble reigne d'Engleterre, et de Fraunce, et Dame d'Irlande'* – it was almost over; bar the fruit and wafers, the ritual washing, the grace, the trumpets and the hippocras – spiced wine – and further spices. Elizabeth left 'with God's blessing and to the rejoicing of many a true English man's heart'.

At mass next day Margaret Beaufort sat on the queen's right, as she did when Elizabeth sat in state in the Parliament Chamber; the Duchess of Suffolk was still present. All the lessons of the Wars of the Roses were surely there: divide and conquer, bring into the fold, make the defeated (especially the placatory, conciliatory, figures of the women) part of the victory. The one person who does not appear to have been there was Elizabeth's own mother, which seems the strongest evidence that she was in some degree of disgrace.[8] But perhaps Elizabeth of York's relations with her husband, her role as queen, would get easier as her own loving but (from all the past evidence) forceful mother moved out of the way.

Visiting the queen in July 1488, the Spanish ambassador De Puebla found her 'with two and twenty companions of angel-ical appearance, and all we saw there seemed very magnificent, and in splendid style, as was suitable for the occasion'. The envoy of Ferdinand of Aragon and Isabella of Castile was in England to negotiate the marriage treaty between the infant Prince Arthur and their daughter Katherine. Some time later the ambassador saw Elizabeth and Henry walking in procession to mass and noticed that her ladies 'went in good order' and were much adorned. The Venetian envoy wrote that she was 'a very handsome woman and in conduct very able' – or, as the original Italian has it, '*di gran governo*'. Elizabeth knew how to be a queen of England; she had learnt it at her mother's knee.

While the new queen's motto was 'humble and reverent', that is not necessarily the entire story. Her mother had surely known the value of informal, closet influence, and maybe Elizabeth of York had picked up something from observing the different styles of queenship exercised by Elizabeth Woodville and

Marguerite of Anjou and the varying degrees of warmth with which they were received. Perhaps, too, if she were influenced that way her own style would in turn affect her son Henry, and the expectations with which he would greet his own queens. There is some slight evidence to suggest that Elizabeth did exercise a behind-the-scenes influence on her husband: for instance, a letter from the Pope to Margaret Beaufort saying that Henry had promised to appoint Elizabeth's candidate to the bishopric of Worcester. Another letter, one of only two intercessionary letters from Elizabeth that survive, was written in 1499 to recommend to Ferdinand of Aragon one 'Henry Stuke, who wishes to go and fight against the Infidels . . . Though he is a very short man, he has the reputation of being a valiant soldier.' A further letter concerns the nomination of a chaplain to a vacant living.

Another Spanish report tells of Elizabeth receiving two letters from Ferdinand and Isabella and two from their daughter Katherine: 'The King had a dispute with the Queen because he wanted to have one of the said letters to carry continually about him, but the Queen did not like to part with hers . . . ,' the ambassador relates. It has been taken as evidence of Elizabeth's independence; and though in fact it may sound more like a thoroughly stage-managed display, it shows how highly missives from the Spanish court were valued – that too would make Elizabeth a conscious player in the diplomatic game.

Against that are reports – such as Bacon's comment that she was 'depressed' in status, and the Spanish view that she was beloved 'because she is powerless' – suggesting that Elizabeth had been sidelined like Anne Neville before her. These writers infer that a canny husband had subsumed her rights and powers into his own, while diverting her into a life of ceremonies interspersed by as many as eight pregnancies. Bacon, indeed, even claimed that the king's 'aversion toward the house of York was so predominant in him as it found place not only in his wars and councils, but in his chamber and bed'. (Bacon did also say, more mildly, that though Henry was 'nothing uxurious, nor scarce indulgent' towards his queen, he was none the less 'companionable and respective [considerate], and without jealousy'.) It seems curious, in the light of these comments, that Elizabeth of York is widely assumed to have been happy.

There are two distinct strands of information concerning Elizabeth's personality and situation, and the two do not altogether match up. Writers have traditionally reconciled her apparent contentment, and her husband's dominance, by portraying her as a woman without ambition and almost without volition – 'a placid, domestic sort of creature',[9] as one of them described her.

The problem with that judgement is that this 'placid' ruminant of a woman had been, only a few years earlier, the passionately pro-active girl of Richard's reign, Elizabeth Woodville's daughter. Unless, that is, the Buck letter is regarded as a complete forgery; the *Ballad of Lady Bessy* is totally ignored; and the apparent fears of Richard III's henchmen that she might revenge her family's wrongs on them are set aside. Perhaps the truth is that the construct of successful monarchy the first Tudors set up leaves no room for evidence of dissent; and any dissents of Elizabeth's were probably of the private, domestic kind. A happy marriage – and this one does seem to have been basically happy – has no story.

In August 1498 the Spanish ambassador delivered another set of letters from Spain to Elizabeth, 'the most distinguished and the most noble lady in the whole of England'. She immediately sent for the Latin Secretary to write replies; he was, the man said, always obliged to write such letters to Spain[10] three or four times, because the queen always found some defects in them.

It is possible that Elizabeth's cultural influence has been underestimated; the chivalric influence at her husband's and her son's courts derived from her Burgundian family, and she shared a measure of literary interest with her mother. The renovations at Greenwich, displaying a Burgundian influence, were made following 'a new platt [plan] . . . devised by the Queen'. From certain similarities in their handwriting,[11] it may have been she who taught her second son and her daughters to write, and in spring 1488 Elizabeth's influence could perhaps be seen when a Lady Mistress was chosen for Prince Arthur (at a hefty fee of more than £26 a year) – Elizabeth Darcy, who had presided over the nursery of Elizabeth's brother Edward V.

Elizabeth owned or used several exquisitely illustrated *Books of Hours*, as well as giving them to favoured ladies. One is inscribed: 'Madam I pray you remember me in your good prayers your mistress Elizabeth R.' A copy of the devotional *Scala Perfectionis*, the 'Scale of Perfection', presented to her lady Mary Roos, was signed both by her ('I pray you pray for me/ Elizabeth ye queen') and by Margaret Beaufort. Elizabeth shared with her mother-in-law an interest in religion that led them particularly to St Bridget of Sweden, whose work took pride of place in the collection of English and Latin prayers they commissioned together from Caxton.

Her relationship with Margaret Beaufort is one of the big questions about Elizabeth of York. The Spanish reports asserting that the queen is 'beloved because she is powerless' continued: 'The King is much influenced by his mother and his followers in affairs or personal interest and in others. The Queen, as is generally the case, does not like it.' It also spoke of Elizabeth's 'subjection' to Margaret. There is a strong received impression that the two were antagonistic – or that antagonism was averted only by this supposed placidity on Elizabeth's part – and perhaps it is true that there was bound to be an element of rivalry.

In 1493 Henry drew up household ordinances demonstrating the concern he shared with his mother for the dignity and order of the court. They stipulated that a bishop dining in Margaret's house would be served 'as he is served in the king's presence'; that when Margaret went to church with the king and queen she too should have her cloth of estate. When the king took wine and spices after evensong it should be served with equal state to him, his mother and his sons – the queen presumably residing in her own household, separately. Indeed, it must not be forgotten that part of the anxious parade of state and intimacy accorded to Margaret rather than to Elizabeth was precisely because the queen had her own separate establishment, and status, already; whereas a place had to be created for the sort of 'king's mother' Margaret was determined to be. Perhaps if Margaret had become a queen, a role which she clearly felt Fortune had denied her, she would not have felt the need to press for her rights quite so stridently.

Cecily Neville had likewise played an active part in the first years of Edward IV's reign, but she, while possibly as determined a woman as Margaret, had herself been newly arrived at the independence of widowhood when her son became king. She had not spent years imagining her future role as Margaret must have done; had not played such an active part in bringing her son to the throne; while Elizabeth of York was not – and this may in part explain why Elizabeth Woodville was relegated to Bermondsey – surrounded, as her mother had been, by so very active a family.

Perhaps it is too simplistic a view to envisage Elizabeth of York and Margaret Beaufort as rivals.[12] The Spanish envoy apart, the picture of their hostility depends largely on one particular story of Margaret Beaufort's intervening to block a man who was trying to petition the queen, and his subsequent complaint that he had been set aside by 'that strong whore', the king's mother. Margaret's action could be seen as officious, or protective, or a little bit of both. Perhaps the Spanish envoy had expectations that were unrealistic in England: at home, Isabella of Castile could exercise power quite openly.

Elizabeth and Margaret may indeed have been able to turn to advantage the fact that between them they represented two very different faces of queenship or quasi-queenship. Certainly the two women worked together when necessary: to receive the licence to found a chantry, for instance, or to apply for the rights to the next presentation to a deanery. It is uncertain, even so, how large a part Elizabeth really had to play in these activities – the more so since both partnerships included Margaret's old retainer Reginald Bray. In 1501, several of Margaret's trusted connections were among Elizabeth's officers – but, after all this time their relationships may just have grown entangled to a degree.

They probably collaborated more naturally on family matters, acting in concert, in the years ahead, to prepare for Katherine of Aragon's smooth passage into English life, and to protect Elizabeth's daughter Margaret from the perils of too early a marriage. But all the same, if Elizabeth of York's life was spelt out in big ceremonies and childbirths, she had her mother-in-law at her side in too many of them.

For the first decade or so of their marriage, reports of the royal couple's movements almost always show that Margaret was with them; and she was often with her son when the queen was absent. Margaret was, of course, a woman now past the pressures of childbearing and rearing, which left her free to act almost like a male counsellor. At the palace of Woodstock Margaret's lodgings were linked to the king's by a withdrawing chamber where the two could be together, for work or leisure. In the Tower, again, her rooms were next to the king's bedchamber and the council chamber.

A letter from William Paston describes how the royal trio 'lie at Northampton and will tarry there till Michaelmas', as though they were one indissoluble entity. A letter of Margaret's from 1497 stated that the king, the queen and all 'our' sweet children were in good health – though by this time Queen Elizabeth would perhaps be able to act more independently. As Henry VII found his feet, Francis Bacon would later claim, he reverenced but did not heed his mother. Nevertheless, to keep a balance between the two women closest to him must always have been a juggling act.

This test of diplomacy can be seen in operation immediately after Elizabeth's coronation, at the end of 1487, when the court spent Christmas at Greenwich. On Twelfth Night the king and queen wore their crowns, though the closest thing Margaret Beaufort could be allowed was 'a rich Coronal'. When the king wore his formal surcoat and the queen hers, Margaret dressed 'in like Mantel and Surcoat as the Queen'.

Distinctions were, however, made. Margaret had to walk slightly behind and 'aside the queen's half train'. After mass, as the king and queen dined in state, the king's marshal ended the formalities by making 'Estate' to the king and queen and 'half Estate' to the king's mother – the same as to the Archbishop of Canterbury. A letter from Henry VIII's day[13] would concede that Katherine of Aragon, after the divorce, could keep the royal privilege of Maundy Thursday alms-giving; not as queen, but only 'in the name of Princess Dowager, in like manner as my Lady the Kings graunt-dame did in the name of the Countess of Richemount and Derby'.

When the court moved on to Windsor for Easter 1488, and the royal trio wore their Garter robes to chapel on St George's Day, the queen and the king's mother were censed after the king; but only the king and queen kissed the Pax. Elizabeth of York was in one sense the senior partner here – she was the one who had ridden in her first Garter procession decades before. Here, once again, her ceremonial presence was probably more important for Henry's legitimacy than was usual for a queen, irritating though that may have been to Margaret. When the two women were accorded the order of the Garter together, a song was composed to celebrate their togetherness: it was as if everyone needed to parade this odd duality, and to reassure the protagonists.

Despite his later reputation for miserliness Henry made frequent and generous payments to dancers, entertainers of all kinds, and especially musicians at his various palaces: Windsor, Westminster, Greenwich, Eltham, Sheen. It seems to have been an interest that he and Elizabeth, who kept her own minstrels, shared. The pair travelled together perhaps more often than was usual, which could be ascribed to affection, or to suspicion if Henry felt he needed to keep an eye on Elizabeth – or on any Yorkists who might be drawn to her, anyway. But it was certainly an economy, since a second household functioning quite independently would inevitably cost more. The Great Wardrobe accounts show him not only making her presents such as robes furred with miniver, but supplying household essentials such as beds and hammers.

Some regard the gifts of cash and communion cloths, gowns and gold wire as evidence of intimacy and affection; but they could be seen another way. Despite the lands settled on her, Elizabeth's finances were not run like those of preceding queens and Henry often had to bale her out, undermining her independence, even though her signature on each page of her Privy Purse accounts shows that she had by no means chosen to abnegate this responsibility. Her lands and fee farms, yielding some £1900 in 1496, plus an annuity the king had extracted on her behalf from the town of Bristol of another £100, still amounted to less than half the income that Elizabeth Woodville had enjoyed in her day. Often in debt, borrowing money on the security of her plate, she was dependent on an ongoing stream of gifts and loans from the king.

The only surviving records of Elizabeth's Privy Purse expenses date from later in the reign. Nonetheless, many of the sums disbursed must have been duplicated every year. The monetary recognition of the endless presents of food – pippins and puddings, peascods and pomegranates, warden pears and chines of pork. Wine and woodcocks, rabbits, quails and conserves of cherries, a wild boar and tripes. The small practical purchases a great household requires – baskets and bellows, bolts and barehides, two barrels of Rhenish wine and the perpetual 'boathire', for transporting people and property from one palace to another along the great watery highway that was the Thames. There were clothes for herself – a gown of russet velvet and white fustian for socks – and her servants: three doublets of Bruges satin for her footmen at 20d the piece, as well as money to the keeper of her goshawk for meat for his bird and his spaniels (27s 8d).

In Lent, almond butter was brought to her – the rich man's substitute, at a time of year when dairy fats were not allowed. She made many acts of charity. Money to nuns in the Minories, by the Tower, whose abbess had sent her rosewater; the burying of a man who was hanged, and money given to another whose house had burnt down. Support for one of the children who had been 'given' to her, and contributions towards the enclosed life of an anchoress. Funding for one John Pertriche, son of 'Mad Beale', right down to payment for the man who cured him of the French pox.

One story in the Venetian state papers does fit with the conventional picture of Henry's miserliness. On 9 May 1489 the papal envoy wrote to the Pope: 'we have, moreover, opened the moneybox[14] which the king was pleased to have at his court: we found in it £11 11s, which result made our heart sink within us, for there were present the King, the Queen, the mother of the King and the mother of the Queen, besides dukes, earls and marquesses, and other lords and ambassadors, so that we expected to have far more.'

The reference to Elizabeth Woodville is interesting. After her exile or retreat to Bermondsey she is supposed to have visited court on only one or two specific occasions, one of them being the visit of a kinsman the following November at the time of her daughter's next confinement. But this extra, less well-known record of her presence some six months earlier suggests that, while she undoubtedly did live largely in retirement, her public appearances might have been more frequent, if not always conspicuously noted.

In autumn 1489 Elizabeth of York did indeed take to her chamber again. (It is possible she had also given birth, the year before, to another son, Edward, who lived only a few hours. Other sources suggest the birth of such a child but set the date considerably later.)

> Allhallows-eve the Queen took to her chamber at Westminster royally accompanied; that is to say, with my lady the Queen's mother, the Duchess of Norfolk, and many other going before her . . . the Queen's chamberlain, Sir Richard Pole [the son of Margaret Beaufort's half-sister], in very good words, desired in the Queen's name all her people to pray that God would send her a good hour, and so she entered into her chamber which was hanged and ceiled with rich cloth of blue arras with fleur-de-lis of gold.

This time Elizabeth flouted the protocol her mother-in-law had enshrined by receiving a great embassy from France, which included a member of her mother's Luxembourg family, after her retreat and 'in her own Chamber. There was with her her Mother Queen Elizabeth, and my Lady the King's Mother, but there entered no more than been afore rehearsed [some four dignitaries], saving my Lord the Queen's Chamberlain, and the Garter Principal King of Arms', said the chronicler reassuringly. Elizabeth's daughter was born just as her tiny son Arthur was being made knight and invested as Prince of Wales. The baby was named for her godmother and grandmother Margaret Beaufort.

Eighteen months later came another, even more significant, confinement for Elizabeth. Prince Henry, the future Henry VIII, was born on 28 June 1491. But the months immediately following brought the start of a new trouble, which would haunt the new dynasty for the rest of the decade.

TWENTY-TWO

The Edge of Traitors

Abate the edge of traitors, gracious Lord,
That would reduce these bloody days again.
And make poor England weep in streams of blood!
Richard III, 5.5

The autumn of 1491 saw the appearance of Perkin Warbeck, a pretender to the throne far more dangerous than Lambert Simnel. Bernard André and Polydore Vergil, with their Tudor-inspired hatred of Margaret of Burgundy, suggest that Warbeck may have had his birth in that country – certainly birth in his adult, royal identity. Bacon tellingly uses the imagery of witchcraft, saying that 'the magic and curious arts' of the Lady Margaret 'raised up the ghost' of the boy Duke of York to walk and vex King Henry. But it was once again Ireland that first saw a pretender hailed as Richard, Duke of York, Elizabeth Woodville's younger son – a claim that, however improbable, cannot be conclusively disproved even today.

By the summer of 1492, when Elizabeth of York was preparing to give birth to another baby, Perkin Warbeck was in France, treated as an English prince and used (just as Henry Tudor had been used before him) as a tool of diplomacy. Indeed, the tall, glowing young man – so like his supposed

277

father Edward IV – seems to have owed a lot of his credibility to the fact that he looked and behaved like a king or at least a prince. The same, at the beginning of his reign, had been said of Henry.

At this timely moment, in early June, Elizabeth Woodville died at her convent in Bermondsey. The event cannot have been wholly unexpected; now in her mid-fifties, she had been predeceased by almost all of her many siblings. On 10 April she had made her will:

> Item. I bequeath my body to be buried with the body of my lord at Windsor, without pompous interring or costly expenses done thereabout. Item. Whereas I have no worldly goods to do the queen's grace a pleasure with, neither to reward any of my children according to my heart and mind, I beseech God Almighty to bless her grace, with all her noble issue; and, with as good a heart and mind as may be, I give her grace my blessing, and all the aforesaid my children.

She willed that 'such small stuff and goods as I have be disposed truly in the contentation of my debts, and for the health of my soul, as far as they will extend . . .'. Less than a decade earlier, walls had to be broken down to get her extensive goods into sanctuary.

A surviving manuscript record shows that her burial was certainly as unostentatious as she had requested. 'On Whit-Sunday, the queen-dowager's corpse was conveyed by water to Windsor, and there privily, through the little park, conducted into the castle, without any ringing of bells or receiving of the dean . . . and so privily, about eleven of the clock, she was buried, without any solemn dirge done for her obit.' The only gentlewoman to accompany her was one Mistress Grace, described as 'a bastard daughter of king

Edward IV'; which suggests Elizabeth Woodville had enough generosity of spirit to make a friend of a girl she might well have resented.

'On the Monday', so the account records disapprovingly, 'nothing was done solemnly for her' except the provision of a hearse 'such as they use for the common people', with wooden candlesticks and tapers 'of no great weight'. Elizabeth of York was not able to take charge of her mother's funeral, having entered her confinement (she would call her new daughter Elizabeth). On the Tuesday (the next daughter, Cecily, also being absent and represented by her husband) the three remaining unmarried daughters of Elizabeth Woodville arrived – Anne, Katherine and even eleven-year-old Bridget from a Dartford convent where she had been placed. With them came Elizabeth Woodville's daughter-in-law the Marchioness of Dorset and her niece; also the gentlemen, led by Dorset himself. Finally the dirge got under way.

'But neither at the dirge were twelve poor men clad in black, but a dozen divers old men, and they held old torches and torches' ends.' Still, the queen dowager herself had said that she wanted it that way. The grave had spared Elizabeth Woodville the agonising doubts that Warbeck's mounting credit and credibility might have inspired. We shall never know what conversations Elizabeth of York and her husband had about the pretender, but a century or so later Bacon would have Warbeck in his character of Richard, declaring that on his delivery from the Tower he resolved to wait for his uncle's death 'and then to put myself into my sister's hands, who was next heir to the crown'. It is an interesting hint that Elizabeth of York's reaction to this putative brother was a matter for speculation even in this near-contemporary day.

At the beginning of October 1492 Henry launched an expedition against France – to protect his former refuge of Brittany from possible annexation by the French, and to punish them for their support of Warbeck. Margaret Beaufort, unsurprisingly, made a major financial contribution. In the event Henry spent only a brief time across the Channel: like Edward years earlier, he was happy to be bought off by a sizeable French pension. Before he sailed from England he did acknowledge that Elizabeth of York's finances were 'insufficient to maintain the Queen's dignity', and gave her reversion rights to her grandmother's property whenever Cecily Neville eventually died.

So Elizabeth was left as her mother had been left, and government was nominally vested in her six-year-old son. Arthur was at Westminster, while Elizabeth seems to have been with her other children at Eltham, the nursery for her younger children; handy for London, an old favourite of her father's and near her own favourite residence of Greenwich. But her absence from Westminster at this moment shows that she did not have even the limited powers that had been invested in Elizabeth Woodville long before. Nor did Margaret Beaufort, presumably: the times were changing and not, for half a century yet, in favour of a woman's authority.

In November a major new player appeared on stage in the Perkin Warbeck drama. It was, predictably, Margaret of Burgundy, who some believed had been behind Warbeck from the very start, but who now met him openly. Despite Maximilian's accord with Henry, the Low Countries had never ceased to be a refuge for Henry's enemies. Nor had Margaret ceased to have contact with Ireland and Scotland, those traditional springboards for an English invasion. She had, indeed, been planning – spreading the rumours that a prince survived, rallying support – even before Warbeck appeared in public. Vergil said that she had found the boy herself – a suitable candidate for instruction. Bacon wrote that she had long had spies out to look for 'handsome and graceful youths to make

Plantagenets'. The French king told his Scottish counterpart that Warbeck had been 'preserved many years secretly' by Margaret. In a letter to the Pope, begging for recognition of her 'nephew's' claims, she gave a garbled version of the biblical story of Prince Joash in the second Book of Kings, snatched from harm to be brought up secretly in the house of an aunt. Certainly Warbeck was now welcomed in Burgundy as a prince, and as Margaret's close kin. Indeed, Vergil wrote that she received him 'as though he had been revived from the dead . . . so great was her pleasure that the happiness seemed to have disturbed the balance of her mind'.

Margaret wrote to Queen Isabella in Spain that when Warbeck/Richard appeared in Burgundy she immediately recognised him as her nephew. She had been told of his existence when he was in Ireland, but had at that time thought the tale 'ravings and dreams'; then he had been identified in France by men she sent who would have known him 'as easily as his mother or his nurse'. When Margaret herself at last met him, she said, 'I recognised him as easily as if I had last seen him yesterday or the day before . . . . He did not have just one or another sign of resemblance, but so many and so particular that hardly one person in ten, in a hundred or even in a thousand might be found who would have marks of the same kind. . . .' She had, however, last seen the actual Duke of York in England when he was a child, some dozen years earlier.

'I indeed for my part, when I gazed on this only male Remnant of our family – who had come through so many perils and misfortunes – was deeply moved, and out of this natural affection, into which both necessity and the rights of blood were drawing me, I embraced him as my only nephew and my only son.' It was perhaps emotionally important that she was now, after Elizabeth Woodville's death, his only mother. She intended

– as the Latin is translated – to nourish and cherish him. The language was that one might use for a young child.

Warbeck/Richard wrote to Isabella too – vaguely, of the 'certain lord' who had been told to kill him but 'pitying my innocence' had preserved him. He seemed however to have got his 'own' age slightly wrong, though his praise of his 'dearest aunt' rang true enough. Isabella was unimpressed, but concerned about the fresh potential for unrest in the country where her daughter Katherine of Aragon was to marry. She wrote, woman to woman, to Margaret suggesting she should not be taken in. But Isabella's caution would not necessarily be followed by the other rulers of Europe: a prince or pretender could always prove an invaluable pawn of diplomacy.

The news that the Duke of York was alive, said Bacon, 'came blazing and thundering over into England', breeding murmurs of all sorts against the king, and 'chiefly they fell upon the wrong that he did his Queen, and that he did not reign in her right, wherefore they said that God had now brought to light a masculine branch of the house of York that would not be at his courtesy, howsoever he did depress [suppress] his poor lady'.

In 1493 Henry was writing about 'the great malice that the Lady Margaret of Burgundy beareth continually against us', in sending first the 'feigned boy' Lambert Simnel and now another 'feigned lad'. He was invoking a concept popular at the time: that of the she-wolf or, as Edward Hall would later imagine Margaret, the 'dog reverting to her old vomit'. Hall memorably described Margaret as being 'like one forgetting both God and charity' in her malice against Henry, seeking 'to suck his blood and compass his destruction'; not just a she-wolf like Marguerite of Anjou, but a vampire as well. Hall (and Bacon after him) followed Vergil, who claimed that Margaret, driven by 'insatiable hatred and fiery wrath', continually sought Henry's destruction – 'so ungovernable is a woman's nature especially when she is under the influence of envy', he glossed. Vergil was probably swayed by Henry VII's own perception of events, and Henry may well have been influenced by Louis of France – he who had cast doubts on Margaret's chastity even before her marriage, just as he had impugned the chastity of Cecily.

Margaret of Burgundy, Bacon sneered, had 'the spirit of a man and the malice of a woman'. Being 'childless and without any nearer care', she could devote herself to her 'mortal hatred' of Henry and the house of Lancaster: a hatred, Bacon claimed, that she now extended even to Henry's wife, her niece. Certainly Margaret did not seem to regard Elizabeth's role of queen consort as elevating the family's status in any way. Her letter to Isabella had spoken of how her family were 'fallen from the royal summit', suggesting the situation could be redeemed only by a 'male remnant'. Or perhaps she thought that for one who had been, in Vergil's words, 'the means of the king's ascent to the throne', a mere consort's role was inadequate.

By this time Henry had discovered an alternative identity for the supposed prince – Perkin Warbeck, a boatman's son from Tournai. That summer of 1493 an embassy was sent to Burgundy, warning Philip (now old enough to hold at least theoretical rule when his father Maximilian succeeded to the grander title of Holy Roman Emperor) that he was giving house room to an impostor. One of the envoys (Warham, the future archbishop), joked unpleasantly to the childless Margaret that in Simnel and Warbeck she had produced 'two great babes not as normal but fully grown and long in the womb'. While Philip, and probably Maximilian behind him, raised men for the pretender, Margaret provided money. Not that she entirely lost her head over the affair: her 'nephew' was to pay his 'aunt' the remaining part of her dowry as soon as he came into his own – her promised wool rights, the manor of Hunsdon and the town of Scarborough.

In October 1494, in England, Henry VII created his second son Henry Duke of York – the title the younger prince in the Tower had borne. Arthur, as Prince of Wales, had been sent the previous year to take up residence in Ludlow, just as Elizabeth of York's eldest brother had done. Prince Henry's new title was a riposte to Warbeck; perhaps, too, a sop to any disaffected Yorkists and a reminder that through his wife the king had annexed also the Yorkist claim. Celebratory tournaments were designed as a chivalric fantasy centring on the queen, just as earlier tournaments had focused on Elizabeth Woodville and her jousting family. Margaret Beaufort was with the king and queen as they left Woodstock for the ceremonies in the capital; she was still with them three weeks later as they processed away from Westminster.

The queen was prominent in her state, the jousters on the first day wearing her crest as well as the king's livery; but subsequent challengers could be seen in Margaret Beaufort's blue and white livery, and she was one of the ladies who advised on the prizes, which were presented by her namesake, the 'high and excellent princess', little Margaret. In January 1495 Henry offered this daughter[15] in marriage to the king of Scotland – the son of Elizabeth Woodville's erstwhile prospective bridegroom.

The queen's sisters were being married off too; Anne to the grandson of one of Richard III's leading adherents, who might thus be reconciled to Henry's regime; and Katherine, by way of reward, into the notably Lancastrian Courtenay family. Connections of the various women were, after all, still involved in machinations against Henry. In February Sir William Stanley – Margaret Beaufort's brother-in-law, the man whose intervention had made all the difference at Bosworth – was found to have had contact with Warbeck and executed. Later that year the royal couple visited William's brother, Margaret's husband, at Lathom, 'to comfort [the king's] mother, whom he did always tenderly love and revere'.

A servant of Edward's sister Elizabeth had been among those indicted in these years; and several of those in trouble over the Warbeck affair were neighbours of, or had been servants of, Cecily Neville's.[16] Cecily left money in her will to a Master Richard Lessy who had been involved in the Perkin Warbeck affair, specifically to help him pay the fine levied for his trangression, and requested that the king might curtail the charge; several of the others to whom she left legacies had connections with Burgundy and with Duchess Margaret. It showed that Henry could never really feel secure about his wife's Yorkist connections, however amicable their personal relations might be.

On 31 May 1495, at Berkhamsted, Cecily died, being, as her will declared,[17] 'of whole mind and body, loving therefore be it to Jh'u [Jesu]', surrendering her soul into God's hands and the protection of the saints; and her body, subject to Henry VII's permission, to be buried at Fotheringhay beside that of 'my most entirely beloved Lord and husband, father unto my said lord and son [Edward IV]'. She left a series of bequests to the Fotheringhay college – everything from mass books to ecclesiastical vestments – and to the abbey at Syon 'two of the best copes of crimson cloth'.

She asks, as was usual, that any debts should be paid; rather touchingly 'thanking our Lord at the time of making of this my testament [that] to the knowledge of my conscience I am not much in debt'. But it is the personal bequests that are interesting: an acknowledgement to the king; legacies to officers of her household; to 'my daughter of Suffolk' her litter chair with all the 'cushions, horses, and harnesses' belonging to it; to her granddaughter Anne a barge with all its accoutrements and 'the largest bed of bawdekyn [a silk fabric with metal threads, like a less costly cloth of gold], with counterpoint of the same'. Her grandson Prince Arthur, heir apparent to the Tudor dynasty, got her tapestry bed decorated with the Wheel of Fortune.

Cecily's granddaughter and godchild Bridget was left the *Legenda Aurea* on vellum, and her books on Saints Katherine and Matilda. A psalter with a relic of St Christopher went to Elizabeth of York, a portuous or breviary 'with clasps of gold covered with black cloth of gold' to Margaret Beaufort. It was yet another exemplar of how religion forged links between women who might find there a new lease of life after their years of marriage and childbearing were over, and after they were freed from their husbands' enmity.

TWENTY-THREE

Civil Wounds

Now civil wounds are stopped; peace lives again.
That she may long live here, God say amen.
Richard III, 5.5

In late June 1495, Perkin Warbeck's fleet set sail across the Channel for a first invasion attempt. His men landed on the coast near Deal but, lacking support, were forced to set sail again for Ireland; in November he made for Scotland and the court of King James. The two young men took to each other and, as Warbeck settled into the Scottish court, the king even married him to the beautiful Katherine Gordon, his own 'tender cousin'. Warbeck was awaiting more arms from Margaret in Burgundy, but financial support even from that quarter seemed to be drying up since the country's new young ruler, Philip, had withdrawn his support. It was a salutary reminder that cooler issues of broader Burgundian policy and of pay ran alongside Margaret's emotional enthusiasm. In the treaty which, in February 1496, restored the damaged trading relations between Burgundy and England, Margaret was bound over not to give aid to Henry's enemies, and she appeared to comply.

That autumn Elizabeth of York's daughter and namesake had died of 'atrophy', aged three – or 'passed out of this transitory life', as her monument in Westminster Abbey described it. On 18 March 1496 another daughter, Mary, was born.[18]

Amid fears of an invasion, Margaret Beaufort and her son now toured her Dorset estates, winding up at the improved and impressive castle of Corfe, traditionally a Beaufort property. Tensions were still running high. It was in that year that she sent a letter to the Earl of Ormond thanking him for a gift of gloves sent from Flanders – 'right good', she said, but too big for her hand. 'I think the ladies in that parts be great ladies all, and according to their great estates they have great personages' – a crack from the petite Margaret Beaufort about the solidly built Margaret of Burgundy. In September 1496 James of Scotland and his protégé Warbeck rode south with a 1400-strong army; but it was little more than a raiding party and they soon returned across the border.

Henry had instituted new forms of taxation to fund a campaign against Scotland when, in the early summer of 1497, news came of trouble at the opposite end of his kingdom. The Cornishmen were in rebellion against the tax and calling for the dismissal of Henry's money-raisers Morton and Bray – Margaret Beaufort's former men. The news caught the royal party at Sheen; the queen and her son Henry moved to London and Margaret Beaufort's house of Coldharbour. A week later, as news came of the rebels' approach as close as Farnham, Elizabeth of York – like her mother before her, and with her own memories – took to the Tower for refuge. The main battle was as close as Blackheath, only a mile or two from the royal nursery palace of Eltham – but fortunately, on 17 June it was Henry who emerged the victor.

At the end of the summer, however, Warbeck, urged on by James, was back, this time leaving Scotland by sea. His wife set sail with him – shades of Anne and Isabel Neville – which may indicate that Scotland was finally tiring of its puppet princeling; that this was to be a last throw of the dice. They landed in Cornwall, the site of the recent May rebellions, where, sending the ladies to St Michael's Mount for safety, Warbeck/Richard declared himself king.[19] As Henry marched west Elizabeth and her young son went east, on pilgrimage to Walsingham. It got them out of the way of danger, without looking too panicky. But Warbeck seems to have been the one who was really unnerved – by the first fighting, along with the news that Henry was on the way. Fleeing into sanctuary, he was persuaded to surrender and confessed to being a fraud. The confession was widely circulated in Europe: Margaret in Burgundy must have heard it. Coincidentally or otherwise, that summer she was taken ill. Vergil wrote that news of the capture 'made her weep many tears for her prince'.

Warbeck wrote to his real mother, Katherine Warbeque, telling her the story of how he had left home for Antwerp and there been taken into the service of Sir Edward Brampton – the man sent to negotiate a marriage for Richard III in Portugal – who had taken him to that country. From here a new employer, Pregent Meno, had taken him to Ireland where he was first taken for a Plantagenet. It was a curious story, made more curious by the fact that both Brampton and Meno had come into King Henry's service; by the doubt expressed by many that a boatman's son could so convincingly play the prince; and, perhaps, by the handling the pseudo-royal couple received.

Warbeck's wife Katherine Gordon is interesting for the light her treatment[20] casts upon Henry VII, and perhaps on Elizabeth too. Katherine – like Elizabeth Woodville before her – had to be 'much talked to' before she would relinquish the privileges of sanctuary. But from the start it was obvious that she would be dealt with kindly. It may have been just the single most striking example of the way in which women were often regarded as exempt from the penalties levied on their menfolk, or something more personal – a reputation for beauty that had gone before her. Henry's letters spoke of her as being 'in dole' – mourning; and literal mourning, rather than just grief for her husband's capture. This may have been for a lost or stillborn child. When she was able to travel Henry sent black clothes in which she could do so: satin dress, riding cloak – everything down to hose and shoes. Vergil said that when Henry saw her he was much taken or, as Hall put it, 'began then a little to fantasy her person'. His concern took an overtly paternal form, providing all the practical necessities of life as well as sober matrons to accompany her 'because she was but a young woman'.

When Henry (so his pet writer, blind Bernard André, wrote in a private volume for the king's own pleasure) arranged a meeting with her husband, Katherine, 'with a modest and graceful look and singularly beautiful, was brought into the king's presence in an untouched state'. Henry, as André tells it, made a long speech to this quasi-maiden – apparently considered, since the man she thought she had married never existed, to have attained the state of honorary virginity almost as a queen did before her coronation – telling her that life ahead would have 'many possibilities'. As Warbeck was forced to repeat his confession to her Katherine burst out into a torrent of lamentation and recrimination, 'soaked through with a fountain of tears'. Only one man could now be her saviour – Henry himself, naturally.

It was natural that Katherine should be taken into the queen's household, the obvious place for one of her undisputed noble birth. Perhaps, too, there was an implication that there had never been a grain of truth in Warbeck's pretensions, so there was no danger in putting Katherine into a position where she could give Elizabeth dangerous information or conspire with her Yorkist connections in any way. It is probably also true that Henry could now feel sure his wife was too committed to the future of her own offspring to be moved by any older loyalty. Certainly Elizabeth seems to have accepted Katherine as one of her ladies, with the high place appropriate to her rank. If Elizabeth had any other reason for warmth towards the girl who had thought to be her sister-in-law, she concealed it. And if, conversely, she had any suspicion of her husband's feelings for Katherine, it would seem she was prepared, as her mother had done, to turn a blind eye. (After the queen's death – and the funeral at which she laid the fourth pall, right after the queen's sisters – Henry was said to have kept Katherine so close it was rumoured they had married. In fact, remaining in England after Henry's death, she made three more marriages with English gentlemen, retaining a particular friendship for the daughter of Queen Elizabeth's sister Cecily.)

The noble Katherine was one thing. But, extraordinarily, even Warbeck was brought to court and treated with surprising leniency. The Venetian ambassador reported only that he and Katherine were forbidden to sleep together, implying that otherwise he was handled courteously.

It has often been suggested over the years that Perkin Warbeck did indeed have Plantagenet blood in his veins – not as the legitimate Duke of York, but as a Plantagenet bastard. True, Edward IV and his brother Richard had acknowledged other illegitimate children; but the decision to do so must to some degree have depended on the mother's position. And the bastard child of a royal woman might be a different story.

It was thought even at the time that Warbeck might possibly be Margaret of Burgundy's illegitimate son.[21] In 1495 Maximilian had apparently said so, and Maximilian was close to her. This may well have been just another example of a man using a

woman's reputation as an expendable tool of political expedi-
ency – the idea has to be seen in the context both of earlier
slurs on her reputation and of the regularity with which such
slurs were cast upon a woman who transgressed in any way.
But the time of a pregnancy would have been in 1473 when
she had disappeared for two months to the palace of Ten-Noode,
commonly used for recuperation.

Elizabeth of York, who must now have seen Warbeck, though
not necessarily at close quarters, appears never to have made
any public comment (unless her kindness to Katherine Gordon
were a comment of sorts). On 11 October at Woodstock the
family certainly put on a good, united display for the visiting
Venetian envoy, who found Elizabeth 'at the end of the hall,
dressed in cloth of gold', with her mother-in-law on one side
of her and Prince Henry on the other.

Margaret Beaufort was still travelling incessantly with her
son. In the summer of 1498 she and the king were together at
London, Westminster, Sheen and Windsor (where Margaret
ordered brooches for her grandchildren), then on a tour of
eastern counties. Her house was now a gathering place. Her
carver Henry Parker remembered how, when serving her at
New Year, he had twenty-five knights following him; how the
men at her table included her husband and her half-brother
Lord Welles as well as the Bishop of Lincoln, while Cecily Welles
(Elizabeth of York's sister) shared her own cloth of state. 'In
her hall from nine of the clock till it was seven of the clock at
night as fast as one table was up another was set, no poor man
was denied at that said feast of Christmas if he were of any
honesty.' It was an almost royal liberality. Margaret seems to
have had a genuine liking for Cecily, the young woman
who was at once her niece-in-law and (through marriage to
Lord Welles) her sister-in-law, arranging permission for her
to worship with Margaret's own household.

When Lord Welles died, Margaret took care of her; and when she made an unsanctioned second marriage with a man of much lower rank, interceded with the angry king to ensure that Cecily was allowed to keep a good portion of her estates. Both Cecily's daughters died in or before 1499, and maybe Margaret found it easier to relate to those who shared her awareness of sorrow.

Her household had its lighter side, too – she employed a fool named Skyp, for whom high-heeled shoes had to be bought, and 'Reginald the idiot'; gave money to visiting dancers, and turned the house over one Christmas to an 'abbot of misrule'. One April she had a 'house of boughs' built in which to dine. And once she paid a man to go on pilgrimage for her – because she herself was too busy playing cards.

In 1498 the ongoing negotiations for a marriage between Prince Arthur and Katherine of Aragon showed how far into the club of European royalty the Tudors had come. Elizabeth herself wrote to Queen Isabella. To her 'cousin and dearest relation' she 'wished health and the most prosperous increase of her desires'; Katherine she described as 'our common daughter'. 'Hence it is', the letter concluded, 'that, amongst our other cares and cogitations, first and foremost we wish and desire from our heart that we may often and speedily hear of the health and safety of your serenity, and of the health and safety of the aforesaid most illustrious Lady Katherine, who we think of and esteem as our own daughter, than which nothing can be more grateful and acceptable to us.' This arrangement had been another instance of Elizabeth and her mother-in-law working together:

The Queen and the mother of the King wish that the Princess of Wales [Katherine] should always speak French with the Princess Margaret [the daughter of Mary of Burgundy, raised in France] who is now in Spain, in order to learn the language, and to be able to converse in it when she comes to England. This is necessary, because these ladies do not understand Latin, and much less, Spanish. They also wish that the Princess of Wales should accustom herself to drink wine. The water of England is not drinkable, and even if it were, the climate would not allow the drinking of it.

That year the Spanish envoy de Ayala was reporting to Ferdinand and Isabella that a marriage between the Scottish king and Henry's daughter had many 'inconveniences'. The English king said that his wife and mother-in-law joined forces to protect their daughter and granddaughter Margaret, who 'has not yet completed the ninth year of her age, and is so delicate and weak [*feminina*] that she must be married much later than other young ladies. Thus it would be necessary to wait at least another nine years.' Besides his own doubts, Henry said, 'the Queen and my mother are very much against this marriage. They say if the marriage were concluded, we should be obliged to send the Princess directly to Scotland, in which case they fear the King of Scots would not wait, but injure her, and endanger her health.' If her granddaughter and namesake took after Margaret Beaufort in stature, the elder lady was clearly determined she should not share her fate.

The year 1498 also saw an attempt by Perkin Warbeck to escape. Vergil wrote that friends pushed him into it and his wife may have urged it – but it is also possible that he had been lured into it by servants of King Henry, now anxious (since Warbeck's presence was proving a hindrance to the Spanish match) to find an excuse to do away with him. Afterwards he was kept in much stricter conditions, and indeed moved to the Tower. This move was shortly followed by the arrival of a trade delegation from Burgundy headed by the Bishop of Cambrai and bearing, so said the Spanish ambassador, a formal apology to King Henry from Margaret, perhaps humbling herself in a last attempt to get clemency for her protégé. The bishop asked if he might see the young man. When taxed with having deceived his benefactress, Warbeck 'swore to God that Duchess Madame Margaret knew as well as himself that he was not the son of King Edward'. The Spaniard reported that Henry wanted to proceed against the duchess, but that Philip of Burgundy and his new wife would not allow it. If Margaret were a mother of sorts to Warbeck she had played that part, too, to Philip; and now Burgundy's ruler stood by her.

At the end of February 1499, Elizabeth of York gave birth to another son at Greenwich. Margaret Beaufort was again the godmother, making generous presents to the midwife and nurses, and a christening gift worth £100. But maybe some frailty in the baby Edmund – who died sixteen months later – was linked to concern over his mother's health. The Spanish envoy wrote to his monarchs that 'There had been much fear that the life of the Queen would be in danger, but the delivery, contrary to expectation, has been easy. The christening was very splendid, and the festivities such as though an heir to the Crown had been born.'

In 1499 the great Renaissance scholar Erasmus was taken by his friend Thomas More to visit the royal nursery at Eltham, and described what he found: nine-year-old Henry ('already with a certain royal demeanour'), flanked on his right by eleven-year-old Margaret, and 'on the left Mary was playing, a child of four. Edmund was an infant in arms.' It sounds as solid a family group as, a generation before, the York family; although, as in the York family, the eldest son had been taken to live outside his mother's direct care and be trained in kingship. With the threats from pretenders receding, the Tudors seemed to be breaking through into a new era of stability. Perhaps now Margaret Beaufort felt she could safely turn her attention elsewhere.

At the turn of the century Margaret spent lavishly on a new series of buildings against the gates of her principal residence, Collyweston in Northamptonshire: a council chamber, a building where those who came to deal with legal matters could receive attention without impinging on the domestic side of the household, and a prison. Margaret Beaufort's house was now not only a palace – with jewel house and presence chamber, library and pleasure grounds – but an administrative centre for the king's authority in the Midlands and further north.

In earlier reigns a measure of control in the north had been deputed by Edward IV to his brother Richard, and by Richard to his nephew John. But Henry VII was an only child, and in the absence of other near relations he turned, as so often before, to his mother. Her brief may have been different from the one given to military men, but there is no doubt that Margaret's was the ultimate authority in deciding the fate of every litigant who came before her council, whether it were a question of money owed between individuals or alleged disrespectful remarks made about the Tudor dynasty. In the early sixteenth century, and again in the early seventeenth, debates at the Inns of Court in London cited Margaret when suggesting that a '*feme sole*' could, through royal commission, be made a justice of the peace; the king's attorney declared that he had seen 'many arbitraments' made by her.

With men like the old 'Kingmaker' Earl of Warwick and Lord Hastings gone, power in the Midlands had fallen largely into the hands of the Stanley family. But the Stanleys were proving themselves dubiously trustworthy, despite being his mother's in-laws. Henry needed someone on whom he could place complete reliance. That may be one reason why in 1499 Margaret Beaufort took another step towards independence.

At the beginning of the year, with the permission of her husband Stanley, the Earl of Derby, she undertook a vow of chastity. To do so would not be an unusual choice for a widow: in these years an increasing number were choosing to become a vowess, which entailed undergoing a ceremony of cloaking and veiling before a bishop and taking a vow of chastity, but without going to live in a convent, taking vows of poverty and obedience, or renouncing the goods and concerns of the lay state. But for a woman with a living husband, Margaret's action was highly unusual.

She was now basing her establishment at Collyweston rather than at Lathom or Knowsley, the houses she had shared with him. There was no actual breach in their relationship – rooms were reserved for him at Collyweston – but he was in no position to resist. Not only was this a recognition of a state of affairs that had probably long existed, it was also to some degree a matter of state, since Margaret's new administrative role required that she should be associated only with those of certain loyalty.

Also from this year, instead of signing her letters 'M Richmond' Margaret took to signing them with the quasi-regal 'Margaret R' – the 'R', of course, capable of being interpreted either as Richmond or as Regina. It was as if she were now crowned queen dowager, as well as being independent of any husband – even the one who had given her her son. But a letter to Henry probably written at this time is signed, from Collyweston, 'your faithful true bedewoman, and humble mother, Margaret R'. There was certainly no diminution in the ardently expressed devotion which breathes from the document itself – addressed to 'My own sweet and most dear King and all my worldly joy'.

The bulk of the letter is concerned with 'my matter which so long hath hanged' – a decades-old attempt to extract from the French ducal house of Orléans a sum of ransom money the Beauforts believed was still owed to Margaret's grandfather. But there was still time among the information and instruction to assure Margaret's 'dear heart' that if she should finally receive the money, 'there shall never be that or any good I have but it shall be yours . . . And Our Lord give you as long good life, health and joy, as your most noble heart can desire, with as hearty blessings as our Lord hath gven me the power to give you.' Margaret's increased independence had only heightened her attachment.

In May the proxy marriage between Arthur and Katherine of Aragon had taken place, but Katherine's Spanish parents were still worried about any threat to the English throne from 'doubtful royal blood'. Nor, all too visibly, were all the old York interests reconciled to the Tudor dynasty: in July Suffolk, the younger son of Edward IV's sister Elizabeth and younger brother of the Earl of Lincoln who had died fighting for Lambert Simnel, decamped abroad. He was persuaded back – this time – and Bacon said that, though he went to Flanders, Margaret of Burgundy was 'growing by often failing in her alchemy weary of her experiments'. But shortly afterwards another young man appeared claiming to be Clarence's son the Earl of Warwick. Henry realised his only safety lay in ridding himself of any such claim.

On 23 November 1499 Perkin Warbeck was executed, as shortly afterwards was the real Warwick, Queen Elizabeth's unfortunate cousin. Henry said the executions were necessary 'because the Duchess Margaret of Burgundy and the King of the Romans [Maximilian] would not stop believing that Perkin was the true and legitimate son of King Edward, and Duke of York; and the duchess had given him so much authority and credit, that it had to be done'. The fact was, of course, that it had to be done to facilitate the Spanish marriage, which, it was hoped, would move the Tudor dynasty on into the next century.

To Margaret in Burgundy Henry's words must have cut deep – as, of course, they were meant to do. At some point in that year she commissioned a painting, derived from Rogier van der Weyden's painting of the Deposition. There are plenty of other portraits of Margaret from which to recognise her long-nosed face: she is the Mary Magdalene lamenting at the feet of the deposed Christ, her crimson velvet cloak and cloth of gold robe caught by a belt trimmed with daisies – marguerites – and ornamented by a white rose. Indeed, her whole posture seems designed to draw attention to the flower which had become Warbeck's symbol in his royal identity.

TWENTY-FOUR

Like a Queen Inter Me

> yet like
> A queen and daughter to a king inter me.
> *Henry VIII*, 4.2

As the new century dawned, a new generation would be coming to the fore. Among Henry and Elizabeth's children Prince Arthur was now thirteen and Margaret ten, fast approaching the age of marriageability; while the increased geographical distance of Margaret Beaufort from the court may have come as a relief to her daughter-in-law. In May Elizabeth went with Henry to Calais for forty days. It was partly to escape the plague, especially bad that year, and partly a matter of diplomacy: a meeting had been planned with Philip of Burgundy. The king took ushers, chaplains, squires, a herald, clerks, grooms and pages as well as guards – and so did she.

A month later the royal couple met Philip outside the walls of Calais at St Peter's church, decorated for the occasion with tapestries and with scented flowers strewn on the floor. Philip had recently married Katherine of Aragon's elder sister Juana; a new tie between Burgundy and the new English dynasty to replace Duchess Margaret's adherence to the old one. The Spanish envoy reported that: 'The King and the Archduke had a very long conversation, in which the Queen afterwards joined. The interview was very solemn, and attended with great splendour.'

The royal couple landed back in Dover on 16 June, but their pleasure at returning home was short-lived. Three days later their baby son Edmund died at Hatfield, and the heartbreakingly tiny coffin had to be carried through the London streets to a royal burial in Westminster Abbey.

There is, for once, no record of Margaret Beaufort having joined the Calais party. The Spanish ambassador had commented on the speed with which the trip was arranged: so perhaps Margaret was simply at Collyweston, too far away to join the party and outside the plague zone. If there was any element of her being left behind to deal with domestic affairs in Henry's absence she may have been determined not to be wholly left out, for early next year she was writing her own letter from Calais 'this day of St Anne's, that I did bring into this world my good and gracious prince, king and only beloved son'.

Once again, her letter was addressed to 'My dearest and only desired joy in this world', and signed as from Henry's 'humble servant, bedewoman, and mother'. The first part of the document concerned, again, what Henry had next to do in support of his mother's long-standing Orléans claim, pursuance of which may have been what brought her across the Channel. 'I wish, my dear heart, an [if] my fortune be to recover it [the money], I trust you shall well perceive I shall deal towards you as a kind, loving mother; and, if I should never have it, yet your kind dealing it is to me a thousand times more than all that good I can recover.' It was as if the common pursuit of money (and the power – or security – that came with it) had evolved into a shared language between mother and son.

In the same letter Margaret asked her son to enter into a small subterfuge to help her maintain good relations with her husband Stanley. Stanley's son, who held offices on her lands in Kendal, had been retaining Margaret's tenants to himself; rather than claim her own rights directly but tactlessly, she suggested the king send her a letter ordering that all her tenants be retained only in the name of little Henry, Duke of York, which would be 'a good excuse for me to my lord and husband'. Perhaps, now Margaret was officially independent of him, Stanley was feeling a little jealous of his rights.

In May 1501 the Portuguese ambassador was writing home: 'the queen was supposed to be with child; but her apothecary told me that a Genoese physician affirmed that she was pregnant, yet it was not so; she has much embonpoint and large breasts.'

Elizabeth too had troubles with her extended family. In August 1501 her cousin Suffolk decamped again, this time permanently, and made his way inevitably into the Burgundian sphere of influence. Caught up in the fall-out were Elizabeth's nephew Dorset (the son of her half-brother, now succeeded to his father's dignities) and her brother-in-law Courtenay, who was arrested and sent to the Tower. The queen's financial records show her taking on responsibility for her sister Katherine and her Courtenay children: payment for their 'diets' and servants (two women and a groom at 14s 4d a week) for bringing them to London, for their rockers, for their doctor – and, when medicine failed, for the burying of one small boy.

Suffolk's timing was particularly galling in that it all but coincided with Katherine of Aragon's long-awaited arrival in the country. Elizabeth's officers were involved at every stage of her grand arrival in London from Plymouth, where she had landed. The ceremony was to be extraordinary, but Henry the puppet master couldn't wait for the curtain to go up on his play. He hastily took his son Arthur south to intercept the Spanish bride on her journey – against the protests of her scandalised staff, who declared she had gone to bed. On his return to Richmond the king immediately reported back: 'he was met by the Queen's Grace, whom he ascertained and made privy to the acts and demeanour between himself, the Prince, and the Princess, and how he liked her person and behaviour.' Margaret Beaufort's *Book of Hours* recorded the progress of Katherine's journey, and her town house at Coldharbour was being fitted out with expensive fabrics and other luxuries to entertain the wedding party. New ovens, freshly glazed windows, new liveries and Beaufort badges for the servants, and a carpet of 'imagery work' for Margaret's own chamber had been ordered. Her comfortable London house even boasted a conservatory, to provide fresh herbs in the winter.

On 10 November the king and queen left Richmond on their separate barges for Baynard's Castle, to be at hand for the festivities. On 12 November Katherine entered London, with an escort of lords. The king and Prince Arthur watched from a haberdasher's house; and, so another contemporary document, *The Receyt of the Ladie Kateryne*, described it, 'in another chamber stood the Queen's Good Grace, my Lady the King's Mother, My Lady Margaret, my Lady her sister [Mary], with many other ladies of the land, not in very open sight, like as the King's Grace did in his manner and party'. What Elizabeth saw as she peeked out of the window was a blooming fifteen-year-old with 'fair auburn' hair, and 'rich apparel on her body after the manner of her country', and 'a little hat fashioned like a cardinal's hat of a pretty braid with a lace of gold'.

Next afternoon Katherine was taken to Baynard's Castle, with a 'right great assembly', to meet Queen Elizabeth, who welcomed her 'with pleasure and goodly communication', dancing and 'disportes'. On 14 November the king and queen – with the king's mother – stood 'in secret manner' in St Paul's to watch the wedding ceremony from behind a lattice.

It was arranged that the bridal couple should process along a walkway six feet above the ground to the specially constructed stage where their marriage would be solemnised – so that everyone could see.

Elizabeth watched while her son Henry escorted the bride into the church and her sister Cecily carried Katherine's train. The Duchess of Norfolk led those who prepared the bed. Later, what did or did not happen in it would become a source of great controversy: Arthur (so it was reported almost thirty years later) boasted the next morning that he had 'been this night in the midst of Spain' but Katherine declared that she had remained as 'untouched and pure' as when she came from her mother's belly. But at the time no one seems to have doubted that everything had gone as it should.

The celebrations proceeded as custom dictated, with mass followed by tournaments and pageants, dancing and feasting. At one moment the ten-year-old Henry, 'perceiving himself to be encumbered with his clothes', cast off his gown and danced in his jacket 'in so goodly and pleasant manner that it was to the King and Queen right great and singular pleasure'. At the Sunday banquet Elizabeth, with her sisters and of course her mother-in-law, sat at a table in the upper part of the Parliament Chamber, 'the table of most reputation of all the tables in the Chamber' – another reminder that this chivalric world was hers by virtue not only of her sex but of her family history. After more tournaments and more spectacles, on the following Friday an armada of barges transported the royal party and their attendants to Richmond.

The new Tudor palace of Richmond had been built on the site of the palace of Sheen, destroyed by fire in 1497. Its richly decorated rooms, the royal apartments glowing with gold leaf offering both luxury and a new measure of privacy, looked out on to gardens of topiary and statues of heraldic beasts, 'the which gardens were apparelled pleasantly for his Highness and certain Lords there ready set, some with chess, and some with tables, byles [*sic*], dice and cards. The place of butts was ready for archers; and there were bowling alleys and other pleasant and goodly disports for every person as they would choose and desire.' It was an ideal place in which to continue the festivities. The wedding party watched as, on a specially rigged platform, a Spaniard showed off 'many wondrous and delicious points of tumbling, dancing and other sleights'. After evensong and supper, the hall was decked out with carpets and cloth of gold cushions, and a great display of plate. A richly decorated portable stage in the shape of a tower was dragged in by sea horses: it was occupied by ladies in disguise and a choir of children. Coneys and white doves were set free to run or fly about the hall, to everyone's 'great laughter and disport'. After 'courtly rounds and pleasant dances' came the void of 'goodly spices and wine', served by a host of nobles.

That account, preserved by Leland, was written to praise, but it does paint an impressive picture. It is miles away from the days when a fleeing Marguerite of Anjou, another foreign princess brought over to become England's queen, had been reduced to living off a single herring. That was the point, presumably.

The new couple set out for Arthur's seat at Ludlow just before Christmas and only a few weeks later, in January 1502, Richmond saw the celebration of Princess Margaret's marriage to the king of Scotland. After mass in the new palace chapel, the queen's great chamber was the site of the proxy wedding. Once again there is no mention of Margaret Beaufort being present, though the party did include little Princess Mary.

King, queen and princess were asked whether they knew of any impediment to the match. Margaret, according to the account of the Somerset Herald, 'wittingly and of deliberate mind having twelve years complete in age' affirmed that she contracted the match; and 'incontinently', after the ceremony was concluded, 'the Queen took her daughter the Queen of Scots by the Hand, and dined both at one Mess covered [using covered dishes]'. Two queens together: it is a pity Elizabeth Woodville could not be there. Jousts and a supper banquet followed. Next morning the new queen of Scots came into her mother's great chamber and 'by the voice of' the officer of arms gave thanks to all the noblemen who had jousted for her,[22] and distributed praise and prizes 'by the advice of the ladies of the court'. Margaret was left in her mother's charge, but it was agreed she would be sent north by the beginning of September 1503.

But three months after the wedding came tragedy. On 2 April 1502 Prince Arthur died at Ludlow after a short illness. The letter arrived at Greenwich so late in the night that the council did not immediately inform the king but summoned his confessor, who broke the news early next day.

> When his Grace understood that sorrowful heavy tidings, he sent out for the Queen, saying, that he and his Queen would take the painful sorrows together. After that she was come and saw the king her Lord, and that natural and painful sorrow, as I have heard say, she with full great and constant comfortable words besought his Grace, that he would first after God, remember the weal of his own noble person, the comfort of his realm, and of her. She then said that my Lady his Mother had never no more children but him only, and, that God by his Grace had ever preserved him, and brought him where that he was. Over that, how God had left him yet a fair Prince, two fair Princesses, and that God is where he was and we are both young enough [to have more children] . . .

After that she was departed and come to her own Chamber, natural and motherly remembrance of that great loss smote her so sorrowful to the heart, that those that were about her were fain to send for the king to comfort her. Then his Grace of true gentle and faithful love, in good heart came and relieved her, and showed her how wise counsel she had given him before; and he for his part would thank God for his son, and would she should do in like wise.

It was positive evidence of Henry and Elizabeth's relationship.

Katherine of Aragon, the youthful widow, was left in painful uncertainty about her fate; she herself was said to be 'suffering' – in other words, ill. It was Elizabeth who sent 'a litter of black velvet with black cloth' to bring her back to the capital by slow stages (there was, after all, the possibility of a pregnancy). By late May she had reached Croydon, and Elizabeth was careful to remain in reassuring contact for all that she herself was planning to journey in the other direction.

That summer Elizabeth went on a progress into Wales, although she must surely have known that, at thirty-six, she was once again pregnant. She and the king had now lost two of their three sons within the space of a year, and even if she had decided that the time for childbearing was past it may now have appeared worth the risk. The timing of her journey does seem odd, given that she had no particular history of long solitary trips, but perhaps all the arrangements were in place before she knew of her condition. An event that occurred in late spring may possibly have played a part in Elizabeth's desire to spend some time away from court. On 6 May one Sir James Tyrell was executed in connection with the Suffolk conspiracies, and his death paved the way for subsequent declarations that he had in his last days confessed to having, at Richard III's instigation, murdered the Princes in the Tower.[23] If such a confession were indeed made, and if Elizabeth believed it, it may have stirred up painful memories. If she had any cause to doubt it – as many have done – it could have operated on her yet more powerfully.

Before Elizabeth even set out from Woodstock she was unwell, but she still managed to depart in early August. Choosing this moment to visit the part of her husband's realm where her son the Prince of Wales had died a few months earlier might, to modern minds, seem linked to her grief for him. But whether sixteenth-century parents, in an age of rearing at one remove for the high-born and frequent child mortality for all, had the kind of relationship with their children that is commonplace today is uncertain. In any case Elizabeth visited not Ludlow but Raglan, home of the Herbert family. William Herbert, Earl of Pembroke, had raised Henry Tudor as a boy; but now his son was married to the queen's cousin Anne, daughter of the Duke of Buckingham and of the queen's aunt Katherine Woodville, Anne's sister Elizabeth Stafford being one of the queen's chief ladies.

At Raglan Castle Elizabeth may have found some escape from recent strains, including the myriad minor complications of the actual journey as recorded in her Privy Purse expenses: repairs for her litter; local guides; twenty pairs of shoes for her footmen – it was a long way to walk. There were grooms and ostlers to be organised, and arrangements to be made for food and drink along the way. The expenses mention a cart and 'load of stuff' which had to travel overland on the journey home, rather than crossing the Severn. The effort it took to carry a queen and her retinue was staggering: not just the provisioning of what was effectively a small army on the march, not just the hasty upgrading of the houses where she was to sleep, but arrangements for the jewels and robes which maintained the queen's majesty.

These Privy Purse expenses, from 1502–3, provide a rare glimpse into daily life and emotional reality. In December by Elizabeth's 'commandment' three yards of cloth were given 'to a woman that was norice [nurse] to the Prince brother to the Queen's grace'. In the same month 12 pence were given to a man who said Earl Rivers (Elizabeth Woodville's brother Anthony) had lodged in his house just before his death. Alms were bestowed twice that year on an old servant of King Edward's; and there were entries for upkeep of the queen's sister Bridget in her convent. The records detail payment to a messenger carrying a command from the queen in April 1502 that the Duchess of Norfolk should receive the wife of Edmund de la Pole 'late Earl of Suffolk' – Elizabeth's traitorous cousin, who had rebelled against Elizabeth's husband. There were payments, of course, for the maintenance of the Courtenay children, whose mother was the queen's sister Katherine but whose father had been implicated in the Suffolk rebellions. A queen was supposed to be the caring face of her husband's regime and of course Elizabeth would care for her family; there was no suspicion of any insurgency. But all the same, one wishes that comparable records had survived for other years, so that we could know whether this kind of support to old Yorkists had been her standard practice, or whether it was new in any way.

A great many of the entries record only part payment from Elizabeth – to tailors, saddlers, goldsmiths – and some of the money was long due. Her gowns were being mended and she bought shoes with cheap tin buckles; she was pledging plate and borrowing money. Henry may have been keeping her short of funds – or perhaps such details reflect the casual relationship with cash of the aristocracy in any century.

The Privy Purse expenses end with a list of payments to women: a pension to the queen's sister Katherine, a sum to her sister Anne's husband for her keep. There were salaries to some half-dozen more ranging from Elizabeth Stafford (£33 6s 8d) to Agnes Dean, the queen's laundress (66s 8d) and the rockers of Katherine Courtenay's children. The lists reveal a web of female connections. Besides payments to those who had been kind to her mother's family, there are payments to some who would ease her daughters' way. The Dame Jane Guildford who received £23 6s 8d in Elizabeth's final wage bill would become one of Margaret Beaufort's close attendants and then, a decade later, would escort Elizabeth's daughter Mary to marry the old king of France; this was the same 'mother Guildford' for whose continued company and counsel Mary would beg hysterically.

Black clothing was paid for in June 1502 after the death of Prince Arthur, and in connection with her expected child, offerings were made at the time of the Feast of the Blessed Virgin on 7 and 8 December; the 13th lists a reward to a monk who brought to the queen 'Our Lady girdle', traditionally worn by women in childbirth. She had ordered a 'rich bed' decorated with red and white roses and with clouds, had purchased linen and interviewed childbed attendants. Then she took boat to Richmond for Christmas; there she played cards, listened to music and paid a messenger who had brought a gift from her mother-in-law. That season, Henry's pet astrologer William Parron had beautifully illustrated and bound what must at the time have seemed a suitable and seasonal prophecy: that Henry would father many sons and Elizabeth live until she was eighty. It was not to be.

Elizabeth spent one January week at Hampton Court, but on the 26th she went to the Tower. On 2 February she gave birth to a baby girl in what would seem a premature delivery. The Privy Purse expenses record the payment that gives the first urgent alarm: 'Item to James Nattres for his costs going into Kent for Doctor Hallysworth physician to come to the Queen by the King's commandment.' There were entries for boat hire from the Tower to Gravesend and back: for two watermen to wait there while the doctor was hastily fetched; and for horse hire and guides 'by night and day'. There is no record of whether the birth itself went smoothly, of how any fever first came upon her, of any attempted remedies. But on 11 February 1503 she died. It was her thirty-seventh birthday.

Elizabeth's body, once sealed in lead by the king's plumber, was placed in a wooden chest for its progress through the London streets to Westminster. No expense was spared for the ceremony, or for the velvet-clad effigy[24] which would be placed on her coffin. 'Item to Master Lawrence for carving of the head with Fedrik his mate, xiij*s* iiii*d*. Item to Wechon Kerver and Hans van Hooh for carving of the two hands, iiij*s* . . . Item for vij small sheep skins for the body . . . ij*s* iiij*d*.'

And Elizabeth was to have the grandest of resting places, even though work on the building which was to house her tomb had begun only weeks before. At the beginning of the century Henry VII had commissioned a wonderful new Lady Chapel; a monument to his family designed, he hoped, ultimately to house the body of Henry VI, canonised into a Lancastrian saint. The old chapel on the site had been pulled down and also, John Stow wrote, an adjoining tavern called, ironically, the White Rose. The first stone had been laid on 24 January 1503. It would be another fifteen years before the tomb that Elizabeth would share with her husband was finally completed; in the meantime her body was placed in a temporary vault in the crossing of the Abbey, in front of the high altar.

As always, there are stories to be deduced from the records of the burial ceremonies. Though the queen's sisters Katherine and Anne took a prominent part in the funeral procession

Bridget, the youngest, must still have been at her convent at Dartford; and Cecily, though next in age to Elizabeth, was absent either for the offence her second marriage had caused the king or perhaps because of the sheer distance of her residence. Instead, place in the procession after Katherine and Anne went to Lady Katherine Gordon, the widow of Perkin Warbeck, by virtue of her own connections to Scottish royalty.

King Henry's retreat into grief was profound and he became seriously ill. Margaret Beaufort moved into Richmond to take care of her son, ordering medicines for him and a sustaining supply of sweet wine for herself. Thomas More's *A Rueful Lamentation of the Death of Queen Elizabeth* vividly imagined Elizabeth's farewell to the world.

> If worship might have kept me, I had not gone.
> If wit might have me saved, I needed not fear.
> If money might have helped, I lacked none.
> But O good God what vaileth all this gear?
> When death is come thy mighty messenger,
> Obey we must, there is no remedy,
> Me hath he summoned, and lo now here I lie.

Besides having Elizabeth bid a respectful farewell to Margaret Beaufort, and a heartbreakingly affectionate one to her children, More's poem also warned King Henry, in curiously modern terms, that: 'Erst were you father, and now must ye supply/The mother's part also.' He may not have found it easy. Even in adulthood his son Henry VIII, who evinced little sign of warm feeling towards his father, remembered his mother's death bitterly enough to recall that 'hateful intelligence' as a standard for melancholy. In the wake of Elizabeth's death there must have been adjustments all round in a diminished family. But as the months passed, life went on.

In summer 1503 the thirteen-year-old Princess Margaret was sent north, as promised, to finalise her marriage to James of Scotland. On 27 June she and her father travelled from Richmond to Margaret Beaufort's Collyweston, whose gardens had been extended and fitted out with new summerhouses to entertain the royal party. On 8 July she set out again, to be crowned in Edinburgh on 3 August, not yet 14 years old. (Out of the six children she would bear James, five would die in infancy; perhaps her mother and grandmother had been right to worry about her health.)

The long account of the journey north, written by that same Somerset Herald who had described Margaret's proxy marriage ceremony eighteen months earlier, makes fascinating reading. There is a melancholy, elegiac tone about a document avowedly written 'to comfort the hearts of age for to hear it, and to give courage to the young to do thereafter in such case to come'.

Everything was splendidly done; Margaret was sent off 'richly dressed, mounted upon a fair palfrey'. The list of towns, of official receptions and leave-takings (the bride always 'richly dressed') is exhausting. Margaret must have been tougher than reputed in order to have survived it, even if she had not 'killed a buck with her bow' at Alnwick. But there is no doubt the ceremonial must have been impressive: this was, of course, a publicity exercise.

Minstrels were sent along to make sure no one missed Margaret's entry into and departure from the various towns, and a party of gentlemen was ordered 'to make space, that more plainly the said Queen and her company might be better seen'. As she passed into Scotland her servants sometimes had to force a way for the carriage; but the 'great quantity' of people flocking to see her had at least brought 'plenty of drink' for those prepared to pay for it.

The description of Margaret's initial meetings with her

husband at Hadington Castle shows, with unusual clarity, the stages of two people getting to know each other under these trying circumstances. As James was brought to her great chamber she met him at the door, and the two 'made great reverences, the one to the other, his head being bare, and they kissed together'. The greeting to the rest of her party being done, they 'went aside, and communed together by long space' – though it is doubtful how much a thirteen-year-old girl and an experienced womaniser of thirty can really have had to say to each other.

Next day James found Margaret playing cards in her room; she kissed him 'of good will' and he played for her on the clavichord and the lute 'which pleased her very much'. The next day again, seeing that the stool where she was seated for supper 'was not for her ease', he gave her his chair. Things were looking good, surely. The two did appear to have some things in common – an interest in music as well as in hunting – and there were still several days to go before their marriage was completed. But, this was an account written to glorify, and although Margaret may have been lucky by comparison with, for example, her grandmother Margaret Beaufort, married at an even earlier age, a letter back to her father Henry in England none the less breathes homesickness.

After formal thanks to all the ladies and gentlewomen who had accompanied her, she asks her father to give credence to the bearer of the letter to whom she had showed more of her mind than she could write, and asks him to take care of one Thomas, who had been her mother's footman. Describing the intimacy that had sprung up between the Earl of Surrey and her new husband, and how her own chamberlain, committed to 'my cause', could hardly get a look in, she can only write that 'I pray God it may be for my poor heart's ease in time to come.' An inexperienced young girl trying to negotiate the politics of a foreign court, she added: 'I would I were with your Grace now, and many times more.' It was the common lot of princesses, but that cannot have made it any easier.

Among the previous generation of York women, 1503 ended on the same sad note with which it had begun. On 23 November Margaret of Burgundy died. Whatever personal grief she had felt for the loss of Perkin Warbeck she had remained a central figure at the Burgundian court: the dowager whose presence was in demand for diplomatic functions; the devoted mother figure who would care for the children of the new duke and duchess whenever they were called away. Indeed, Duke Philip spoke of 'how, after the death of our late lady mother, she behaved towards us as if she were our real mother . . .'. She had become, almost, the Plantagenet who got away: safe from the precautionary violence that in decades to come the Tudors would continue to wreak on other remaining scions of the family.

At some unrecorded time between January 1503 and May 1504 Edward IV's other sister Elizabeth also died – the mother of Lincoln and Suffolk, the last of Cecily Neville's brood. The ground was being cleared. Of the women who had figured earlier in this story, there was only one survivor. It was, inevitably, Margaret Beaufort.

TWENTY-FIVE

Our Noble Mother

Tell me, how fares our noble mother?
Richard III, 5.3

It was an end, of course, but perhaps also a beginning. Lady Margaret Beaufort had now – with Elizabeth of York dead, Princess Margaret gone north and Princess Mary still a child – become England's first lady. Perhaps she no longer felt she had to struggle so hard now that her position was acknowledged by everybody.

Before the end of the decade John Fisher,[25] the cleric with whom she developed an increasingly close relationship in the last few years of her life, would be called on to preach her memorial sermon. All England, he would say, 'had cause of weeping' for her death:

The poor creatures that were wont to receive her alms, to whom she was always piteous and merciful. The students of both the universities to whom she was as a mother. All the learned men in England to whom she was a very patroness . . . . All the good priests and clerks to whom she was a true defenderess. All the noble men and women to whom she was a mirror and exemplar of honour. All the common people of this realm for whom she was in their causes a common mediatrix, and took right great displeasure for them.

Fisher, perhaps inevitably under the circumstances, painted a portrait of a saint; whatever Margaret Beaufort's virtues, she was not that. Fisher's assurance that she was never guilty of avarice or covetousness carries less conviction than his description of how her servants were kept in good order, suitors heard, and 'if any factions . . . were made secretly amongst her head officers, she with great policy did bolt it out and likewise any strife or controversy'. The image of Margaret ruling her household with a rod of iron and a measure of surveillance is not hard to conjure up. More personal still, perhaps – even in an age when the spectre of death was considered a good companion for the living – was Fisher's description of how Margaret would not only comfort in sickness any of the dozen poor people she maintained, 'minstering unto them with her own hands', but 'when it pleased God to call any one of them out of this wretched world she would be present to see them depart and to learn to die.'

Fisher also gave a description of Margaret's exhausting daily round of devotions, reminiscent of those recorded for Cecily Neville some years before. They began before dawn with the matins of our lady and the matins of the day 'not long after v [5] of the clock'. She attended four or five masses a day 'upon her knees' before dinner (10 a.m. on 'eating days', 11 on fasting days); after dinner she 'would go her stations' at three altars; then say her *diriges* and commendations, and her evensongs before supper. 'And at night before she went to bed she failed not to resort unto her chapel, and there a large quarter of an hour to occupy her in devotions': all this, even though so much kneeling was difficult for her 'and so painful that many times it caused in her back pain and disease'. She was probably suffering from arthritis.

Fisher describes her habit of saying every day when she was in good health the crown of our lady 'after the manner of Rome', kneeling each of the sixty-three times she heard the word 'ave'; and her meditations from French devotional books 'when she was weary of prayer'. He talks of her 'marvellous weeping' at confession, which at many seasons she made as often as every third day; and how when she was 'houselled' or received the Eucharist, nearly a dozen times a year, 'what floods of tears there issued forth from her eyes'.

It is a picture of, for that time, perfect piety: wholly obedient to Rome, and partaking of all the old rituals though perhaps not uninfluenced by the more individual, more interior style of religious practice beginning to make its way over from the continent. Margaret would surely have been horrified by any suggestion that the inevitably questioning nature of her own intelligent interest – her readiness to challenge the Church authorities over matters of property and patronage when necessary – could have sown the seeds of her grandson Henry VIII's future actions. But it is hard not to see in Fisher's words a woman who had learnt through bitter experience that life was not to be trusted, even if you might still rely on God's mercy; and hard not to be touched when Fisher recalls how the 'merciful and liberal' hands which gave comfort to the poor were so afflicted with cramps as to make her cry out: 'O blessed Jesu help me. O blessed lady succour me.'

Margaret's one-time carver Henry Parker confirmed Fisher's picture of the extraordinary devotions – 'as soon as one priest had said mass in her sight another began'. But he adds that at dinner (and 'how honourably she was served I think few kings better') she was always 'joyous' at the beginning of the meal, hearing tales to make her merry, before moving on to more serious and spiritual mental fare. None the less – despite her fondness for muscatel, her habit of keeping wine and spices in a locked cupboard in her own chamber for a nightcap – Fisher wrote of her 'sober temperance in meats and drinks'. For 'age and feebleness', he wrote, she might have been exempted from the fast days appointed by the Church, but chose instead to keep them 'diligently and seriously', and especially all through Lent 'restrained her appetite to one meal and one fish' a day. 'As to hard clothes wearing she had her shirts and girdles of hair, which when she was in health every week she failed not certain days to wear . . . [so] that full often her skin as I heard her say was pierced therewith.'

Like Cecily Neville Margaret owned – and commissioned Wynkyn de Worde to print – Walter Hilton's writing on the 'mixed life', which combined a spiritual programme with more worldly concerns. Like her frequent opponent, Cecily's daughter Margaret of Burgundy, she was particularly attached to the reformed order of Franciscans, the Observants. Margaret of Burgundy had probably been responsible for their establishment in England after 1480; in 1497 Margaret Beaufort was granted confraternity by the order.

A disproportionate amount of the surviving information on Margaret Beaufort comes from these final years of her life, thanks in part to her involvement with the Cambridge colleges in whose archives much of it is preserved. But perhaps that ever more active engagement was not coincidental – perhaps it was now, when she had been shaken by the death of one she can never have expected to predecease her, that Margaret realised it was time to follow her own interests and make her own legacy.

King Henry's retreat immediately after Elizabeth's death showed he was indeed devastated: he would continue, religiously, to keep the anniversary of her demise, and from this time on there would be a marked lessening in the cheer of his court. But Henry was now a widower; just as his son Arthur's wife Katherine of Aragon was now a widow. For a moment it may have seemed a good way of resolving the equation and keeping Katherine's dowry and the Spanish connection in the country: good to Henry, anyway. Her mother Isabella in Spain was horrified when she heard the rumours: such a marriage between father and daughter-in-law would be 'a very evil thing – one never before seen, and the mere mention of which offends the ears – we would not for anything in the world that it should take place'. It is an interesting sidelight on Henry's character that his instructions to his ambassadors, when later he was considering other candidates, made it plain he was not prepared to marry an ugly second wife. They were to make a careful note of breath, breasts and complexion: a roundabout tribute to Elizabeth of York.

In the event Katherine was betrothed shortly afterwards to Prince Henry, amid much debate as to whether she was betrothed as Arthur's widow in the fullest sense, or as the virgin survivor of an unconsummated marriage: it was a debate which would display its full ramifications later in the century. Henry argued indefatigably over the question of Katherine's dowry, but in this and other negotiations he was now manoeuvring from a position of decreased security.

The death of Elizabeth of York, so soon after that of the near-adult, heir Prince Arthur, put fresh question marks over a regime that had, after all, been in power for less than twenty years. Any persons tethered by loyalty to the old Yorkist dynasty of which Elizabeth had been, pretenders apart, the last embodiment might now consider themselves free. Too many of the men (and women) who had been involved in the rebellions against Henry had surnames like Neville, or else were under the young Duke of Buckingham's sway. Margaret Beaufort's one-time ward, son of Richard III's nemesis, Buckingham had turned out to be another who gazed at the throne with covetous eyes. Henry VII was known to be ill, and his sole surviving son was at this moment only eleven years old. Had the king died now it would have been a matter of another minority – or another man's opportunity.

In 1504 Henry's officers were discussing a conversation that had earlier taken place between 'many great personages' about the succession and the future of the country. Some spoke of Buckingham as a possible next king, some of Suffolk; but none of them 'spoke of my lord prince'. An agent of Suffolk's at the court of the Holy Roman Empire had been assuring Maximilian that, should Henry VII die, young Prince Henry could in no way prevail against his own claim. This insecurity probably affected the way Henry VII comported himself once the warmth and influence, and the political authority, that he had gained from his wife were no longer his.

That summer of 1503 Reginald Bray died – Henry's greatest officer, and one who had had his start under Margaret Beaufort. Rather than replace him by making any other individual as powerful Henry increasingly kept power in his own hands, raising new men in status but trusting no one completely. It may have given him less time for other things. A letter he wrote to his mother around this time makes excuse that he had 'encumbered you now with this my long writing, but me thinks that I can do no less, considering that it is so seldom that I do write . . . '. Henry was also becoming ever more obsessed with money – an accusation that could of course also be brought against his mother. Perhaps Elizabeth had been instrumental in his earlier comparative liberality.

The following summer Margaret's husband Stanley died, which allowed her greater access to her own funds. She took the opportunity to confirm her vows of chastity:

In the presence of my Lord God Jesu Christ and his blessed Mother the glorious Virgin St Mary and of all of the whole company of Heaven & of you also my ghostly father I Margaret of Richmond with full purpose and good deliberation for the weal [welfare] of my sinful soul with all my heart promise from henceforth the chastity of my body. That is never to use my body having actual knowledge of man after the common usage in matrimony the which thing I had before purposed in my lord my husband's days.

But despite her powerful religious interests she did not turn to a semi-retired and contemplative life as others had done. She had different duties.

She now felt it necessary to abandon her recently established power base of Collyweston for a variety of houses often borrowed from the bishops whose perks of office they were; Margaret was prepared to take advantage of everything the Church had to offer. She wanted to be nearer to her son and his court, even if there were some frictions between them: Henry was in the process of taking her beloved, and convenient, Woking away from her to convert it to royal use. The matter recalled Cecily and Fotheringhay – which, indeed, was one of the properties Margaret now used, cleared and cleaned for her convenience.

One thing Margaret did have was that other ever more absorbing field of independent interest: patronage, especially of Cambridge University. Her benevolence had originally been a little more widely spread: in the closing years of the fifteenth century Oxford too had hailed her as the princess 'of rank most exalted and of character divine' who would exceed all others in her patronage. However, the influence of John Fisher – as well, perhaps, as its proximity to her geographical areas of influence – had led her to the other establishment.

Margaret's support for Queens' College in Cambridge

(which Marguerite, Anne and Elizabeth Woodville had supported before her) could be taken as part of her ongoing bid for the regal role. Her long-standing interest in Jesus College, too, was shared by the whole royal family. But what came next was all her own. She took the underfunded 'God's House' in Cambridge and turned it into Christ's College: not her only enduring legacy in that city, but the one that can be most clearly identified with her. The college statutes of 1506 show that she reserved for her own use a set of four rooms there, located between the chapel and the hall and with windows giving a direct view down into either. From this position she could partake of the college devotions in privacy, perhaps fancy herself part of this masculine seat of learning, and keep an eye on daily college business. Her heraldic devices – a portcullis and a 'yale' – are still prominently modelled on the oriel outside her former lodgings. The mythical Yale was a goatlike creature with the ability to twist its horns in different directions so as to keep one of them safe in a fight. It symbolised proud defence and was highly appropriate for the wary Tudors.

Margaret not only ensured that Fisher could use her rooms when she was not in residence, but arranged for a country property to be used by the scholars whenever plague came to the city. Margaret is known to have visited Cambridge in 1505, 1506, 1507 and less certainly 1508. Nor did her work there cease with the foundation of Christ's. As early as 1505 Fisher drew her attention to the lamentable state of the ancient hospital of St John the Evangelist; and though in the event it would be her executors who oversaw the difficult process of converting it into St John's College, a place to be 'as good and as of good value' as Christ's, here too her arms can still be seen resplendent above the porter's lodge.

There is a story of how, looking out of her windows at

Christ's once, she saw the dean punishing a lazy scholar and cried out '*lente, lente*' (gently, gently). But that softer side of her character is not often visible; life had not taught her to display it readily. After Elizabeth of York's death, however, Margaret was certainly involved to some degree in the upbringing of Prince Henry. The excessive interest his father now took in the young prince meant he was never going to be sent off to Ludlow where his brother had died, but as heir to the throne he was still in need of a more adult and masculine establishment. Here, as everywhere, his grandmother's hand can be seen, and the composition of his new household showed a considerable degree of cross-fertilisation with hers. His bede-roll – a portable prayer manual, meant to be pored over daily – suggests not only a genuine piety but a particular interest, which Margaret shared, in the crucifixion itself: the wounds and the holy name of Jesus. His love of chivalry might have originated in the York side of the family, but here too Margaret played a role: in 1504 two of the four young men added as 'spears' to the prince's household came from hers, and she would send him a gift after he had distinguished himself 'running at the ring' in the tourney.

There is no evidence of her having fulfilled any such sympathetic function for Katherine of Aragon – however much the girl may have stood in need of it, caught as she was between her father's and her father-in-law's diplomacy. At the end of 1504 the death of her mother Isabella of Castile reduced Katherine's diplomatic value, representing as she now did only a less valuable alliance with her father's Aragon rather than with a united Spain. In June 1505 Prince Henry was instructed to repudiate his official marriage with her, leaving Katherine once again without clear prospects in a strange land.

Isabella's own kingdom of Castile, her share of Spain, descended not to her husband Ferdinand but to her daughter

Juana, Katherine's elder sister. This created a battle for control between Juana's husband Philip of Burgundy and her father Ferdinand, who had no intention of giving up so easily. There is evidence that Juana made valiant if ineffectual efforts to take control into her own hands and rule as her mother had done, but the real tussle was between the two men. Juana has been given the sobriquet 'the Mad',[26] but though her behaviour could sometimes be erratic the slur was probably little more than a pretext used by the men of her family to set her aside.

In January 1506, the wintry weather gave England a first-hand view of Juana and her problems and blew an unexpected bonus on to Henry's shores. Juana and Archduke Philip, on their way to Spain to claim her inheritance, were shipwrecked on the Dorset coast. On hearing the news at Richmond Henry immediately sent word to his mother at Croydon and set about preparing a dazzling welcome for guests who, despite their gracious reception, were also now in a sense hostages. The reluctance of her male connections to support the isolated Katherine was dramatised when she invited her brother-in-law Philip to join her in a dance, and got only a resounding snub. It was the precocious Princess Mary, not yet in her teens, who saved the situation by dancing with Katherine herself. (It was common practice for women to dance together.) Philip's attitude to Juana was also made plain. He purposely kept her away from Henry's court until he himself was firmly established as the star visitor, which left Katherine only a few hours to spend with the sister she was never likely to see again. Other factors apart, the last thing Philip would have wanted was for Katherine either to encourage Juana in independence or to get too much evidence of her sanity.

Philip was taken also to visit Margaret Beaufort at Croydon. Here the archduke's minstrels performed for the king's mother, and Prince Henry received a grandmotherly present of a new horse with fine gold and velvet trappings, the better to show off in front of a Burgundian guest who was a leading exponent of martial chivalry.

King Henry's main topic of negotiation with his guest was a treaty of mutual defence between England and Burgundy – something which made an Aragonese alliance with Katherine even less necessary. One subtext was Henry's determination to regain custody of Suffolk, who was still enjoying Burgundian hospitality. He won – for all that Philip initially demurred, apparently invoking the memory of Margaret of Burgundy to whom he said he still owed a loyalty. And King Henry, when he met her, appeared to have been considerably more impressed with Juana than Juana's own husband, lending her, when the time came to resume her journey, Elizabeth of York's 'rich litters and chairs'.

Suffolk was brought back to imprisonment in England: he would eventually be executed, but by Henry VIII rather than his father. Indeed, a number of compromised figures were treated with a leniency that may owe something to their female connections. In other directions, however, the king was proving himself a harsher ruler than in earlier days. He now had two new and dauntingly aggressive money collectors, Empson and Dudley, who used every tactic of law and intimidation to extract revenue and caused, so Bacon heard from an earlier chronicle, 'much sorrow' from the autumn of 1506. Perhaps this was what John Fisher meant when he wrote that Margaret Beaufort detested avarice and covetousness in anyone, but most especially in any that belonged to her. Her own love of money was tempered by possibly a softer heart, and surely a stronger morality.

But if there were any differences of opinion between Margaret and her son, they would now regularly be subsumed into concerns over the king's health. Early in 1507 he fell ill with an infection of the throat or chest – perhaps an abscess or tuberculosis. Lady Margaret moved in to Richmond to be by his side, just as she had done in 1503; and, just as she had done then, she buried her worries in the practicalities, ordering not only a supply of medicinal materials but also mourning garb which in the event proved unnecessary.*

That May the tournaments with their elaborate springtime pageantry were all about the young Prince Henry and the ravishing sovereign of the joust, his budding sister Princess Mary. After Elizabeth's death Mary had probably spent some of her time in Margaret Beaufort's care, whether at court or at Eltham – where even the swans in the moat now wore enamelled badges bearing the Beaufort portcullis. By the summer the king was sufficiently recovered to be set on a new courtship. Philip of Burgundy had died unexpectedly in the autumn of 1506, leaving Juana, the queen of Castile, a widow. From Henry's viewpoint she was almost as desirable a prospect as Elizabeth of York had been – beautiful, and carrying with her a kingdom. The Spanish ambassador wrote that the English 'seem little to mind . . . her insanity, especially since I have assured them that her derangement of mind would not prevent her from bearing children'.

Ferdinand, of course, was never going to be prepared to give England such a controlling hand in Spanish affairs, and within two years Juana had entered into the incarceration, nominally because of her mental health, that would last almost half a century. But in

---

* Also in 21 February 1507, several years after her marriage, Margaret in Scotland gave birth to a son, so it is possible her husband James, unlike Edmund Tudor long ago, had delayed consummating the marriage until she was mature. She was none the less dangerously ill after the birth, but her husband went seven days on foot to a famous shrine to pray for her recovery. This child, like several others, died young; but Margaret's one surviving son would go on to become King James V, father to Mary Queen of Scots. Margaret's husband, however, died at Flodden in 1513, fighting against an English army. After his death she was appointed regent for her baby son, albeit that some argued this was against Scottish tradition. But after making a controversial second marriage to the Earl of Angus she was demoted to a lesser title, albeit one with resonance in her family – that of 'My Lady the King's mother'.

the meantime Juana's sister Katherine got involved, at Henry's request, in the negotiations and delivered to her father-in-law a 'letter of credence' which declared her her father's ambassador. Katherine, of course, had every reason to desire her sister's presence at Henry's side – it might not only help her free herself from limbo but relieve her endless money worries. The disputes about her dowry had dragged on, and she sent frantic pleas to her father that she was spending not on frivolities but on necessities.

It would soon become clear that Henry VII was in no state to contemplate anything so arduous as another marriage. In the chill early spring of 1508 his illness returned and Margaret Beaufort was back at Richmond with her orders and her sweet wine. Once again Henry recovered – strong enough by the summer to resume normal activities – but it was clear what the future would be. The Spanish envoy Fuensalida wrote that the young Prince Henry was still kept 'in complete subjection to his father and his grandmother and never opened his mouth in public except to answer a question from one of them'. But whether or not this was a true picture, he would soon be called upon to carry forward the Tudor dynasty.

The great diplomatic game of arranging marriages went on, with his children Henry and Mary the two cards Henry VII still had to play. Three marriages had been discussed while Philip of Burgundy was in England: of Prince Henry to Philip's daughter; of King Henry to Philip's sister; and of Princess Mary to Philip and Juana's son Charles, the boy who would become the most powerful ruler in Europe. The first two never took on much colour of reality, but on 17 December 1508 a betrothal between Charles and Mary was celebrated amid great festivities. This would be a match indeed, since Charles was heir through his mother to the Spanish territories and through his father to the Holy Roman Empire. The bride made, in perfect French, a lengthy speech from memory; the king kept his watchful eye on even the smallest detail of the pageantry and, as the printed souvenir had it, the red rose (Lancaster's rose) looked set to bloom throughout the Christian world.[*]

The times were repeating themselves. There had been another father, Edward IV, obsessed by his daughter's marriage as the last months of his life approached. In January 1509, as the air of triumph died away, so too did this last spurt of the king's energy. The annual pattern must have been horribly familiar but this time there was a difference; and there would be no rally as the dank, sapping air of early spring warmed into new life at last. Henry seemed to know it. His religious observance took on a hysterical note; observers recorded how he 'wept and sobbed by the space of three quarters of an hour' in penance, how he would crawl to the foot of the monstrance to receive the mass. It was the end of March when Margaret Beaufort had herself rowed upriver from Coldharbour, where she had been nursing her own health. She brought to Richmond her favourite bed and a quantity of 'kitchen stuff', clearly prepared for a long stay. It would not, in the end, be that long: on 21 April Henry died.

He had named his mother chief executrix of his will. When the king's death was followed by what was in essence a massive cover-up – a two-day pretence that he was still alive, until a smooth succession of power could be established – there can be no doubt that Margaret Beaufort was at the heart of it. The account left by Garter Herald Thomas Wriothesley made that clear: the busy councillors were being 'over seen by the mother of the said late king'. Margaret, like Elizabeth Woodville after Edward IV's death, could not afford the time to mourn her private loss; she too was having to cope with a minority – though

---

[*] Mary's marriage to Charles would not in the end proceed. She would instead be married by her brother Henry VIII to the ageing French king Louis XII, and dance him into his grave.

this time, blessedly, there was only a matter of weeks to go before, in June, the heir would reach his eighteenth birthday.

As the young King Henry VIII, now at last proclaimed, moved to the Tower in preparation for his coronation, his grandmother briefly stayed behind at Richmond from where, notable even amid this stream of business, orders were sent out to arrest Empson and Dudley. The seizure of these hated officials would be one of the defining moments that set the seal on the new king's popularity. Coincidentally or otherwise, Margaret Beaufort had once been crossed in a property deal by Dudley.

The interim council, which would keep firm hands on the reins of government until Henry was crowned, is likely to have had her fingerprints all over it. Stow's *Annales* would state that the young king 'was governed by the advice of his grandmother in the choice of the privy council he appointed at the commencement of his reign'. Edward Herbert in the seventeenth century would write that Henry trusted his grandmother's choices for counsellors 'and took their impressions easily', suggesting even that it was she who held them together during her life, though afterwards they might fall out among themselves. As Henry VII was buried according to his wishes beside Elizabeth of York, 'our dearest late wife the queen', Margaret Beaufort, in ensuring her grandson's smooth accession, had struck another blow on behalf of the Tudor monarchy.

She moved at once to claim back her old home of Woking, which her grandson made over to her on 19 May. But it is unlikely that, had she lived longer, she would have won lasting influence. The influence she had enjoyed under Henry VII had been based not only on a similarity of temperament (and sheer gratitude on his part) but on the fact that he had arrived in England as an outsider, in urgent need of trusted allies. It was very different for Henry VIII. Margaret had a vital role to play in that tense moment of succession, but young men do not usually wish to be governed by old women, as Elizabeth I would discover in the last years of her reign. The new king seemed, moreover, to take after his mother and his mother's York ancestors, right down to his height and splendid appearance. In the long term he would remorselessly stamp out any Yorkist threats to his throne, but his first instinct on acceding to it was to treat his Yorkist relations kindly.

Perhaps it was memories of his mother, and of the happiness she had brought his father, that made him so anxious to be married himself. Henry's wedding to Katherine of Aragon took place fast and privately; the joint coronation less than a fortnight later was to be huge and public, a fit celebration of what some now see as the end of the long war. 'The rose both red and white/In one rose now doth grow', as Henry's one-time tutor, the poet John Skelton, put it.

The ceremony took place on 24 June, the crowd hacking up the carpet just as they had done when Henry VIII's mother had been crowned twenty-two years earlier. Just as before, Margaret Beaufort, with Princess Mary, watched the procession from behind a lattice in the window of a rented house in Cheapside. She did so with 'full great joy', Fisher recorded, though the old lady kept up her usual reminders that 'some adversity would follow'. She had, at least, set aside her usual convent attire of black and white and ordered dresses of tawny silk for her entourage to wear on the occasion. Maybe she felt vindicated when a sudden shower forced the drenched bride to shelter under the awning of a draper's stall. Margaret enjoyed the coronation banquet, but afterwards felt unwell. Henry Parker records that 'she took her infirmity with eating of a cygnet'. But Margaret was now sixty-six, and it was soon clear that this was no mere case of surfeit, but a serious illness.

She, who had always sought so desperately to control all the details of her life, had not neglected her own obsequies. In fact, some of her instructions and bequests would be a source of controversy, not least among her servants who were unhappy with the leading role John Fisher was given in handling her legacy. But her tidy mind and attention to detail were reflected even in the date of her death. Margaret Beaufort died on 29 June, the day after her grandson's eighteenth birthday.

Tidily again, she died in the precincts of Westminster Abbey where she would be buried. Fisher described how on her deathbed 'with all her heart and soul she raised her body . . . and confirmed assuredly that in the sacrament was contained Christ Jesu'. If prayers, pity upon the poor, and pardons granted by divers popes could assure her future in the next world, he said, then it was 'great likelihood and almost certain conjecture' that she was indeed in the country above. But he touched too on that other side of her personality, the side that lived always in fear: 'for that either she was in sorrow by reason of the present adversities, or else when she was in prosperity she was in dread of the adversity for to come'. The focus of his sermon was a comparison of Margaret to the biblical Martha: he cited the nobility of her nature and the excellence of her endeavours, and compared the painful death of Margaret's own body to the way Martha 'died for the death of her brother Lazarus'. It is true, of course, that the one she loved most had gone before her. But perhaps Fisher also saw in Margaret some echo of Martha's resentment: the woman who complained to Jesus that her sister Mary, whose life was so much easier, was yet more appreciated than she.

Fisher's long character analysis contains some flashes that bring Margaret to life. He recalled that she was never forgetful of any service done to her; and wary of 'any thing that might dishonest [dishonour] any noble woman'; that she was of a wisdom 'far passing the common rate of women'; 'good in remembrance and in holding memory'; 'right studious' in books in French and English, even the ones that were 'right dark'. Fisher touched on the way that, 'for her exercise and for the profit of others', she was herself responsible for translating several devotional works from the French: *The Mirror of Gold for the Sinful Soul*, as well as the fourth book of the *Imitation of Christ*. Her linguistic ability would be mirrored by her multi-lingual great-granddaughter, Elizabeth. As a purchaser and patron she did much to popularise translations of religious literature and to encourage printing in England, giving a seal of royal approval to the new industry.

Despite Fisher's repeated assurances of her generosity and liberality, her freedom from concupiscence, Margaret died hugely wealthy. The paperwork from her executors mentions bequests to the 'King's good grace that now is, King Henry VIII; the queen that now is, the princess of Castile', as Mary was now called. The extensive list of memoranda concerning various properties now 'in the king's hands by the death of his grandmother' shows just how far Margaret's grasp had stretched: from Kent to Kendal, from Devon to Dartford. Where cash was concerned, it was noted that she left 'Ready money £3,595. 8s. 9½d. Obligations £783. 6s. 8d.' It was a comforting balance tipped the right way: in the financial realm at least, Margaret had known how to find her security.

An inventory of the goods left in her closet, hard by her bedchamber, reveals her interests and concerns, her physical frailty and her ability to command luxury. There were spectacles, but made of gold; combs of ivory; cramp rings worn to ward off pain; silver pots for powdered medicines; a small gilt shrine to hold reliquaries; two service books bound in velvet; and a small gold goblet with the Beaufort emblem of a portcullis on the cover. A pile of paperwork included bonds, details of the jointure made to her by Thomas Stanley, annuities arranged for dependants, and the king's patent for founding a preacher's position in Cambridge.

In her wardrobe at her death were seven gowns of black velvet with ermine trimming, as well as an old scarlet Garter gown. The nun-like appearance of her late portraits, with the widow's wimple and white barb, is deceptive: Margaret had not put away the pleasure and pomp of dress. Black fabric was expensive, because it required a large quantity of dye. In the keeping of one of her gentlewomen were pearls and rubies; 'a serpent's tongue set in gold garnished with pearls'; two books whose images were mounted in gold leaf; a piece of the holy cross set in gold and one of 'unicorn's horn'.

Here is something that was previously lacking: the tangible, human details of daily life. Combined with the personal emotion that she, unlike the other women in this story, expressed in her letters, they form the materials of modern biography. Shakespeare never wrote a voice for Margaret Beaufort;[27] and indeed it is hard to envisage her fitting into his parade of betrayed and bitter women. Her papers and her writing contain clear evidence not of a dramatic creation, but of a real personality. It is a world different from today's – more than five centuries different – but one that is brought vividly alive.

EPILOGUE

The tomb Lady Margaret's executors commissioned in Westminster Abbey looks oddly austere today. But it is among the most convincingly human of the Abbey's monuments, albeit that of a woman who in life tended to command either pity or respect rather than sympathy. The hands of the bronze-gilt figure are those old, arthritis-ridden ones that John Fisher described, and old too are the deep brackets around the mouth. The sculptor was the quarrelsome Italian Pietro Torrigiano, the man who broke Michelangelo's nose, and for a fee of 20 shillings Erasmus composed the inscription around the ledge.

Margaret's head rests on a cushion, at her feet (so the contract for the carving stated) 'a beast called a Yale'. The arms around the base of the tomb are those she shared with her first husband, Edmund Tudor; those of her son Henry VII and his queen; of her dead grandson Arthur; of her grandson Henry VIII and Katherine of Aragon; of her parents and grandparents; those she shared with her last husband, Stanley; those of Henry V and Katherine of Valois, even; but no visible sign of her second husband, Stafford, happy though her life with him seems to have been. He was commemorated in the masses she had ordered to be said for him at the Abbey – but the tomb was about the dynasty.

This tomb and its companion were not finished until well into Henry VIII's reign. The contract for the figure on Margaret's tomb was only drawn up on 23 November 1511, and her executors' accounts record: 'First paid the 27th day of December in the 4th year of the reign of King Henry VIII to M. Garter the king of heralds for making and declaring my lady's arms in viii 'scochyns' [escutcheons] for my lady's tomb, and delivered to the Florentine: 8s 4d.' It was probably his figure of Margaret which won Torrigiano the commission to sculpt the figures for the more important royal tomb – that of Henry and Elizabeth – which is one of the glories of Westminster Abbey. The figures lie side by side in unemotional gilt splendour, on a plinth of Italian marble. They are gazing upwards to God, and God sees them clearly: two gold images, almost sanctified by their beauty. Static and stationary, in their tranquillity they emphasise the message of the Henry VII Chapel that the Tudors were here to stay.

Above the tomb of Henry and Elizabeth are the Beaufort portcullis, the Tudor rose and, the French fleur de lis. Leland called the chapel '*miraculum orbis universali*', the wonder of the entire world: not only for its myriad carvings – the saints in their ranks, the beasts of heraldry – and its stained glass, now long lost, but for the soaring arches of the roof. It was the last great gasp of Perpendicular Gothic, built just as a new world was coming into being. Henry VII's dream of seeing Henry VI canonised and 'translated' here had never become reality, but both he and Margaret Beaufort had poured money into the project – some £20,000, equivalent to about £7 million today.

Elizabeth lies with eyes open and hands folded in prayer, wearing a fur-lined robe and with her feet resting on a royal lion. Torrigiano can never have seen Elizabeth of York – the image was only completed fifteen years after her death – so this may be either a standardised royal image or one guided by her effigy. The result has been called the finest Renaissance tomb north of the Alps, with gilded putti and curling foliage jostling the greyhound and the Tudor dragon. But the point – the point of the whole chapel – is the dynasty.

In the south aisle of the chapel are three free-standing tombs. With Margaret Beaufort lie two of her descendants: her great-great-granddaughter Mary, Queen of Scots; and her great-granddaughter Margaret Lennox, the mother of Mary's husband Lord Darnley. It is a distinctly crowded setting, given the quantity of white marble beneath which the Scots queen was reinterred in the seventeenth century. In the north aisle are two more of Margaret Beaufort's great-granddaughters, the two English ruling queens Elizabeth and Mary. Since Henry VIII lies at Windsor – with Edward VI merely placed beneath the altar in Henry VII's chapel – this has wound up being a monument not only to the Tudors as such, but to the distaff side of history: a 'Lady' Chapel in honour, appropriately, of the Virgin Mary.

None of the other women in this story has a tomb as visible as these in Westminster Abbey. Elizabeth Woodville, interred with so little ceremony, at least got to share, almost unnoticed, her husband's tomb at Windsor. Anne Neville is known to be buried in Westminster Abbey, but the site is not recorded. And though Cecily Neville is buried as she planned at Fotheringhay, the place never became what she had intended, a memorial to the Yorkist dynasty; indeed, by Elizabeth I's day the tombs had fallen into such disrepair that she ordered to be them tidied away. Even Margaret of Burgundy's tomb in Malines was ransacked in the sixteenth century – by local iconoclasts, Spanish troops or English mercenaries – and today no trace of any memorial remains. Margaret of Anjou was buried as she requested with her parents at Angers – evidence that the war in the country which should have been her marital home had not gone her way.

Everything that is known about these women suggests that their main imperative was dynastic – genetic. And the blood of Elizabeth Plantagenet and Henry Tudor – and therefore the blood of Margaret Beaufort, Elizabeth Woodville and Cecily Neville – still runs in Britain's royal family. This legacy would surely outweigh whatever personal price they had to pay. Amongst the women of this Cousins' War, Margaret Beaufort fought hardest and most successfully for her bloodline. She is also the only one to leave another sort of legacy – a legacy of works.[1]

The links between these women and their descendants would continue long after they were dead. The deadly dispute between cousins continued for the next century, with its contests mostly fought away from the battlefield, in arenas where women could compete more visibly. Elizabeth of York's granddaughter 'Bloody' Mary would dispute the throne with her kinswoman Jane Grey (descended from Elizabeth's younger daughter Mary); Elizabeth Tudor would be forced to execute the Queen of Scots, descended from Elizabeth of York's elder daughter Margaret. But out of their combined experience, out of the different models of female agency they embodied, would be born something more productive.

England's consort queens, from the Conquest to the Tudors, demonstrate a gradual move towards mere domesticity[2] – from the time when a strong woman 'will be counted among the men who sit at God's table' to one when any sign of such 'manful' strength was a source of profound unease. And yet, in the century ahead, the idea of the strong woman (something then seen almost as a third sex) was about to reach its apogee. Elizabeth I, perhaps the country's greatest monarch, played upon all the ambiguities of gender, not least in her famous speech at Tilbury. She reconciled, at least for her own lifetime, the problem with which Marguerite of Anjou had grappled in vain: that of reconciling the requirements of rule and the pressure to be 'womanly'.

That later Elizabeth, of course, was a woman whose undoubted contribution was neither genetic nor dynastic. That has been, to all women since, her lasting legacy. If Elizabeth of York was Elizabeth I's physical progenitor, then perhaps she could trace back to Marguerite a different kind of ancestry. Perhaps, even – however cruelly the wars had told upon her – that fact gives to Marguerite, too, a share in the ultimate victory.

SELECT BIBLIOGRAPHY

Primary Sources

André, Bernard, *Vita Henrici Septimi* in *Memorials of King Henry VII* ed. J. Gairdner, Rolls Series (London, 1858)

Antiquarian Repertory, The: A Miscellaneous Assemblage of Topography, History, Biography, Customs and Manners (vol. 4), ed. Francis Grose and Thomas Astle (1807)

Calendar of Papal Registers vol. 13, part I, ed. J.A. Twemlow (1955)

Calendars of Patent Rolls: Henry VI 1452–61 (HMSO, 1897); *Edward IV 1461–67* (HMSO, 1899); *Edward IV and V and Richard III 1476–85* (HMSO, 1901)

Calendar of the Close Rolls Edward IV, vol. i, 1461–68 (HMSO, 1949)

Calendar of State Papers Milan, i, 1385–1618, ed. Allen B. Hinds, (HMSO, 1912)

Calendar of State Papers Spanish, i, 1485–1559, ed. G.A. Bergenroth (1862)

Calendar of State Papers Venetian, i, 1202–1509, ed. Rawdon Brown (1864)

Chronicles of London, ed. C.L. Kingsford (1905 repr. Gloucester 1977)

Commynes, Philippe de, *Mémoires*, trans. A.R. Scoble (1855–6); also trans. M. Jones (Harmondsworth, 1972)

Crowland, *Ingulph's Chronicle of the Abbey of Croyland with the Continuations by Peter of Blois and Anonymous Writers*, trans. Henry T. Riley (1854)

Crowland Chronicle Continuations, The, 1459–1486, ed. and trans. Nicholas Pronay and John Cox (Sutton, 1986)

Ellis, Sir Henry, *Original letters illustrative of English history; including numerous royal letters; from autographs in the British Museum, the State*

Paper Office, and one or two other collections (Three series: 1824, 1827, 1846)

English Chronicle of the Reigns of Richard II, Henry IV, Henry V and Henry VI, ed. J.S. Davies (Camden Soc., 1856)

English Historical Documents, general editor David C. Douglas (Eyre & Spottiswoode 1953–70). *vol. 4 1327–1485*, ed. A.R. Myers, *vol. 5 1485–1558*, ed. C.H. Williams

Fisher, John, *The English Works of John Fisher*, ed. J.E.B. Mayor (1876)

Great Chronicle of London, The, ed. A.H. Thomas and I.D. Thornley (originally published for the Library Committee of the Corporation of the City of London 1938, facsimile edition Sutton, 1983)

Gregory's Chronicle: in *Historical Collection of a Citizen of London*, ed. J. Gairdner (Camden Soc., new series, 17, 1876)

Hall, Edward, *The Union of the Two Noble Families of Lancaster and York*, originally printed 1552, 1558, 1550 – modern edition, ed. H. Ellis (1809)

Historie of the Arrivall of Edward IV, ed. J. Bruce (Camden Soc., 1838)

Leland, John, *De Rebus Britannicis Collectanea*, ed. T. Hearne (1774)

Malory, Sir Thomas, *Le Morte darthur: The Winchester Manuscript*, ed. Helen Cooper (OUP, 1998)

Mancini, Dominic, *The Usurpation of Richard III (Dominicus Mancinus Ad Angelum Catonem De Occupatione Regni Angliae Per Riccardum Tercium Libellus)*, ed. C.A.J. Armstrong (Clarendon Press, Oxford, 1936)

More, Thomas, *Complete Works (vol. 2)*, ed. Richard S. Sylvester (Yale University Press, 1963)

New Chronicles of England and France, The, aka *Fabian's Chronicle*, ed. H. Ellis (1811)

Nicolas, Nicholas Harris, *Privy Purse Expenses of Elizabeth of York: Wardrobe Accounts of Edward the Fourth: With a Memoir of Elizabeth of York* (1830)

Paston Letters, The, ed. J. Gairdner (1904)

Pizan, Christine de, *A Medieval Woman's Mirror of Honour: The Treasury of the City of Ladies*, trans. Charity Cannon Willard, ed. Madeleine Pelner Cosman (Bard Hall Press and Persea Books, 1989)

Stonor Letters, Kingsford's Stonor Letters and Papers 1290–1483, ed. C. Carpenter (CUP, 1996)

Vergil, Polydore, *Three Books of Polydore Vergil's English History;
Comprising the Reigns of Henry VI, Edward IV, and Richard III* (1844)

*Wills from Doctors' Commons: A Selection from the Wills of Eminent Persons
etc.*, ed. J.G. Nichols and J. Bruce, (Camden Soc., old series, 83, 1863)

NB A number of these original sources are now also available online,
notably the different versions of the *Ballad of Lady Bessy*, and the
texts of the *Arrivall* and *Gregory's Chronicle* cited above. Useful
sites are those of the Richard III Society's online library
(http:www.r3.org/bookcase) and of British History Online
(http://www.british-history.ac.uk).

Quotations from Shakespeare are from the texts printed by Cambridge
University Press.

Secondary Sources

Armstrong, C.A.J., 'The piety of Cicely (*sic*) Duchess of York, a Study in
late Medieval Culture' in D. Woodruff (ed.), *For Hilaire Belloc, Essays
in hour of his 72nd birthday* (Sheed & Ward, 1942)

Ashdown-Hill, John, *The Last Days of Richard III* (History Press, 2011)

Ashdown-Hill, John, *Eleanor: The Secret Queen* (History Press, 2009)

Bacon, Francis, *The History of the Reign of King Henry VII*, ed. Brian
Vickers (CUP, 1998)

Bagley, J.J. *Margaret of Anjou, Queen of England* (Herbert Jenkins, 1948)

Baldwin, David, *The Lost Prince: The Survival of Richard of York* (Sutton, 2007)

Baldwin, David, *Elizabeth Woodville: Mother of the Princes in the Tower*
(Sutton, 2002)

Buck, George, *History of King Richard the Third*, ed. A.N. Kincaid
(Sutton, 1979)

Bullough, Geoffrey (ed.), *Narrative and Dramatic Sources of Shakespeare*,
vol. 3 (Routledge and Kegan Paul, 1960)

Castor, Helen, *Blood and Roses: The Paston Family and the Wars of the
Roses* (Faber & Faber, 2004)

Castor, Helen, *She-Wolves: The Women Who Ruled England Before
Elizabeth* (Faber & Faber, 2010)

Chrimes, S.B., *Henry VII* (Eyre Methuen, 1972)

Cooper, Charles Henry, *Memoir of Margaret, Countess of Richmond and Derby* (Cambridge, 1874)

Coss, Peter, *The Lady in Medieval England 1000–1500* (Sutton, 1998)

Crawford, Anne, *Letters of the Queens of England* (Sutton, 2002)

Crawford, Anne, *Letters of Medieval Women* (Sutton, 2002)

Crawford, Anne, *Yorkists: The History of a Dynasty* (Hambledon Continuum, 2006)

Cunningham, Sean, *Richard III: A royal enigma* (The National Archives, 2003)

Davies, Katharine, *Elizabeth Woodville: The First Queen Elizabeth* (Lovat Dickson, 1937)

Dockray, Keith, *Edward IV: A Source Book* (Sutton, 1999)

Dockray, Keith, *Henry VI, Margaret of Anjou and the Wars of the Roses: A Source Book* (Sutton, 1997)

Dockray, Keith, *Richard III: A Source Book* (Sutton, 1997)

Duffy, Eamon, *Marking the Hours: English People and their Prayers* (Yale University Press, 2011)

Dunn, Diana, 'Margaret of Anjou, Queen Consort of Henry VI: A Reassessment of her Role, 1445–1453,' in Rowena E. Archer (ed.) *Crown, Government and People in the Fifteenth Century* (Sutton, 1995)

Fields, Bertram, *Royal Blood: King Richard III and the Mystery of the Princes* (Sutton, 2006)

Fox, Julia, *Sister Queens: Katherine of Aragon and Juana Queen of Castile* (Weidenfeld & Nicolson, 2011)

Gillingham, J. (ed.), *Richard III: A Medieval Kingship* (Collins & Brown, 1993)

Goldstone, Nancy, *The Maid and the Queen: The Secret History of Joan of Arc and Yolande of Aragon* (Weidenfeld & Nicolson, 2012)

Goodwin, George, *Fatal Colours: Towton 1461 – England's Most Brutal Battle* (Phoenix, 2012)

Gregory, Philippa, David Baldwin and Michael Jones, *The Women of the Cousins' War: The Duchess, the Queen and the King's Mother* (Simon & Schuster, 2011)

Griffiths, Ralph A. and Roger S. Thomas, *The Making of the Tudor Dynasty* (Sutton, 1987)

Griffiths, Ralph A. and James Sherborne (eds), *Kings and Nobles in the Later Middle Ages* (Sutton, 1986)

Hanham, Alison, *Richard III and His Early Historians 1483–1535* (OUP, 1975)

Hardyment, Christina, *Malory: The Life and Times of King Arthur's Chronicler* (Harper Perennial, 2006)

Harris, Barbara J., *Edward Stafford, Third Duke of Buckingham 1478–1521* (Stanford University Press, 1986)

Harvey, Nancy Lenz, *Elizabeth of York* (Weidenfeld & Nicolson, 1973)

Haswell, Jock, *The Ardent Queen: Margaret of Anjou and the Lancastrian Heritage* (Peter Davies, 1976)

Hicks, Carola, *The King's Glass: A Story of Tudor Power and Secret Art* (Chatto & Windus, 2007)

Hicks, M. A., *False, fleeting, perjur'd Clarence: George, Duke of Clarence 1449–1478* (Sutton, 1980)

Hicks, Michael, *Anne Neville: Queen to Richard III* (Tempus, 2007)

Hicks, Michael, *Edward V: The Prince in the Tower: The Short Life and Mysterious Disappearance of Edward V* (Tempus, 2007)

Hicks, Michael, *Warwick the Kingmaker* (Blackwell, 1998)

Hilton, Lisa, *Queen Consort: England's Medieval Queens* (Weidenfeld & Nicolson, 2008)

Hookham, M. A., *The Life and Times of Margaret of Anjou* (1872)

Hughes, Jonathan, *The Religious Life of Richard III: Piety and Prayer in the North of England* (Sutton, 2000)

Hutchinson, Robert, *Young Henry: the Rise of Henry VIII* (Weidenfeld & Nicolson, 2011)

Ingram, Mike, *Battle Story: Bosworth 1485* (The History Press, 2012)

Johnson, P.A., *Duke Richard of York 1411–1460* (OUP, 1988)

Jones, Michael K., *Bosworth 1485: Psychology of a Battle* (Tempus, 2002)

Jones, Michael K. and Malcolm G. Underwood, *The King's Mother: Lady Margaret Beaufort, Countess of Richmond and Derby* (CUP, 1992)

Kingsford, C.L., *English Historical Literature in the Fifteenth Century* (Clarendon Press, 1913)

Lander, J.R., *The Wars of the Roses* (Palgrave Macmillan, 1990)

Laynesmith, J.L., *The Last Medieval Queens: English Queenship, 1445–1503* (OUP, 2004)

Lewis, Katherine J., Noel James Menuge and Kim M. Philips (eds), *Young Medieval Women* (Sutton, 1999)

Leyser, Henrietta, *Medieval Women: A Social History of Women in England 1450–1500* (Weidenfeld & Nicolson, 1995)

McKendrick, Scot, John Lowden and Kathleen Doyle, *Royal Manuscripts: The Genius of Illumination* (British Library, 2011)

Marks, Richard and Paul Williamson (eds), *Gothic: Art for England 1400–1547* (V&A Publications, 2003)

Mattingly, Garrett, *Catherine of Aragon* (Jonathan Cape, 1942)

Maurer, Helen E., *Margaret of Anjou: Queenship and Power in Later Medieval England* (Boydell Press, Woodbridge, 2003)

Myers, A.R. and Cecil H. Clough, *Crown, Household and Parliament in Fifteenth Century England* (Hambledon Press, 1985)

Nenner, Howard, *The Right to Be King: The Succession to the Crown of England 1604–1714* (Macmillan, 1975)

Norton, Elizabeth, *Margaret Beaufort: The Mother of the Tudor Dynasty* (Amberley, 2010)

Okerlund, Arlene, *Elizabeth Wydeville: The Slandered Queen* (Tempus, Stroud, 2005)

Okerlund, Arlene Naylor, *Elizabeth of York* (Palgrave Macmillan, 2009)

Palmer, Richard and P. Michelle Brown (eds), *Lambeth Palace Library: Treasures from the Collection of the Archbishops of Canterbury* (Scala, 2010)

Penn, Thomas, *Winter King: The Dawn of Tudor England* (Allen Lane, 2011)

Perry, Maria, *Sisters to the King* (André Deutsch, 1998)

Pollard, A.J. (ed.), *The Wars of the Roses* (Macmillan, 1995)

Ross, Charles, *Edward IV* (Eyre Methuen, 1974)

Ross, Charles, *Richard III* (Eyre Methuen, 1981)

Royle, Trevor, *The Wars of the Roses: England's First Civil War* (Little, Brown, 2009)

Rubin, Miri, *The Hollow Crown: A History of Britain in the Late Middle Ages* (Allen Lane, 2005)

Seabourne, Gwen, *Imprisoning Medieval Women: The Non-Judicial Confinement and Abduction of Women in England, c 1170–1509* (Ashgate, 2011)

Seward, Desmond, *The Last White Rose* (Constable, 2011)

Seward, Desmond, *The Wars of the Roses* (HarperPress, 2008)

Starkey, David (ed.), *Henry VIII: A European Court in England* (Collins & Brown, 1991)

Starkey, David, *Henry: Virtuous Prince* (HarperPress, 2008)

Strickland, Agnes, *Lives of the Queens of England*, vols III, IV (1841, 1842)

Sutton, A.F. and P.W. Hammond (eds), *The Coronation of Richard III: The Extant Documents* (Sutton, 1983)

Sutton, A.F. and Livia Visser-Fuchs, *The Reburial of Richard Duke of York, 21–30 July 1476* (Richard III Society, 1996)

Thurley, Simon, *The Royal Palaces of Tudor England: architecture and court life 1460–1547* (Yale University Press, 1993)

Tremlett, Giles, *Catherine of Aragon: Henry's Spanish Queen* (Faber & Faber, 2011)

Walpole, Horace, *Historic Doubts on the Life and Reign of King Richard III* (first published 1768), in Paul Kendall (ed.), *Richard III: the Great Debate* (Folio Society, 1965)

Weightman, Christine, *Margaret of York: The Diabolical Duchess* (Amberley, 2009)

Weir, Alison, *Britain's Royal Families: The Complete Genealogy* (Pimlico, 2002)

Weir, Alison, *The Princes in the Tower* (Pimlico, 1997)

Weir, Alison, *Lancaster and York: Wars of the Roses* (Pimlico, 1998)

Williams, Marty Newman and Anne Echols, *Between Pit and Pedestal: Women in the Middle Ages* (Markus Wiener, Princeton, 1994)

Williamson, Audrey, *The Mystery of the Princes: An Investigation into a Supposed Murder* (Sutton, 1978)

Wolffe, Bertram, *Henry VI* (Eyre Methuen, 1981)

Woolgar, C.M., *The Senses in Late Medieval England* (Yale University Press, 2006)

Wroe, Ann, *Perkin: A Story of Deception* (Vintage, 2004)

Articles

Chamberlayne, Joanna L. (Joanna Laynesmith), 'A paper crown: the titles and seals of Cecily Duchess of York', *Ricardian*, vol. 10, no. 133, June 1996

Cron, B.M., 'Margaret of Anjou and the Lancastrian March on London 1461', *Ricardian*, vol. 11, no. 147, December 1999

Hanham, Alison, 'Sir George Buck and Princess Elizabeth's Letter: A Problem in Detection', *Ricardian*, vol. 7, no. 197, June 1987

Kincaid, Arthur, 'Buck and the Elizabeth of York Letter', *Ricardian*, vol. 8, no. 101, March 1988

Laynesmith, Joanna, 'The King's Mother: Cecily Neville', http://www.richardiii.net/r3_mother.htm

Laynesmith, Joanna, 'The King's Mother', *History Today*, vol. 56, issue 3, 2006

Maurer, Helen, 'Whodunit: The Suspects in the Case', http://www.r3.org/bookcase/whodunit.html

Sutton, Anne F. and Livia Visser-Fuchs, 'The Device of Queen Elizabeth Woodville: A Gillyflower or Pink', *Ricardian*, vol. 11, no. 136, March 1997

Visser-Fuchs, Livia, 'Where Did Elizabeth of York Find Consolation?', *Ricardian*, vol. 9, no. 122, September 1993

Williams, Barrie, 'Elizabeth of York's Last Journey', *Ricardian*, vol. 8, no. 100, March 1988

NOTES

There is very little, from the cupidity of Elizabeth Woodville to the culpability of Richard III, on which the historians of the middle and late fifteenth century agree. There is just one subject, however, on which they are unanimous: the inadequacy of their sources. J.R. Lander wrote that these were 'notoriously intractable' – and it is especially true when it comes to dealing with women, who fought in no battles and passed no laws. Charles Ross, biographer of Edward IV, lamented that 'any discussion of motive and the interplay of personality in politics [were] matters generally beyond the range of the unsophisticated and often ill-informed and parochial writers of the time'.

The fifteenth century saw great change in the writing of history. The monastic Latin chronicle, with a couple of honourable exceptions, was in decline; and though the baton was being passed to secular chroniclers – city merchants and the like, writing in the vernacular and often anonymously – their records were erratic and often confusing. In an age which showed few signs of a sense of authorship or provenance, the chroniclers and antiquaries frequently repeated and adapted each other. The writing of humanist history in the Italian style only started in England at the beginning of the sixteenth century with Polydore Vergil and Sir Thomas More, as did the keeping of state papers. And though the records of state departments such as the Chancery, the Exchequer and the law courts have been the subject of extensive recent study they do not satisfy the biographer's thirst for motive and feeling.

The records of royal life provide few personal letters of the kind found in the Paston papers. Perhaps the fact that aristocratic letters were usually dictated militated against the written expression of intimate feeling; not only that, but the times were dangerous and a friend could so easily become an enemy. There is, too, the fact that in the civil war most reports were written very definitely from one side or the other. As Lander put it, introducing his book on the Wars of the Roses: 'Many of the letters and narratives quoted in this book purvey biased opinion, wild rumour, meretricious propaganda and the foulest of slander as well as historical truth.' Not just what someone writing after the event thought had happened, but, even more invidiously, what they wanted others to think had happened. Brief introductions are given below to some of the most important contemporary writers, in an attempt to offer the reader some idea of their likely starting point. For a more extensive discussion see Keith Dockray's introductions to his *Source Books*, or the chapter 'Writing History' in *English Historical Documents*, vol. v.

Any work of synthesis, such as this largely is, inevitably owes a great deal to existing individual studies. Six of the seven women here have already been the subject of biographies, from the great Victorian works of Cooper, Hookham and the like to the sometimes less considerable works of the mid-twentieth century. More recently Michael K. Jones and Malcolm G. Underwood in *The King's Mother* have produced a wealth of new detail on Margaret Beaufort, while Helen Maurer's book on Margaret [*sic*] of Anjou has explored the whole question of queenship and power. Both Elizabeth Woodville and Elizabeth of York have benefited from new biographies by Arlene Okerlund; and Christine Weightman was able to bring a knowledge of continental sources to bear on her biography of Margaret of Burgundy (or 'Margaret of York'). With these I would couple, as of prime importance, Joanna Laynesmith's *The Last Medieval Queens: English Queenship, 1445–1503*; while Lisa Hilton's *Queens Consort: England's Medieval Queens*, and Helen Castor's *She-Wolves: The Women Who Ruled England Before Elizabeth* provide an invaluable context.

Michael Hicks has been brave enough to confront the sometimes daunting lack of information for a biography of Anne Neville; but there has, at the time of writing, been no published study of Cecily Neville, though Joanna Laynesmith (née Chamberlayne) has written several valuable articles, and Michael K. Jones used his book on the psychological background of Bosworth to explore his controversial but fascinating theories. It is possible that the uncertainty surrounding several crucial points is enough to prohibit a biography as such: therefore the source notes given here for Cecily are more extensive than for the other women in this book.

Prologue

1   **Elizabeth of York's funeral:** *The Antiquarian Repertory*, vol. 4, pp. 655–663
2   **matter as much as the battlefields:** Leyser, *Medieval Women* p.167

cites Philippa Maddern in the *Journal of Medieval History 14* (1988) on the important role of the Paston women in the 'bloodless battles of land transactions, county rumour-mongering and client maintenance'.

Part I 1445–1460

1 **fifteen-year-old:** Earlier writers have Marguerite born in 1429 rather than 1430 but this perception was corrected in an article of 1988 by C.N.L. Brooke and V. Ortenberg, 'The Birth of Marguerite of Anjou', *Historical Research, 61* (pp. 357–8).

2 **Polydore Vergil:** *c.*1470–1555, Italian Renaissance scholar who came to England in 1501–2 and a few years later was invited by Henry VII to write a history of England – the *Anglica Historia,* not completed until the reign of Henry VIII. When considering his views on, for example, events as controversial as those of Richard III's reign it is disconcerting to realise he can have had no first-hand knowledge of them: the more so, since his writings have been among the most influential in blackening Richard's name. None the less, although writing in a Tudor, which effectively meant a Lancastrian, age, Vergil set conscientiously about his task, collecting memories and canvassing opinions; and his work is widely seen as marking a turning point in the writing of English history. Keith Dockray, moreover, points out that where the civil wars are concerned so many of the surviving records were written from a Yorkist viewpoint that Vergil serves as a useful corrective in recreating the Lancastrian perspective.

3 **took stock of her:** One report goes that Henry had earlier instructed his ambassadors to have portraits taken of other potential brides 'in their kirtles simple and their faces, like as you see their stature and their beauty and colour of skin and their countenances'. He had an aesthetic appreciation, unworldly though he may have been.

4 **chivalry:** A concept which, embodied in the courtly tournament and in popular literature, recurs time and again in the lives of the women of the late fifteenth century, serving simultaneously to elevate and to contain them. See Leyser, *Medieval Women,* p. 248: that it was once a standard practice to contrast the bloody epics of

the early medieval period with the later, 'heroine-centred' romances 'showing women in the courtly worlds of the later Middle Ages as the privileged and adored mistresses of all they surveyed. More recent criticism has come to make this view seem singularly naive; the romance heroine on her pedestal is, if anything, worse off than her epic predecessor who had at least some part to play in the thick of the fighting . . . .' Many of Marguerite's problems would come from the uncertainty of her position between these two worlds. See also Epilogue, note 2.

5 **queenship:** What did it mean to be a queen in the late fifteenth century? The models were contradictory. A book printed by Caxton in 1475, the *Game and Playe of the Chesse*, by the Dominican Jacobus de Cessolis, had been written almost two centuries earlier, but the publication of this new English edition suggests that its vision was still in currency. A queen, de Cessolis wrote, ought to be chaste and wise, 'secret' – i.e. discreet – 'and not curious in nourishing of her children'. 'A Queen ought to be well mannered and amongst all she ought to be timorous and shamefast [shamefaced].' Good advice for any woman, no doubt – but not wholly adequate for a queen when the turmoils of the time might well force her to take a part in public affairs.

Christine de Pizan repeatedly writes of her 'princess' also as someone who may have the business of state thrust upon her. 'The lady with great responsibilities in government has little time free from ruling. Lords often give over their rule to their ladies when they know them to be wise and good and when they themselves are obliged to be absent. Such women have enormous responsibility and authority to govern their lands and serve as council chief.' It was in part expectations like these, which Marguerite would bring across the Channel with her, that would so trouble her new country – for all that de Pizan carefully presents her lady's rule as being only that of her lord's deputy. By the same token a tract written in France in the fourteenth century, and translated in the fifteenth, *The III Consideracions Right Necesserye to the Good Governaunce of a Prince*, urged a queen to 'have good and due regard to such things as toucheth the profit and the honour of her lord and herself. And she should take in hand no great matters without license or

"congie" [permission] of her lord' . . . which did however imply
that she could take on such matters if necessary. This was clearly a
position of responsibility without power: the queen could function
only through her influence on the king, and while this often served
its purpose, allowing her acknowledged if informal influence, it
could rebound on her if the situation changed. Marguerite's biographer Helen Maurer makes a distinction between power, which
women could wield either through influence or through armed
force, and authority – the recognition of their right to exercise
power – which they would be denied until the next century.

6 **the 'Wars of the Roses':** The beginning and end points of which are
a matter for dispute. The preferred option now tends to be from
1455 to 1485 – the battle of Bosworth – or possibly 1487 and the
battle of Stoke. None the less, some have seen this conflict as
starting as early as 1399, with the seizure of Richard II's throne by
Henry IV; while others point out that 1471, with the death of
Henry VI and his son, saw the end of any conflict between York and
what could properly be called the house of Lancaster.

7 **Crowland Abbey chronicles:** 'Crowland' is a convenient way of referring to the important chronicles compiled at Crowland – or Croyland
– Abbey in the Fens. The chronicle begun by one 'Ingulph', giving
the history of the abbey from 655, was later taken over by a series of
'continuators'; the identity of the second continuator who chronicled
the years from 1459 to 1486 (which, he declares, was the time of
writing) is a matter of debate. The most popular candidate is John
Russell, Bishop of Lincoln (Richard III's chancellor for much of his
reign, but needing now to ingratiate himself with the new king Henry
VII); or possibly a member of Russell's staff. Other candidates,
however, have been suggested: from a clerk in Chancery whose writings only later found their way to the abbey, to an unknown
Crowland monk working from a secular source. It has often been
pointed out that the second continuator, whoever he was, displays a
certain animus against Richard III. But the more one reads the
records for this period, the more does a certain amount of bias seem
inevitable; and Crowland must rank as a very significant source.

8 **through the male line:** The question of inheritance through a
female line would prove a recurrent issue in this century, despite

the fact that it had long ago provided the basis for the Neville family's power: after one Robert Fitz Meldred of Raby had married the daughter of Geoffrey de Neville, their son took the rich mother's Neville name and founded this branch of the Neville family. See Young, Charles R., *The Making of the Neville Family 1166–1400*, Boydell Press, 1996.

9 **jointly to choose a confessor:** For what information exists on Cecily's early married life, see Crawford, *Yorkists*, pp. 1, 3, 5.

10 **Cecily's expenditure:** For Cecily as a 'late medieval big spender' see Jones, *Bosworth 1485*, p. 59.

11 **debate . . . about Edward's birth:** These are the facts on which Michael K. Jones bases his argument that the suggestion Edward was not York's son was in fact true. He points out (*Bosworth*, p. 67) that York was away from Rouen on campaign exactly nine months before Edward's birth on 28 April 1442; has, indeed, found new documentation which shows the duke was away for longer than had been previously thought – from mid-July until after 20 August. But the baby would have had to be only a matter of weeks late or premature to put the argument in jeopardy, even disregarding the possibility of conjugal visits during a campaign fought only 50 miles away. See Crawford, *Yorkists*, pp. 173–8 for the facts that weigh against the theory. Jones also suggests that Cecily's later piety was that of the reformed rake; but this theory, though fascinating, can only be speculative.

12 **Edward took after his mother:** Edward's different appearance would later be held up as evidence of his illegitimacy. But the same grounds would also be used by Richard III to infer the bastardy of Edward's brother Clarence, who himself had been the first to accuse Edward of bastardy; and Clarence was born some years and several siblings down the line, and in a different country.

13 **no sign of querying his son's paternity:** and this as the all-important heir. As Horace Walpole put it (in *Historic Doubts*) in the eighteenth century – a time of notably lax aristocratic morality – 'Ladies of the least disputable gallantry generally suffer their husbands to beget the heir'.

14 **Mancini:** Dominic Mancini was an Italian visiting England for the first half of 1483 and writing a report on English affairs for his patron Angelo Cato, one of the advisers of the French king Louis.

These comprised Richard III's takeover of the country, as well as a certain amount of background. He left England in July 1483, though he seems to have tried to update his information right up until the point when he handed in his report at the beginning of December. It is unclear how good his sources were – though one may possibly have been John Argentine, physician to the boy king Edward V – or even how much English he spoke. None the less, because he was writing in the year the events he described took place his testimony is invaluable. It is perhaps worth noting that, though his report is usually known as the 'Usurpation' of Richard III, its Latin title actually referred to the '*Occupatio*', i.e. occupation or seizure of the throne, rather than to its '*usurpatio*'.

15 **relayed by . . . Charles of Burgundy:** When it reached Louis of France, so the report runs, he enjoyed it so much that he pretended deafness, so it might be repeated to him. But the sixteenth-century historian Pierre de Bourdeille, Seigneur de Brantome, reported in his *Memoirs* that Louis was a collector of 'bawdy-tales of loose-living ladies . . . [He] had a very low opinion of women, and believed none to be chaste.' A story concerning the notoriously pious Cecily, mother to Louis' rival Edward, would surely have been a particularly effective passport to his favour. Pierre de Bourdeille, *The Lives of Gallant Ladies*, Pushkin Press, 1943, p. 325.

16 **Jean de Waurin:** Jean or Jehan de Waurin (*c.*1398–*c.*1474) was born a Frenchman but wound up at the court of Burgundy, where he was commissioned to write a history of England, ending in 1471. A single copy of his *Recueil* survived in the library of Louis de Gruuthuyse, q.v.

17 **Marguerite, whose father:** Although some said now that Marguerite was not even her father's legitimate daughter, an accusation hurled against her by Edward in Shakespeare's *Henry VI Part 3*, along with the charge that when he married her Henry VI 'took a beggar to his bed'.

18 **Shakespeare has Marguerite pleading:** *Henry VI Part 2*, Act 3, Scene 2.

19 **a high-spending queen:** Myers and Clough in *Crown, Household and Parliament in Fifteenth Century England*: studies on 'The Household of Queen Margaret of Anjou, 1452–3'; 'Some Household Ordinances of Henry VI'; as well as on 'The Household of Queen Elizabeth Woodville, 1466–7'.

20 **Margaret [Beaufort] had been raised at her own family seat:**
Though another theory (see Hardyment, *Malory*, p. 244) suggests that
she was at least partly raised in Alice Chaucer's household at Ewelme.

21 **Cecily . . . wrote to Marguerite:** Crawford, *Letters of Medieval Women*,
pp. 233–5. On the birth of her son Richard Cecily writes of an
'encumberous labour, to me full painful and uneasy, God knoweth'.

22 **Thomas More:** More's *History of King Richard the Third* brings into
sharp focus many of the issues which bedevil the historical sources
for the late fifteenth century. That focus is all the sharper not only
for More's own later reputation as a figure of probity, but for the
extremely attractive (and quotable) nature of his writing – full of
lengthy reported speeches and the kind of human drama not always
found in other sources of the day.

The first question is whether More can be regarded as a
contemporary, given that he – born in 1478 – is describing the
events of 1483. (His mention of Richard's birth, like his descriptions
of Richard's brother's marriage, are all part of the back story to his
main theme.) But this apart, the long impassioned speeches he gives
to Elizabeth Woodville and her opponents over the surrendering of
the younger of the Princes in the Tower could in any case not
credibly have been relayed to him verbatim even by someone who
was present. They give point to the observation that his *History* is as
much a matter of literary creation as factual narrative – a conscious
warning against the dangers of tyranny owing a good deal to
classical models. (Unless – a suggestion mooted by R.S. Sylvester,
editing the sixteen-volume Yale edition of More's works – he was
drawing on a now-lost piece of writing by someone, possibly John
Morton, in whose household the youthful More spent some time.)

Morton (whose own experience would help account for More's
anti-Richard bias) has most often been suggested as More's probable
source of information: other theories, however, have been raised.
Jones (*Bosworth*, pp. 63–4) postulates that 'Jane' Shore, whom More
evidently knew, may have given him some information, though she
would hardly have been privy to the speeches mentioned above; Weir
(*The Princes in the Tower*, p. 170) points out that More was in close
touch with a nun in the Minoresses' convent of Aldgate, the inmates
of which might have had important information to give him

concerning the fate of the princes (the daughter of Sir Robert Brackenbury and two female relatives of Sir James Tyrell: see Part v, note 23 on p. 375 for Tyrell's supposed confession). It is More's testimony concerning the fate of the princes which has been more influential even than Vergil's in blackening the reputation of Richard III: none the less, supporters of King Richard can choose between simply blaming him for calumny, and speculating that the reason he left his narrative unfinished, ending at the point of the murder, may have been that he had come to realise this version of events was a lie. Assuming, of course, that he did indeed abandon it at this point . . . *The History of King Richard III* was printed only two decades after his death, at which time it was described merely as having been found among More's papers and was in his hand, so that even the authorship could – the crowning uncertainty – be seen as unclear.

23 **honour or dishonour:** Helen Cooper writes in her introduction to the OUP edition of Malory's *Morte d'Arthur*: 'Malory's Arthurian world operates by the principles of a shame culture, where worth is measured in terms of reputation, "worship", rather than by the principles of a guilt culture.'

24 **several of the early Norman queens:** The two Matildas – the Conqueror's wife and daughter-in-law – exercised this kind of power, as did Eleanor of Aquitaine, while in 1253 Henry III had named his queen Eleanor of Provence regent during his absence.

25 **process was completed:** Maurer in *Margaret of Anjou* states on p. 78: 'There has been a tendency among historians to acknowledge Margaret's [*sic*] emergence as a political actor but then to shy away from looking at it too closely. A part of the problem lies in the traditional habit of regarding the Wars of the Roses from the perspective of its male protagonists.' See also Maurer, pp. 81–2.

26 **two sides of the same unnatural coin:** This is the theory by which Richard, in *Henry VI P*art 3, 5.5 accused her of having usurped her husband's breeches, i.e. his masculinity.

27 **Anne Neville:** Another aspect of Neville power was that it was northern. Anne Neville was, of course, great-niece as well, eventually, as daughter-in-law to Cecily.

28 **perhaps physically:** The famous thirteenth-century tract *Holy Maidenhead* paints a horrifying picture of maternity: 'a swelling

in your womb which bulges you out like a water-skin, discomfort in your bowels and stitches in your side . . . the dragging weight of your two breasts, and the streams of milk that run from them. . . . Worry about your labour pains keeps you awake at night. Then when it comes to it, that cruel distressing anguish, that incessant misery, that torment upon torment, that wailing outcry; while you are suffering from this, and from your fear of death, shame [is] added to that suffering. . . .' (Leyser, *Medieval Women*, p. 123). The same tract paints an equally damning picture of a wife's lot – the child screaming, 'the cat at the flitch and the dog at the hide, her loaf burning on the hearth and her calf sucking, the pot boiling over into the fire – and her husband complaining.' (Leyser, p. 146). But at least that is a position with which Margaret Beaufort would not have to cope. The tract may have been written specifically for an audience of enclosed religious women: later in life Margaret Beaufort would be recorded as fitting out a cell for at least one anchoress, at Stamford in Lincolnshire, and making her gifts of wine and apples.

29   **Bernard André:** Also known as Andreus, 1450–1522, French Augustinian friar who was appointed Poet Laureate in the first few years of Henry VII's reign; became his official 'historiographer' (and inevitably apologist); and played a role in the education of his sons. *Vita Henrici Septimi* in *Memorials of King Henry VII*, ed. J. Gairdner, Rolls Series, London, 1858.

30   **a new marriage had to be arranged for her:** Or perhaps – since she did, after all, ride out to be present at the negotiations – her modern biographers are right to suggest she took a hand in arranging it herself. Earlier biographers of Margaret Beaufort preferred to stress her piety and resignation.

31   **unmanly and cruelly was entreated:** *English Chronicle of the Reigns of Richard II, Henry IV, Henry V and Henry VI*, p. 83.

32   **'submitted her unto his grace':** *Gregory's Chronicle*, p. 206.

33   **relief of [Cecily] and her infants:** *Calendar of Patent Rolls, Henry VI, 1452–61*, p. 542.

34   **the Countess of Salisbury was personally attainted:** a comparatively novel procedure where a woman was concerned. From the

parliamentary rolls of 1442: 'Also pray the commons . . . that it may please you, by the advice and assent of the lords spiritual and temporal in this present parliament assembled, to declare that such ladies (duchesses, countesses, or baronesses) thus indicted . . . of any treason or felony . . . whether they are married or single, should be held to reply and set for judgement before such judges and peers of the realm as are other peers of the realm. . . .'

35 **chair of blue velvet:** Weightman, *Margaret of York*, p. 45; *Paston Letters*, iii, p. 233.

36 **Hall and Holinshed:** For *The Union of the Two Noble Families of Lancaster and York* Hall (*c.*1498–1547) drew heavily on Vergil and on More; in fact, when More's *History* was first printed, it was described as having appeared earlier in Hall but 'very much corrupt . . . altered in words and whole sentences'. Raphael Holinshed (?–1580) first published the *Chronicles* containing his *History of England* in 1577; his work, more directly even than Hall's, which in large parts it reproduces (a modern age would say plagiarises), is the major source for Shakespeare's history plays. John Stow (1525–1605, mentioned subsequently in text), who contributed to a later edition of Holinshed's work, was also an antiquary who transcribed a number of manuscripts.

37 **pillaged the land:** There is a theory that the whole saga of Marguerite's indifference and her soldiers' outrage originated as Yorkist propaganda. See Cron's article 'Margaret of Anjou and the Lancastrian March on London 1461'.

38 **the ladies were Ismanie, Lady Scales . . . :** That, at least, is the consensus view, though Cron's article (see above) demonstrates how this is a good example of the way information has often to be pieced together from diverging sources. The *Great Chronicle of London* mentions Jacquetta and Lady Scales but not Anne; the *Annales* once attributed to the antiquary William Worcester and the *Calendar of State Papers Milan* mention Anne and Jacquetta but not Lady Scales: another source, the so-called *English Chronicle* edited by Davies, has Anne alone.

39 **her eldest daughter Elizabeth:** The name of Domina Isabella (the Latin 'Elizabeth') Grey occurs among the ladies attending Queen Marguerite at a point when (in so far as the records allow a guess

at dates to be made) the young Elizabeth Woodville had probably recently been married to the Lancastrian John Grey. This reference may well describe another lady; none the less, Thomas More would mention Elizabeth's service with Marguerite as a fact. The nineteenth-century writer Prévost d'Exiles relates a romantic story that Elizabeth had accompanied her husband on the campaign and was, before St Albans, persuaded by Marguerite to visit Warwick's camp as the queen's spy.

40 **The Bishop of Elphin ... sets the glad tidings later:** *Calendar of State Papers Venetian*, p. 103; also *Calendar of State Papers Milan*, pp. 65–6.

Part II 1461–1471

1 **the lands held by his father:** See *Calendar of Patent Rolls Edward IV 1461–67*, p. 131 (1 June 1461), an extremely extensive list of properties (with their 'advowsons, wards, marriages, escheats . . . warrens, chases, fairs, markets, fisheries, liberties, wrecks of sea') granted to Cecily for life 'in full recompense of her jointure'. A later grant describes her holding properties, which carried with them the right to hold a three-weekly court, 'as fully as the king's father had them'. See also *Calendar of the Close Rolls Edward IV, vol. i, 1461–68*, p. 73.

2 **couple were estranged:** When in 1461 Exeter was forced to flee abroad and was attainted, his wife was granted the bulk of his lands; and if this favour came at a price (in 1466 she was required to allow her heiress daughter to marry a son of Queen Elizabeth Woodville), no doubt she felt it was well worth paying.

3 **another . . . issue would raise its head:** see p. 155 below. The possibility of Edward's having been already married is explored at length in Ashdown-Hill's *Eleanor: The Secret Queen*; see also Crawford, *Yorkists*, pp. 178–9.

4 **'to love together':** Against that, an unsanctioned love match in 1469 of Margery Paston with Richard Calle, the family's bailiff, had, her mother claimed, 'struck sore at our hearts'. The bishop hauled in to adjudicate, who by no means thought such a matter too light for him, assured Margery that if she persisted in claiming this marriage,

none of her friends would receive her – 'remember', Margery's mother Margaret urged her son, 'that we have lost of her but a brothel, and set it less to heart . . .'. Love within an agreed marriage was of course another, wholly desirable, thing. A letter in the *Stonor Papers*, from a partner in the firm who had been betrothed to a teenaged Stonor daughter not yet deemed ready to complete the match: 'when I remember your youth, and see well that you are no eater of your meat, which would help you greatly to grow, forsooth then you make me very heavy again. And therefore I pray you, my own sweet cousin, even as you love me, to be happy and eat your meat like a woman. And if you will do so for my love, look what you will desire of me, whatsoever it may be, and by my truth I promise by the help of our Lord to perform it to the best of my power.' The messages here are potentially mixed, of course – but the young Katherine was sufficiently content with her lot to show a 'responsible loving dealing' towards her future partner.

5 **The only Englishwoman to become queen consort since the Conquest:** The closest comparisons would probably be with Matilda of Scotland, wife of Henry I, whose mother came from a Saxon royal house; and Joan of Kent, who made a controversial marriage with the Black Prince, son of Edward III. It could not, however, be held against Matilda that she was not of royal stock; while the Black Prince died before he became king, or Joan queen.

6 **Cecily elaborated her title:** Chamberlayne 'A paper crown'; see also Crawford, *Yorkists*, pp. 175–6.

7 **until de Brezé found her:** Nor were her dramatic adventures over. When she and her son, with de Brezé, had ridden back into Scotland, they fell into the hands of an English spy called Cook who planned to take her to Edward IV. Cook's confederates overpowered the men, dragged them all into a rowing boat and put out to sea where, as dawn broke, Marguerite was able surreptitiously to loosen de Brezé's bonds so that he was able to overpower Cook and they got away.

8 **A queen was allowed . . . to exercise influence:** Men, of course, exercised influence as well, but they had more formalised rules also, which meant that the dangerous, mistrusted interaction of the political and the personal was one step further away.

9 **Messengers . . . bringing instructions from Marguerite:** Malory's biographer Christina Hardyment postulates (*Malory*, p. 419 ff) that he may have been employed as a go-between.

10 **Woking:** In December 1468 the Staffords invited the king to visit Woking; perhaps it was to calm frayed nerves, and to signal continued good intentions, that he accepted. He hunted in the deer park and dined in the hunting lodge under a canopy of purple sarcenet, on a pewter dinner service brought down from London by a hostess who had purchased velvet and Holland cloth to dress for the occasion. The party ate pike, wildfowl, thirteen lampreys and seven hundred oysters, with 'half a great conger for the king's dinner'.

11 **'Worcester':** The chronicler once mistakenly identified as the fifteenth-century antiquary William of Worcester, and now often known as 'pseudo-Worcester'.

12 **Clarence's mother Cecily had now told him this was true:** Jones, *Bosworth*, p. 73. Militating against the theory that Cecily here fell out with Edward is (as Joanna Laynesmith points out in the article cited in the next note) the fact that in a time of danger soon after- wards – a time when he had, however, been reconciled with Clarence – Edward took his family for safety to his mother's house; and that Cecily was recorded as taking part in several family cere- monials in the years ahead. As several writers have also reflected, however, within the context of a family irritation is not the same thing as total alienation – now or in the fifteenth century.

13 **Cecily and her daughters . . . working:** Like so much concerning Cecily's role in the Clarence saga this seems to be, as Jane Austen put it, 'a truth universally acknowledged' rather than one for which it is possible to produce actual proof. For discussion of that role, see Laynesmith, 'The Kings' Mother'; also Jones, *Bosworth*, Chapter 3 for his theory as to Cecily's motives in travelling to Sandwich to see Clarence as he set off for Calais and marriage with Warwick's daughter.

14 **Marguerite held out for fifteen days:** Shakespeare in *Henry VI Part 3*, Act 3, Scene 2 takes full dramatic licence to have Warwick change his allegiance, and Marguerite accept it, in half a dozen lines or the blink of an eye.

15 **Commynes:** Philippe de Commynes or Commines (1447–*c.*1511) made the opposite journey to that of Jean de Waurin. Born in Flanders, he wound up in the service of the French king Louis XI (at which court he may have met the exiled Henry Tudor). His *Mémoires* reflect the insider's view of international relations that he gained in his career as a diplomat, while his analytical style has seen him dubbed 'the first truly modern writer'.

16 **his force met Warwick's at Barnet:** The reports of the battle serve as a good example of how news spread. The battle of Barnet started at dawn 12 miles outside London. Wild rumours were abroad early and by 10 a.m. the city was hearing tales of Edward's victory, but these were disbelieved until, the *Great Chronicle of London* says, a rider raced through the streets displaying one of Edward's own gauntlets, sent as token to his queen. A Norfolk man claimed to have seen the bodies of Warwick and Montague at St Paul's that morning. Wanting to be the first to deliver the news back home, he took a boat after dinner, about twelve, but was captured at sea by merchants of the Hanseatic league and taken to Zeeland where his story was quickly taken to Margaret of Burgundy at Ghent. Margaret wrote a letter describing it to her mother-in-law and presumably also to her husband – who, however, was also getting erroneous news that Edward IV had been killed.

17 **womanly behaviour . . . of the Queen:** Agnes Strickland's early Victorian *Lives of the Queens of England* claimed that Elizabeth's 'feminine helplessness' had drawn forth a 'tender regard' for her throughout the realm, in contrast to the effect produced by the 'indomitable spirit' of Marguerite of Anjou. The comparison might be phrased differently today, but contemporaries clearly agreed.

Part III 1471–1483

1 **Cecily . . . 'sore moved' Sir John to sell her the place:** Castor, *Blood and Roses*, p. 119. She had, after all, grown up in far less commodious establishments: Raby was a palace-cum-fortress rebuilt almost a century earlier, with towers and apartments irregularly grouped round courtyards.

2 **disguised as a kitchen maid:** If that sounds too much like Cinderella in the fairy story, it should be remembered not only that Marguerite is supposed to have travelled disguised as a servant, but that in the turmoils of the 1440s Alice Chaucer had had to go to Norwich disguised 'like a housewife of the country'.

3 **the dispensation:** Anne's biographer Michael Hicks (*Anne Neville*, p. 143 ff) has written on what he believes to be the invalidity of the dispensation and therefore of the marriage; clearly not a subject of debate at the time, but casting an interesting light on Richard's attitudes.

4 **any other choices:** And Hicks, for example (*Anne Neville*, p.111), though without citing actual evidence, portrays it as her own decision to marry Richard.

5 **George Buck:** Sir George Buck, 1560–1622, James I's Master of the Revels, Richard III's first determined apologist, and author of the *History of King Richard the Third*. Buck's account plays a significant part in the history of the next reign (see below, pp. 225–7) at which time it will, however, become clear that information from this source must be treated warily.

6 **Rous:** John Rous, Rows or Roos (d. 1491), Warwickshire cleric and antiquary, the chronicler of Anne Neville's family. His *Rous Roll*, a history of the earls of Warwick, warmly praised Anne's husband, then on the throne as Richard III; later, however, his *History of the Kings of England* vilified the dead king just as ardently. It was this work that first saw the portrait, seized upon by Shakespeare, of a Richard who spent two years in his mother's womb, emerging complete with teeth and long hair.

7 **a declaration of trust:** Cecily, by contrast, spent the summer well away from the seat of power. A letter from Margaret Paston to her son John (*Paston Letters* vol. 5 p. 236) describes how 'my Lady of Yorke and all her household is [*sic*] still here at St Bennet's [an abbey near the Paston home of Mautby in Norfolk] and purposed to abide there still, till the king come from be yonder the sea, and longer if she like the air there'. The *Paston Letters* contain a number of references to Cecily; see, for example, vol. 3 pp. 110, 233, 366.

8 **the reburial at Fotheringhay:** Sutton and Visser-Fuchs, *The Reburial of Richard Duke of York*.

9   **simply watched the ceremony:** Sutton and Visser-Fuchs say Cecily was certainly conspicuous 'for her absence, or for the failure of the texts to refer to her'. They speculate on the possibility that 'Her status as the widow of a man who was being buried almost as a king may have created problems of precedence that were best resolved by her merely watching'; suggesting alternatively that she may have been absent from sickness 'or choice'.

10   **Elizabeth Stonor writes:** Crawford, *Letters of Medieval Women*, pp. 75–7; *Stonor Letters*, pp. 269–71.

11   **One letter perhaps written in 1474:** Crawford, *Letters of Medieval Women*, pp. 133–4. For the possible significance of Syon in the family dynamics, and the shared piety here reflected as a bond between Richard and Cecily, see Jones, *Bosworth*, p. 78. Crawford, *Yorkists*, p. 66, however, sees Edward IV's later decision to call one of his youngest daughters Bridget, 'a name almost unknown in England', as a reflection of Cecily's devotion to St Bridget of Sweden and the Bridgettine abbey of Syon. See note 20.

12   **Cecily's second daughter Elizabeth . . . access of independence:** The Paston letters suggest that John was perhaps dominated by his mother Alice; as possibly, at least in her younger years, was Elizabeth herself, who in any case would have been fairly well occupied with her childbearing. In 1468 the Pastons reported that Queen Elizabeth had been persuaded to write to 'my lady of Norfolk and another letter unto my lady of Suffolk the elder' – Alice. It is noteworthy that the Pastons first found it worth petitioning Elizabeth herself – to intercede in a land dispute – just after Alice's death in 1475. But Elizabeth's awareness of the need for status and finery continued to be at war with her and her husband's comparatively low financial standing. Present when Edward made one of his few gestures to education, at Oxford in 1481, she could be found writing (in, most unusually for any fifteenth-century noblewoman, her own hand) to John Paston, asking if she might have the use of his rooms at Windsor. 'For God's sake, say me not nay.'

13   **the ever-troublesome Scots:** Edward had the option of other marital plans as a peaceable way of dealing with the Scots. A letter of 1477 to his ambassador in Scotland replies to the Scots king's suggestion that Clarence and his sister Margaret should marry a

sister and brother of his own – despite the fact that Edward pleaded both were still in their period of 'doule' or mourning, and that until they were out of it he would not be able to 'feel their dispositions'. It is, however, again a moot point whether he would have wished thus to advance his dangerous brother.

14 **daughter of the great Earl of Shrewsbury:** Eleanor Butler was also, through her mother, niece by marriage to Warwick; and Shakespeare only echoes other sources in having Warwick cast up against Edward 'th'abuse done to my niece' *Henry VI Part 3*, 3.3; speaking also of the difficulty of this king's being 'contented by one wife' *ibid* 4.3.

15 **Thomas More . . . Elizabeth Lucy:** More also has Cecily, at the time of Elizabeth Woodville's marriage to Edward and 'under pretence of her duty towards God', sending for Elizabeth Lucy and putting considerable, though ultimately unavailing, pressure on her to stake her prior claim. The idea of precontract was regularly encountered: the *Mirror for Magistrates* of 1559 would suggest that Humfrey, the old Duke of Gloucester, had attempted to prevent Marguerite of Anjou's marriage on the grounds that Henry VI was precontracted to another lady.

16 **as one author puts it:** Jones, whose theory this is, writes in *Bosworth*, p. 35, of 'a far more collective sense of identity held by medieval society . . . As custodians of an historical pedigree, a family would together determine where the interests of its lineage lay and act to defend it.'

17 **good ladyship:** Both letters in Crawford, *Letters of the Queens of England*, pp. 142–3; see also Crawford, *Letters of Medieval Women*, p. 238, for Cecily's exercise of influence.

18 **[Cecily] can be glimpsed:** See, e.g., the *Calendar of Patent Rolls Edward IV 1467–77*, pp. 89, 151; also *Edward IV and V and Richard III 1476–85*, pp. 218, 459, 522. See also *Calendar of Patent Rolls Edward IV and V and Richard III*, p. 441, and *Calendar of Papal Registers*, vol. 13, part I, pp. 106, 260.

19 **A few years later:** *English Historical Documents, vol. 4, 1327–1485*, p. 837 (from *A Collection of Ordinances and Regulations for the Government of the Royal Household*, ed. J Nichols, 1790), a record believed to have been made some time around 1485, which leaves it open to interpretation whether the events which first pushed Cecily to a religious retirement (if that were indeed the sequence of events)

were those of 1478, 1483 or 1485 itself. It is the dwindling traces of her presence at court which inclines me to the earlier date.

20 **Cecily had chosen . . . the mixed life:** See Armstrong, 'The piety of Cicely Duchess of York'; see also Hughes, *The Religious Life of Richard III*, and Laynesmith, 'The King's Mother: Cecily Neville'.

21 **she had it painted:** This work and a number of others mentioned, including the *Shrewsbury Book* and the *Beaufort Hours*, were shown in a British Library exhibition in 2011–12. See catalogue by McKendrick, Lowden and Doyle, *Royal Manuscripts: The Genius of Illumination*.

22 **their mother too was a patron of Caxton's:** Gregory, Baldwin and Jones, *The Women of the Cousins' War*, suggest (p. 135) she may be the noble lady who, in the interests of her daughters' moral education, commissioned from Caxton a translation of the manual for young ladies, *The Book of the Knight of the Tower*.

23 **her Victorian biographer Mary Ann Hookham:** Hookham also quotes the local historian of the nineteenth century, J.F. Bodin: 'Her blood, corrupted by so many sombre emotions, became like a poison, which infected all the parts that it should nourish; her skin dried up, until it crumbled away in dust; her stomach contracted, and her eyes, as hollow and sunken as if they had been driven into her head, lost all the fire, which had, for so long a time, served to interpret the lofty sentiments of her soul.'

Part IV 1483–1485

1 **his wishes no longer paramount:** This begs the question of whether deathbed codicils to Edward's will (mentioned by both Crowland and Mancini but, if made, since lost) had in any case removed the powers formerly given to her.

2 **even female:** The hint of Richard's double prescience – both as to Edward V's fate and Elizabeth of York's future importance – cannot necessarily this time be put down to hindsight since Mancini's narrative ended, with his visit, in the summer of 1483.

3 **confided to his wife:** Anne's role in events is one of the great imponderables. Shakespeare, in *Richard III*, Act 4, Scene 1, would have a scene of mutual lamentation when the three women – Elizabeth

Woodville, Anne Neville and Cecily – get the first inkling of Richard's plans. But there is no reason to assume this was the reality (it certainly failed to reflect the dissent between Elizabeth and her mother-in-law). Janis Lull, introducing the CUP edition of the play, notes on p. 9 that the triad has been compared to the lamentations of Helena, Andromache and Hecuba in Seneca's *Troades*, and explores also the motif of the three Marys – Mary Magdalene, Mary Salome and Mary the mother of James – in the medieval Resurrection plays.

4 **Margaret Beaufort's ally:** Morton had been one of the protectors involved in the negotiation of Margaret Beaufort's marriage settlements, as well as mediator to Edward IV in her attempt to get her son home.

5 **On 16 June a delegation was sent:** Some sources, Mancini, Vergil and More among them, seem to suggest that the younger boy was surrendered before Hastings' execution; however, the dispassionate evidence of a contemporary letter and an account book suggest the sequence of events followed here.

6 **More's pages need some decoding:** See note 22, p. 354.

7 **Another view:** That of Jones in *Bosworth*: 'The painful turmoil of 1469 was to be mirrored in 1483, as Richard succeeded where Clarence had failed. And as King Richard struggled to overcome the threats from those who opposed this new Yorkist settlement, it was Cecily to whom he appealed for daily blessing in his enterprise. Her role was crucial.' See Chapter 4, 'The Search for Redemption'. It is Jones who cites as evidence the Archbishop's register: *Registrum Thome Bourgchier, Cantanuariensis Archiepiscopi, AD 1454–1486*, ed. F.R.H. Du Boulay, Canterbury and York Soc., LIV, 1957, pp. 52–3. Jones also states (p. 91) that several decades later, in 1535, a conversation between the Spanish ambassador Chapuys and Henry VIII's minister Thomas Cromwell showed that Cecily had made a written confession. The actual statement from Chapuys (CSP Foreign and Dom H8 viii, 281) is that he had told Cromwell that Henry, in seeking a divorce from Katherine of Aragon, was wrong to rely on the statutes of the realm, 'which only depended on the prince's wish, as might be seen by the Acts of King Richard, who . . . caused King Edward himself to be declared a bastard, and to

prove it, called his own mother to bear witness, and caused it to be continually preached so'. From this Jones concludes that Cecily did indeed bear written evidence; that she did so before Shaa preached his sermon; and that she was in London to do it. But this may apportion more weight than Chapuys' statement can really bear. Laynesmith in her article for the *Ricardian* of Autumn 2005, suggests as her own suspicion that Cecily 'did not actively promote Richard's accession, but equally did not oppose it either'. I would be inclined to agree. I am indebted to Dr David Wright for confirming my interpretation of the Latin *Register*.

8 **The right of inheritance to the throne:** Even a hundred years later, when Elizabeth I was dying, there was – to quote the succession historian Nenner (*The Right to Be King*, p. 13) – no agreement as to how the next ruler should be chosen, let alone as to who he or she should be. No one knew 'whether the crown ought to pass automatically at the death of Elizabeth to the next in the hereditary line; whether the next in the hereditary line might be passed over because of a "legal" incapacity to rule; whether the next monarch ought to be determined in parliament; or whether the queen should be exhorted in the waning days of her life to nominate her own successor'.

9 **the grant of [Cecily's] manors and lands:** *Calendar of Patent Rolls Edward IV and V and Richard III*, p. 459.

10 **The list of accounts:** Sutton and Hammond, *The Coronation of Richard III*.

11 **Elizabeth Woodville . . . was so well pleased:** A phrase from Crowland is often cited, which might seem to suggest that Elizabeth had taken a very active and early part in the plotting: 'many things were going on in secret . . . especially on the part of those who had availed themselves of the privilege of sanctuary'. But a fuller quotation describes specifically the people 'of the South and of the West' of the kingdom, 'especially those people who, because of fear, were scattered without franchises and sanctuaries'.

12 **Margaret was on the point of sending . . . Christopher Urswick:** In the end, another messenger would be sent to Brittany, with 'a good great sum of money' raised by Margaret in the city. This next messenger, interestingly, was one Hugh Conway, who had connections not only to Edward IV's household but to the Stanleys.

13 **an outside candidate for villain:** If the Duke of Buckingham had
had the boys killed, then (as Buckingham would surely have calcu-
lated) Richard might indeed have hesitated at least in the short term
to publish the news of their deaths; though one must still ask why
did he not do so later. Henry VII, when the time came, might well
have kept a similar silence. If this were true the guilty man, after all,
was nominally one of Henry's supporters – one of his mother's
close allies.

14 **historians from Vergil and More onwards:** Unless, just possibly,
More broke off his history at the crucial point because he could no
longer subscribe to what he had become convinced was a lie.

15 **Candidates include . . . Margaret Beaufort:** See Maurer's article,
'Whodunit: The Suspects in the Case' for an analysis of the
evidence for the different candidates mooted (who in fact include
even the boys' mother Elizabeth Woodville). Margaret Beaufort is
her personal favourite for the role.

16 **by the vise [advice] of the Duke of Buckingham:** This comforting
theory may have been the one to which Margaret of Burgundy
persuaded herself to subscribe. Of the chroniclers associated with
Burgundy, Molinet blamed Richard but Commynes put at least part
of the guilt on Buckingham. Margaret may, alternatively, have
assumed that any rumours of murder were exaggerated.

17 **evidence . . . is in short supply:** There is, of course, the question of the
bones found in the Tower – but medical examination of them made in
the 1930s could not state with certainty that they were those of the
princes, though the examiners came down on the side of probability.

18 **Some time that month Elizabeth's daughters left sanctuary:**
Vergil says that: 'When the queen was thus qualified, king Richard
received all his brothers' daughters out of sanctuary into the
court'; which might seem to show that they went to court immediately. But a precise timescale was not necessarily the priority of
the contemporary chroniclers: Vergil also implies that all of this
happened after the queen wrote to bring her son Dorset home,
which other evidence shows to have happened a year later.
Crowland writes that Elizabeth Woodville ('after frequent
entreaties as well as threats') 'sent all her daughters out of the
sanctuary at Westminster before mentioned to King Richard' – i.e.

into his charge – implying, however, that this happened rather earlier than other evidence suggests.

19   **quietly allowed to join her:** Even a location for the family's secret residence has been suggested by one of Richard's modern supporters, Audrey Williamson: Gipping Hall in Suffolk, seat of the Tyrell family, whose own tradition suggests that royal children lived 'by permission of the Uncle'. (Williamson, *The Mystery of the Princes*, pp. 122–4). More will be heard of Sir James Tyrell later. This would not only cast a new light on his relations to the princes, but explain why Henry Tudor might later feel the need to put a very different spin on them.

20   **died from natural causes:** This may be another case of arguing from effect to cause. Professor Wright, who in the 1930s examined two children's skeletons found within the Tower, noted that the skeleton of the elder child bore the symptoms of what has been tentatively diagnosed as the progressive bone disease osteomyelitis. But it is not known for certain whether these skeletons were those of the princes; and though the elder prince was known to have been visited by his doctor that summer, any royal person might have a physician in precautionary attendance anyway.

21   **Francis Bacon:** 1561–1626. Best known as Elizabeth I's counsellor and James I's Attorney-General and Lord Chancellor, he turned wholly to writing after being indicted by parliament on charges of corruption. His *History of Henry VII* was published in 1622.

22   **giving away . . . her family lands:** albeit that some of them were to the Queens' College that honours her as a patron. Some thirty years later the *Great Chronicle* would call her 'a woman of gracious fame'; but of that too there is very little evidence.

23   **of similar colour and shape:** For consistency I have used the older translation of the complete *Crowland Chronicle* (*Ingulph's Chronicle of the Abbey of Croyland with the Continuations by Peter of Blois and Anonymous Writers*, trans. Riley, 1854). Here, however, the more recent translation of the work of the 'second continuator' (*The Crowland Chronicle Continuations 1459–1486*, ed. and trans. Pronay and Cox, 1986) differs in significance as well as wording. Their translation from the Latin ('*eisdem colore et forma*') is 'who were alike in complexion and figure', which clearly indicates the women

rather than the garments. (Dress was an important signifier of rank.) Interpretation has hitherto varied – but the real point is that nothing in the original necessarily compels the popular assumption that Richard had given the garments: Buck indeed says that Anne herself instituted the swap.

24 **damning in several ways:** Shakespeare's wooing (*Richard III*, Act 1, scene 2) by Richard of a Lady Anne still lamenting her first husband, whom Richard had killed, in a sense represents a dramatisation of our reaction to this different, but equally shocking, marriage. It might have been unwise for him to comment more directly on the behaviour of one who was grandmother to Elizabeth I.

25 **letter was a total invention:** Against that theory is the fact that Buck gave a specific source for the letter – in the collection of Thomas Howard, Earl of Arundel, in a 'rich and magnificent cabinet, among precious jewels and more monuments' – and he would have been taking a huge risk that other scholars might have called his bluff. For the theory is the fact that Buck, a determined apologist for Richard, was not above 'suppressing evidence and altering record', as one modern historian, Alison Hanham, declared. N. Harris Nicolas in the nineteenth century put it even more directly: 'the character of Buck as a faithless writer is well known'. The great Victorian James Gairdner, on the other hand, was disgustedly inclined to accept the letter, writing that 'the horrible perversion and degradation of domestic life which it implies is only too characteristic of the age' – so different, one can't but add, from the home life of his own dear queen.

26 **article for the *Ricardian*:** Kincaid, 'Buck and the Elizabeth of York Letter'. See also Visser-Fuchs, 'Elizabeth of York's Letter', *Ricardian* Bulletin, Winter 2004 and 'Where Did Elizabeth of York Find Consolation?' and of course Kincaid's introduction to his edition of Buck's *History of King Richard the Third*.

27 **the marriage proposed for Elizabeth:** Details of the Portuguese proposal, and Elizabeth of York's role in it, from Ashdown-Hill, *The Last Days of Richard III*. Ashdown-Hill suggests (p. 32) that rumours about a foreign match for her and one for Richard were

misunderstood (by contemporaries as well as by later historians) as concerning a match between her and Richard.

28 **the Great Chronicle recorded:** Although some internal evidence, confusingly, would suggest that this entry was intended to describe the spring of 1484.

29 **the *Ballad of Lady Bessy*:** The *Ballad of Lady Bessy* (or, *The Most Pleasant Song of Ladye Bessiye*) is believed probably to have been written by Stanley's officer Humphrey Brereton – chiefly because it is hard otherwise to account for the large part Brereton himself plays in the narrative.

30 **his mother Cecily Neville's residence:** Ashdown-Hill, *The Last Days of Richard III*, p. 53, cites R. Edwards, *The Itinerary of King Richard III*, 1983.

31 **The Middle Ages . . . died:** If, of course, they can be said ever to have existed in any definable form. The term is in many ways as spurious as 'Wars of the Roses' and is certainly capable of wildly elastic limits. While in England the battles of Hastings and of Bosworth provide convenient starting and ending points, the period is sometimes seen as beginning with the fall of the Roman Empire, while a school of French historians argued convincingly that for the mass of their population – the illiterate rural poor – they lasted until the industrial revolution.

Part V 1485–1509

1 **starting place of the early modern age:** Rubin in *The Hollow Crown*, p. 322: 'Historians have claimed that a "new" monarchy arose with the coming of Henry VII, that a new age was inaugurated . . . But wise readers should be wary of the "new" . . . Most change, deep change, occurs more slowly, experimentally, cautiously, and through deliberation. It thus often goes unnoticed by those who live it and make it happen.'

2 **said Francis Bacon:** In his *History* of Henry VII. The question of whether a woman's right of inheritance to the throne should automatically pass over her to her sons was of course still an issue in the mid-sixteenth century when Edward VI attempted to will his crown to 'Lady Jane's heirs male', before being forced by the imminence of

his own death to alter it to Jane Grey and her heirs male. See also Castor, *She-Wolves*, pp. 28–9.

3 **silent uncertainty was everybody's friend:** Baldwin in Gregory et al., *The Women of the Cousins' War*, p. 210: 'It is impossible to believe' that those women closest to them – women in positions of power – remained in complete ignorance of the boys' fate. He concludes not only that 'The implication is that they did know but chose to remain silent, something that would not have been necessary if both boys were dead and threatened no one', but that 'the most likely scenario' is that the younger son at least may have been sent to a secure place.

4 **Lincoln's own attempt:** Francis Bacon: 'And as for the daughters of King Edward the Fourth, they thought King Richard had said enough for them [i.e. the people thought that Richard's example showed they were not the inevitable heirs], and took them to be but as of the King's party, because they were in his power and at his disposing.'

5 **discontent with the King:** Elizabeth Woodville's biographer Baldwin suggests as one possibility that she envisaged a papal dispensation allowing Elizabeth of York, with Henry out of the way, to marry her cousin Warwick while she herself became the power behind a monarch believed to be of feeble personality. There is, as he says, no evidence. Another possibility is that Elizabeth knew one of her sons was alive and intended, should the rebellion succeed, to assert his prior claim in place of Warwick's; though this might suggest that she had not been sure of her son's fate earlier, when she allowed her daughter to marry herself and her valuable royal rights into the opposing dynasty.

6 **fundamental role in the Lambert Simnel drama:** Weightman, *Margaret of York*, p. 153.

7 **John Leland:** Best known for his *Itinerary*, describing his findings on journeys through England and Wales. Leland (?1503–1552) was also the antiquary whose *De Rebus Britannicis Collectanea* contains a number of the most important descriptions of key ceremonies in Henry VII's reign. Narratives quoted from this source include Margaret Beaufort's ordinances for the confinement of a queen and the christening of her child (vol. iv, pp. 179–84); the christening of Prince Arthur (pp. 204–15); Elizabeth of York's coronation (pp. 216–33);

the Twelfth Night celebrations of 1487 (pp. 234–7); Elizabeth's taking to her chamber (p. 249); the proxy marriage of Princess Margaret and her journey to Scotland (pp. 258–300).

8 **evidence that she was in some degree of disgrace:** Theories that Elizabeth Woodville's health had gone into some sort of major decline, necessitating her retirement, are contradicted by the fact that the negotiations for her to marry the king of Scots went on for years: see Baldwin in Gregory et al., *The Women of the Cousins' War*, p. 215. But then again, if Elizabeth were seriously suspected of treason it is unlikely Henry would have contemplated giving her access to a foreign army.

9 **placid, domestic sort of creature:** Nicholas Harris Nicolas, editing her Privy Purse expenses in 1830: 'The energy and talents of Henry the Seventh left no opportunity for his Queen to display any other qualities than those which peculiarly, and it may be said exclusively, belong to her sex. From the time of her marriage she is only to be heard of as a daughter, a wife, a mother, a sister, and an aunt; and in each of these relations, so far as materials exist by which it can be judged, her conduct reflects honour upon her memory.'

10 **letters to Spain:** There was also considerable mention in De Puebla's correspondence of Elizabeth's determination to arrange a marriage with an Englishwoman for De Puebla himself, and his efforts to avoid it. Perhaps one of the early lessons Elizabeth had learnt was that marriage as a means of bringing a party to your own side might be the most useful tool of diplomacy.

11 **similarities in their handwriting:** Starkey, *Henry: Virtuous Prince*, pp. 118–20.

12 **Elizabeth of York and Margaret Beaufort as rivals:** Laynesmith argues that between the two – both of whose royal blood had caused their fortunes to seesaw in the years past – 'there probably existed more than cordial relations', equivalent to those between Eleanor of Provence and Eleanor of Castile some 250 years earlier. Elizabeth's biographer Okerlund suggests that Margaret Beaufort may have substituted for the absent Elizabeth Woodville – if Margaret really did have that sort of warm personality?

13 **A letter from Henry VIII's day:** Ellis (ed.), *Original letters illustrative of English history*, series 1, vol. 2.

14 **we have, moreover, opened the moneybox:** *Calendar of State Papers Venetian*, p. 181, 9 May 1489.

15 **Henry offered this daughter [Margaret]:** The elder Margaret, Margaret Beaufort, had always promoted her half-blood family and the autumn of 1494 was also when she arranged for Richard Pole – the son of her half-sister, Edith St John – to marry Clarence's daughter Margaret. This would prove to be setting up trouble: for the Tudor dynasty, but also for Margaret Pole who, as the increasingly paranoid eyes of an ageing Henry VIII focused on her family, would be beheaded in one of the Tower's nastiest execution stories. At the time, however – since it may have seemed unrealistic to keep Margaret Pole for ever unmarried – it may have looked like the safe thing to do, another way of using the marriage tie to secure her within the family.

16 **servants of Cecily Neville's:** Wroe, *Perkin*, pp. 178–9.

17 **as her will declared:** *Wills from Doctors' Commons.*

18 **another daughter, Mary, was born:** Her date of birth is often given as 1495, which is how it is described in the *Beaufort Hours* – but Margaret Beaufort followed the then-current practice of beginning a new year on 23 March.

19 **Warbeck/Richard declared himself king:** Among his otherwise rather vague charges against Henry was that he had married 'by compulsion certain of our sisters' – Elizabeth's younger sisters – to his own friends and kinsmen of unsuitably low degree.

20 **Katherine Gordon . . . treatment:** Wroe, *Perkin*, pp. 374–8.

21 **Margaret of York's illegitimate son:** There is a possible alternative identification, as suggested by Wroe (*Perkin*, pp. 516–18). The childless Margaret took several children under her wing (and indeed even the fertile Elizabeth of York's Privy Purse expenses show upkeep for children who had been 'given' to her). One of Margaret's appeared to have attracted her special interest: Jehan le Sage, a boy of about five when she adopted him in 1478, which makes him around the same age as Richard, Duke of York. Carefully educated and luxuriously clad, he was reared in some seclusion until – at the end of 1485, just when Margaret must have been swallowing the bitter knowledge of the destruction of the house of York – he vanished from the records. It may be pure coincidence that the room

in the country palace of Binche in which he lived was later known as 'Richard's room'. Wroe notes also (pp. 467–71) that the delegation sent to enquire into Perkin's fate was headed by the Bishop of Cambrai; among those who believed Perkin to be Margaret's own son, it was said (p. 209) that he had been fathered by the incumbent of the Cambrai see, whether this man or his predecessor.

22 **jousted for her:** Among the fighters – so John Younge, the Somerset Herald who wrote the description, noted, 'Charles Brandon had right well jousted.' A dozen or so years down the line Brandon would be the husband in Mary Tudor's unsanctioned second marriage.

23 **Tyrell . . . confessed to having . . . murdered:** Such a declaration was never published, nor seen by any of those who mention it. Indeed, though both Vergil and the *Great Chronicle* (both postdating 1502) refer to Tyrell's guilt or at least the possibility of it, mention of the confession, so dramatically utilised by Shakespeare, can be traced back only as far as Thomas More. But in early to mid-August 1483, so the tale runs, Richard had ordered Sir Robert Brackenbury, the man in charge of the Tower, to put the boys to death; but Brackenbury had refused. He did, however, agree to turn the keys over for one night to a less scrupulous man – Tyrell, who enlisted two ruffians called Miles Forrest and John Dighton to do the actual deed.

There are both indications and counter-indications as to the truth of the tale. Those for include the fact that Richard rewarded Brackenbury for deeds unspecified, reappointing him to his post for life in March 1484 'considering his good and loyal service to us before this time, and for certain other considerations especially moving us'; and that Tyrell too prospered under his rule. But in fact Tyrell was not in 1483 the needy man on the make Thomas More depicts – his name has indeed cropped up, as a successful court official, earlier in this tale. Some theories that have the younger prince, at least, released alive also have him hidden at the Tyrell family seat; while the fact that in late 1484 Richard sent Tyrell to Flanders 'for divers matters greatly concerning the King's weal' could be taken to suggest that Tyrell had escorted the boy to safer hiding there.

Indeed, almost every piece of evidence can be taken two ways (even, indeed, the fact that Tyrell had once been in Cecily

Neville's wardship and Audrey Williamson points out, *Mystery*, p. 178, that a Miles Forrest was one of Cecily's attendants). In June 1486 Henry VII issued Tyrell with a general pardon for anything he had done before that date; on 16 July he issued him with another one: almost as if, in the intervening month, Tyrell had, with Henry's knowledge, committed some other heinous crime. (If Henry found the boys alive after Bosworth, it would seem odd that he should have kept them alive for almost a year and then murdered them. Perhaps Elizabeth of York's pregnancy gave an urgent reason to remove any threat to his dynasty. It has even been suggested that Elizabeth Woodville found out what Henry had done, and that this was why she was despatched to her convent so abruptly.) After that time Tyrell continued to thrive under Henry's rule, albeit that the posts Henry gave him kept him out of the country. When Tyrell was finally attainted in 1504 it was only for treason in connection with Suffolk, while Dighton (both Forrest and Brackenbury being already dead) was left at liberty. Bacon says that Henry 'gave out' word of Tyrell's guilt, but there is no sign of his having actually published any confession – which seems incomprehensible. It must go down as yet another mystery – and one of those stories that do not reflect well on the Tudor dynasty.

24 **velvet-clad effigy:** The effigy (or part of it) is still there in the precinct museum – a bald head, long stripped of its wig and crown; a wooden arm and hand. It looks like a monstrous doll – the broken toy of some giant child. The body of straw-stuffed leather fell victim to a World War II incendiary bomb. The flames took no hold in the vaulted stone room, but the damage was done by water from the firemen's hoses. The planks of pear wood around which the torso was built started to separate after their wartime saturation and in 1950 they were 'discarded', as the restorer noted regretfully. But photographs survive and show the 'ragged regiment' of the royal effigies in all their macabre glory. For more information see *The Funeral Effigies of Westminster Abbey*, ed. A. Harvey and R. Mortimer, Woodbridge, 1994.

25 **John Fisher:** John Fisher, Bishop of Rochester (*c.*1469–1535). First holder of the Cambridge Lady Margaret Professorship of Divinity, Vice-Chancellor of that university, Fisher (like Sir Thomas More)

would be best remembered, and indeed canonised, for his refusal to accept Henry VIII as head of the Church of England: a refusal which sent him to the block. For the 'Mornynge Remembraunce' sermon preached a month after Margaret Beaufort's death see *The English Works of John Fisher*, ed. J.E.B. Mayor, 1876.

26 **Juana . . . 'the Mad':** see Fox, *Sister Queens*.

27 **Shakespeare never wrote a voice for Margaret Beaufort:** He never wrote a *Henry VII*, of course, though the co-authored *Henry VIII* takes the story up to the christening of Elizabeth I.

Epilogue

1 **legacy of works:** In Cambridge today, her image is among the parade of academic notables who gaze down over the modern setting of the Graduate Society's café, the only other woman there besides Rosalind Franklin, the 'dark lady' of DNA. Flick through the *Cambridge Guide to Women's Writing in English* and there she is, 'Beaufort, Lady Margaret, English translator of religious texts and literary patron', sandwiched between Simone de Beauvoir and American satirist Ann Beattie.

2 **move towards mere domesticity:** see 'Conclusion' to Hilton, *Queens Consort*.

ACKNOWLEDGEMENTS

This book began with two conversations, each with writers more familiar than I with the pleasures and pitfalls of the fifteenth century. I was discussing with Alison Weir the possibility of basing a book around a place or an event, rather than a person, when the idea of a book on the battle of Bosworth first occurred to me – one from the viewpoint of the women affected. I was discussing that idea with Ann Wroe when she mentioned that she'd always thought how interesting it would be to try to build an entire book around the Privy Purse expenses of one of those women, Elizabeth of York. I wasn't quite courageous enough to take that on, but it did start me thinking about how the surviving records for the lives of the royal ladies might be used in a new way. It was George Lucas of Inkwell Management in New York who, eyeing my first proposal on Bosworth, said that since it was clearly the women than really interested me, why didn't I just write about the women? But even since then, it has been a long journey.

Along the way I have encountered the most extraordinary generosity. Susan Ronald most kindly made available to me her own research on Richard III. Besides Alison Weir, my text was read and improved by Ceri Law, while Julian Humphrys and George Goodwin corrected my blunders on military history, and Dr David Wright checked my interpretation of certain Latin texts. What errors remain are all my own. Above all, thanks are due to Margaret Gaskin who, as so often before, answered the call of old friendship and came to my rescue over everything from questions of attribution to the family tree.

I owe a huge debt to my agent Peter Robinson, to my commissioning editor Arabella Pike, to Essie Cousins and the whole team at HarperCollins. I owe much, also, to those authors whose work on the individual subjects and strands which combine to make up this book has been of such assistance to me. Every effort has been made to contact the owners of any copyright material reproduced, but if any have been inadvertently overlooked the publishers would be glad to hear from them so that the mistake can be corrected in future editions.

INDEX